Aladdin Elaasar

PRAISE FOR "THE LAST PHARAOH"

"This book is stunning in its revelations of Mubarak's stranglehold on every aspect of life in this glorious, long- suffering nation. Connecting one mysterious dot to the next, the author teases the reader from chapter to chapter as he lucidly explains the details of Egypt's worst kept secrets of all…the 'secret' of Mubarak's power and how he plans to rule from his own royal crypt."

- Professor Tate Miller, Monterey Institute of International Studies.

"Let me give you the four scariest words I can't pronounce in Arabic: *Egypt after Mubarak.* Mubarak's *emergency rule dictatorship* is deep into its third decade, making him one of Egypt's most durable pharaohs. His succession plan is clear: Son Gamal tries to replicate Beijing's model of economic reform, forestalling political reform..."

Thomas Barnett, Esquire columnist and author of "*The Country to Watch: Egypt.*"

"U.S. policymakers now face a difficult choice: continuing to support the iron-fisted rule of Mubarak and his likely hand-picked successor, or backing a beleaguered democratic opposition that some believe could open the door to Islamic fundamentalist rule".

- *Voice of America.*

"Equally alarming is the rise of anti-American and anti-Semitic conspiracy theories in Egypt's state media and society. Haunted by the memories of the overnight fall of the Shah of Iran to the Ayatollahs, U.S. policymakers fear a similar event in Egypt. Obama is likely to face an unbelievably bad choice in the largest Arab country. *Elaasar's* book is indeed an eye opener"

- Swiss News Agency

"With so much at stake, the West is slowly coming to grips with a new reality; a reality which no single book or author could possibly address. *The Last Pharaoh* should be indispensable to anyone hoping to understand Egypt's role, not only the Middle East, but the potential for Mubarak's Egypt to impact the destiny of global events".

- The Media Oasis.

"In this remarkably frank and revealing portrayal of Mubarak's Egypt, no reader of this book could ever again think of Egypt as anything less than the potential tipping point of Middle Eastern society."

- Syndicated columnist Ray Hanania.

"When it happens, it will rock the world; octogenarian Mubarak, will leave office, either by his own decision or that of Providence. So far, few in the West have paid much attention. But Egyptians certainly are getting ready, and we should do so as well".

- Georgetown University Professor Michelle Dunne and expert on Arab politics and U.S. policy at the Carnegie Endowment for International Peace.

"That's the bold prediction offered by Elaasar. American policy-makers could soon face the same tough choice on Egypt that they once suffered with Iran's faltering Shah: Step in with maximum effort during a succession crisis or let the chips fall where they may."

-Thomas P.M. Barnett, University of Tennessee's Howard Baker Center.

"*The Last Pharaoh* is nuanced and remarkably thorough. The simplicity of the style and content makes this book required reading for students, journalists, policymakers and general public in order to understand the mechanisms of authoritarianism and despotism in Egypt and Arab countries."

- Political Science Professor, Noureddine Jebnoun,
The University of Montana.

THE LAST PHARAOH

Mubarak and the Uncertain Future of Egypt in the Obama Age

BY
ALADDIN ELAASAR

BEACON PRESS

Paperback edition first Published in 2009 by Beacon Press.

Beacon Press books are available at special discounts for bulk purchases in the United States by corporations, institutions, and other organizations. For more information, please contact the Marketing and Publicity Dept., Beacon Press, at 523 Dearborn Ave., Missoula, Montana 59801, or call (224) 388 1353.

Library of Congress Cataloguing-in-Publication Data
Elaasar, Aladdin
The Last Pharaoh: Mubarak and the Uncertain Future of Egypt in the Obama Age
p.cm.
Includes bibliographical references and index.
1. Egypt-History.I.Title.
International Standard Book Numbers:
ISBN-10: 0615300707
ISBN-13: 978-0615300702

Printed in the United States of America

Note: The author and publisher specifically disclaim any responsibility for any liability for the opinions expressed in this book through direct quote, or else.

Also by Aladdin Elaasar:
"Silent Victims: The Plight of Arab and Muslim Americans in Post 9/11 America"

Book Cover Designer: Neal Wiegert
Front Cover Cartoon: Kjell Nilsson-Maki
Interior Designer and Indexer: Shauna Murphy

The paper used in this publication meets the requirements of the American National Standard for Permenance of Paper for Printed Library Materials Z39.48-1984.

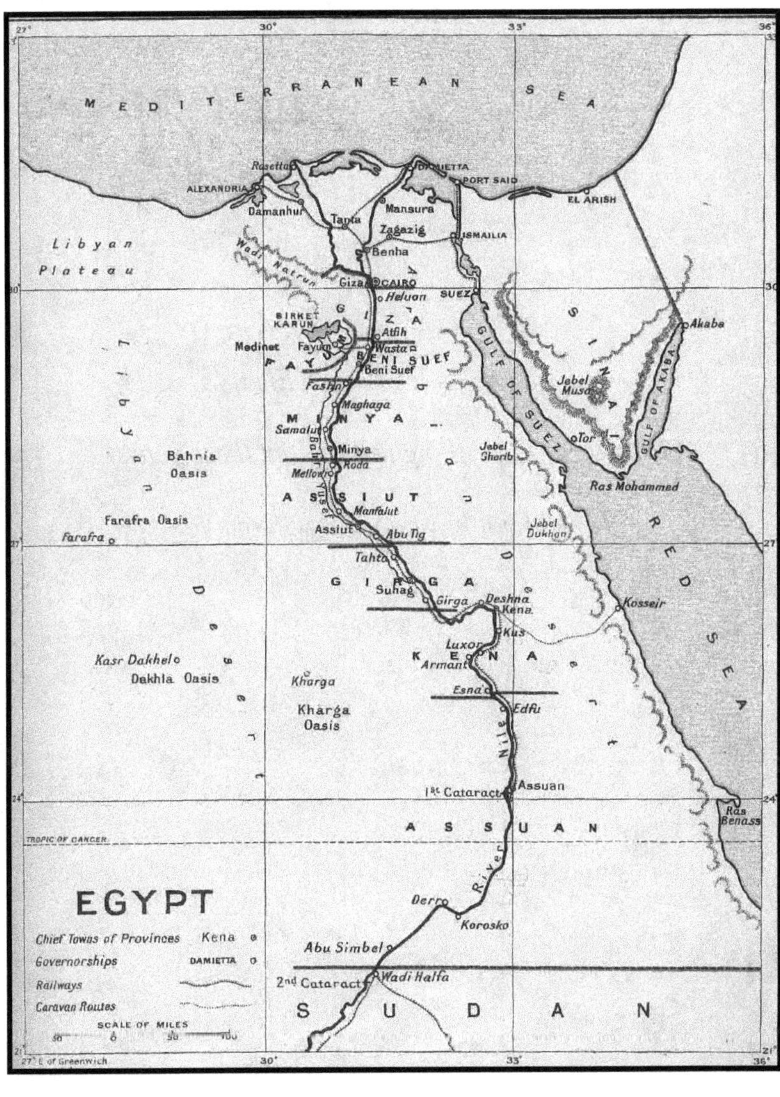
MEDITERRANEAN SEA
Rosetta
DAMIETTA
PORT SAID
ALEXANDRIA
Damanhur
Tanta
Mansura
Zagazig
ISMAILIA
EL ARISH
Libyan Plateau
Wadi Natrun
Benha
Giza
CAIRO
Helwan
SUEZ
BIRKET KARUN
GIZA
Atfih
Akaba
Medinet
Fayum
FAYUM
Wasta
BENI SUEF
Beni Suef
GULF OF SUEZ
SINAI
Jebel Musa
GULF OF AKABA
Fashn
Maghaga
MINYA
Samalut
Tor
Bahria Oasis
Minya
Roda
Jebel Gharib
Mellowi
Ras Mohammed
ASSIUT
Manfalut
Farafra Oasis
Assiut
Jebel Dukhan
Farafra
Abu Tig
Tahta
GIRGA
Suhag
Girga
Deshna
Kena
Kosseir
RED SEA
Kus
Luxor
Kasr Dakhel
KENA
Dakhla Oasis
Armant
Kharga
Esna
Edfu
Kharga Oasis
Nile
Assuan
1st Cataract
ASSUAN
Ras Benass
TROPIC OF CANCER
River
EGYPT
Derr
Korosko
Chief Towns of Provinces Kena
Abu Simbel
Governorships DAMIETTA
Railways
2nd Cataract
Wadi Halfa
Caravan Routes
SUDAN
SCALE OF MILES
27° E of Greenwich
30°
33°
36°

To my beloved wife Elsa

Thanks for everything throughout these years,

I could not have done it without you

NOTE ON TRANSLITERATION

The author's approach to the transliteration problem consists of the following:

Step 1: the 'generally accepted' English transliteration of key names such as *'Nasser'* instead of *'Nasir'*.

Step 2: the use of an apostrophe to delineate hamzas and ains in Arabic.

Step 3: the use of Egyptian dialect in the cases of names – i.e. *'Gamal'* instead of *'Jamal'*. Otherwise modern written Arabic is generally used.

The reader might find some names like *Al-Sharif* spelled *El-Sharif* as mentioned in different resources. The author kept the two variations as quoted from different sources. These variations can also appear as *al-Sharif* or *el-Sharif;* the two variations are the same name for the same person. *Al* or *EL* in Arabic is the definitive article meaning the, which precedes many Arabic family names.

وَإِذْ نَجَّيْنَاكُم مِّنْ آلِ فِرْعَوْنَ يَسُومُونَكُمْ سُوَءَ الْعَذَابِ يُذَبِّحُونَ أَبْنَاءكُمْ
وَيَسْتَحْيُونَ نِسَاءكُمْ وَفِي ذَلِكُم بَلاء مِّن رَّبِّكُمْ عَظِيمٌ (2:49)

And [remember the time] when We saved you from pharaoh's people, who afflicted you with cruel suffering, slaughtering your sons and sparing [only] your women which was an awesome trial from your Sustainer. Quran

قَالَ فِرْعَوْنُ آمَنتُم بِهِ قَبْلَ أَن آذَنَ لَكُمْ إِنَّ هَـذَا لَمَكْرٌ مَّكَرْتُمُوهُ فِي
الْمَدِينَةِ لِتُخْرِجُواْ مِنْهَا أَهْلَهَا فَسَوْفَ تَعْلَمُونَ (7:123)

Said pharaoh: "Have you come to believe in him ere I have given you permission? Behold, this is indeed a plot which you have cunningly devised in this [my] city in order to drive out its people hence! But in time you shall come to know, [my revenge]. Quran

But the LORD inflicted serious diseases on Pharaoh and his household because of Abram's wife Sarai. Genesis 12:17

وَقَالَ الْمَلأُ مِن قَوْمِ فِرْعَونَ أَتَذَرُ مُوسَى وَقَوْمَهُ لِيُفْسِدُواْ فِي الأَرْضِ
وَيَذَرَكَ وَآلِهَتَكَ قَالَ سَنُقَتِّلُ أَبْنَاءهُمْ وَنَسْتَحْيِـي نِسَاءهُمْ وَإِنَّا فَوْقَهُمْ
قَاهِرُونَ (7:127)

And the great ones among pharaoh's people said: "Wilt thou allow Moses and his people to spread corruption on earth, and to [cause thy people to] forsake thee and thy gods?" [pharaoh] replied: "We shall slay their sons in great numbers and shall spare [only] their women: for, verily, we hold sway over them!" Quran

ל וַיָּקָם פַּרְעֹה לַיְלָה, הוּא
וְכָל-עֲבָדָיו וְכָל-מִצְרַיִם,
וַתְּהִי צְעָקָה גְדֹלָה,
בְּמִצְרָיִם: כִּי-אֵין בַּיִת,
אֲשֶׁר אֵין-שָׁם מֵת.

30 And Pharaoh rose up in the night, he, and all his servants, and all the Egyptians; and there was a great cry in Egypt; for there was not a house where there was not one dead.

לא וַיִּקְרָא לְמֹשֶׁה וּלְאַהֲרֹן
לַיְלָה, וַיֹּאמֶר קוּמוּ צְּאוּ
מִתּוֹךְ עַמִּי--גַּם-אַתֶּם,
גַּם-בְּנֵי יִשְׂרָאֵל; וּלְכוּ
עִבְדוּ אֶת-יְהוָה,
כְּדַבֶּרְכֶם.

31 And he called for Moses and Aaron by night and said: 'Rise up, get you forth from among my people, both ye and the children of Israel; and go, serve the LORD, as ye have said.

وَأَوْرَثْنَا الْقَوْمَ الَّذِينَ كَانُواْ يُسْتَضْعَفُونَ مَشَارِقَ الأَرْضِ وَمَغَارِبَهَا الَّتِي
بَارَكْنَا فِيهَا وَتَمَّتْ كَلِمَتُ رَبِّكَ الْحُسْنَى عَلَى بَنِي إِسْرَآئِيلَ بِمَا صَبَرُواْ
وَدَمَّرْنَا مَا كَانَ يَصْنَعُ فِرْعَوْنُ وَقَوْمُهُ وَمَا كَانُواْ يَعْرِشُونَ (7:137)

Whereas unto the people who [in the past] had been deemed utterly low, We gave as their heritage the eastern and western parts of the land that We had blessed. And [thus] thy Sustainer's good promise unto the children of Israel was fulfilled in result of their patience in adversity; whereas We utterly destroyed all that pharaoh and his people had wrought, and all that they had built. Quran

ثُمَّ بَعَثْنَا مِن بَعْدِهِم مُّوسَى وَهَارُونَ إِلَى فِرْعَوْنَ وَمَلَئِهِ بِآيَاتِنَا
فَاسْتَكْبَرُواْ وَكَانُواْ قَوْمًا مُّجْرِمِينَ (10:75)

And after those [earlier prophets] We sent Moses and Aaron with Our messages unto pharaoh and his great ones: but they gloried in their arrogance, for they were people lost in sin. Quran

فَمَا آمَنَ لِمُوسَى إِلاَّ ذُرِّيَّةٌ مِّن قَوْمِهِ عَلَى خَوْفٍ مِّن فِرْعَوْنَ وَمَلَئِهِمْ أَن
يَفْتِنَهُمْ وَإِنَّ فِرْعَوْنَ لَعَالٍ فِي الأَرْضِ وَإِنَّهُ لَمِنَ الْمُسْرِفِينَ (10:83)

But none save a few of his people declared their faith in Moses, [while others held back] for fear of pharaoh and their great ones, lest they persecute them: for, verily, pharaoh was mighty on earth and was, verily, of those who are given to excesses. Quran

"Those leaders who seek to sow conflict, or blame their society's ills on the West: Know that your people will judge you on what you can build, not what you destroy. To those who cling to power through corruption and deceit and the silencing of dissent, know that you are on the wrong side of history".

- President Barack Obama in his inaugural speech.

"One of the saddest episodes in modem history is that one of the richest and most promising regions of the world, with one of the oldest and most authentic civilizations known to man, is becoming the permanent field for local wars and internal strife because of the lack of imagination, the lack of generosity, and the lack of diplomacy shown by its elite."

- Former UN Secretary General, former Egyptian Foreign Minister and Political Science Professor at Cairo University, Boutros Boutros-Ghali.

DEDICATION

This book is dedicated to my late mother, who taught me how to read and write at the age of three. She passed away three years ago. I could not go back home to Egypt to bid her farewell. She spent almost forty years of her life teaching Arabic to thousands of students in Egyptian schools.

This book is also dedicated to the late Egyptian novelist and Nobel Peace Prize Laureate Naguib Mahfouz. Mahfouz' writings embodied and immortalized the spirit of the Egyptian people. Mahfouz's novels and writings have been inspirational to many people worldwide, including me.

PROLOGUE

Egypt has held a special place in the hearts and imagination of poets, writers, and ordinary folks alike. They admire its rich history and glorious past. It has a special place in the hearts of Arabs, Moslems, Jews, and Christians, where Egypt was mentioned as a sacred place in their holy books.

Yet, in spite of having one of the most glorious heritages, Egyptians remain nowadays very pessimistic about the future of their country. Their future seems to be very bleak and uncertain. Contrary to public belief that the Pharaonic era in Egyptian history had ended thousands of years ago, the Egyptians do still have fresh memories of their pharaohs.

The 81 years old President Mubarak of Egypt has been in power since 1981 and was elected for six more years in 2005. Concerns about Mubarak's health draw much greater attention to the question of who will next rule the nation of Egypt. Succession plan for Mubarak's son Gamal is already in place.

Visible signs of discord between the United States and Egypt over a wide array of issues have appeared in recent years. Today, the bilateral relationship has eroded over Egypt's cold peace with Israel, to dealings with terrorist supporting states on its borders.

Equally alarming is the rise of anti-American and anti-Semitic conspiracy theories in Egypt's state media and society. Haunted by the memories of the overnight fall of the Shah of Iran to the Ayatollahs, U.S. policymakers fear a similar event in Egypt. Once thought to be a strong U.S. ally, the Shah lost his grip over power to the zealous clergy sabotaging every effort for peace and stability in the region. Marcos and Suharto, two old dictators considered strong U.S. allies, as well, fell to the angry mobs in the Philippines and Indonesia.

President Obama is likely to find himself facing an unbelievably bad choice in the largest Arab country. Would America intervene militarily to preserve Gamal's faltering rule? Or would America throw up its hands writing Tel Aviv a blank check, and hope that a twenty-first-century Masada can hold out in a Middle East where Iran has the bomb? Is Africa where *al-Qaeda* hides its money, guns, recruits, training camps and its future? Africa would be the last great stand in this *Long War,* where all those impossibly straight borders will inevitably be made squiggly again by globalization's cultural reformatting process. Now this fight heads south...and yes, the *Long War* could be even uglier there.

If that scenario is not frightening enough, there are few others that are even scarier. A scenario where an ambitious general would stage another coup, turning Egypt into a *God-knows-what regime.* Would that general ally himself with Muslim radical groups like the Muslim Brothers, Hamas, or Hezbollah? Would Egypt witness another Khomeini-style revolution?

Considering the alarming rising poverty figures in Egypt and the disparities between the classes, could Egypt be overrun by an angry and hungry mob, *French Revolution-style*? Egypt would then erupt into lawlessness, chaos, or perhaps civil war with the dissolving of the central government, its head figures and its upper class, already preparing for such a turn of events.

If the Muslim Brotherhood were to achieve power in Egypt, Israel's demise would once again become the overt unifying principle for governments in the region. *The difference this time*? It still may be America and the West that would have to intervene.

Whatever the scenario would be, spillover from what could occur in Egypt in the near future would impact many nations. With Hamas taking control in the Palestinian territories, Hezbollah in Southern Lebanon - backed by the Baathists in Damascus and the Mullahs in Tehran; who would all agree on one thing: hatred for America and wiping the state of Israel off the map. The uncertainty and anxiety grows among people of the region.

For that, Western observers are keeping tabs on the situation in Egypt, fearing a domino effect in case of a trigger event occurring in Egypt.

CONTENTS

PART ONE:
THE LEGACY OF THE PHARAOH CONTINUES

PART TWO:
DEMAGOGUES, ZEALOTS AND ANTI-SEMITES

PART THREE:
THE BEGINNING OF THE END

CONCLUSION

CHRONOLOGY

- A unified kingdom founded circa 3200 BC by King Narmer, or Menes.
- First Pharaonic Dynasty circa 3100 BC.
- 19th Dynasty from 1279 BC to 1213 BC.
- The New Kingdom was marked by a number of famous pharaohs including the female Hatshepsut and Akhenaton, founder of the first monotheistic religion, Atonism.
- Ramses II, pharaoh of the Nineteenth Dynasty was born cairca 1302 BC. At age fourteen, Ramses II was appointed Prince Regent.
- The Battle of Kadesh in May 1274 BC - Egyptian forces under Ramses II leadership marched through through Canaan (nowadays Israel) through the Beka'a Valley and approached Kadesh.
- Ramses' army was almost totally destroyed by the surprise initial Hittite chariot attack effectively wining the war. He was compelled to retreat south.
- In 1258 BC, Ramses decided to conclude an agreement with

the Hittite king at Kadesh, Hattusili III, to end the conflict and sign the earliest known peace treaty in history.

- Ramses turned his humiliating defeat into a glorious victory. He was depicted on the walls of his temples as single-handedly smiting, decimating and decapitating the Hittites.

- Ramses II was buried in the Valley of the Kings, Luxor, where his mummy was found in 1881 at Deir el-Bahri.

- The last native dynasty, known as the Thirtieth Dynasty fell to the Persians in 343 BC.

- Ptolemaic and Roman (400 BC - 641 AD). Egypt fell to the Greeks, Romans, Byzantines and Persians again.

- In 629 the Emperor Heraclius drove the Jews from Jerusalem followed by a massacre of Jews throughout the empire.

- Arab Rule, (641 - 1250). The Treaty of Alexandria sealed the Arab conquest of Egypt. More than 40,000 Jews were living in Alexandria alone.

- Rule of the Fatimite Caliphs (909-1169).

- Saladin and the Ayyubid sultans (1169-1250). In 1166 Maimonides settled in Fostat as a physician for Saladin. The title *Ra'is al-Umma* (Head of the Nation), was bestowed upon him.

- Mameluke Rule (1250-1517). The first Mameluke Sultan Baibars doubled the tribute paid by the *ahl al-dhimmah* (Jews and Christians).

- On Jan. 22, 1517, Turkish sultan Selim defeated Tuman Bey, the last of the Mamelukes starting the Turkish rule from (1517-1922). Sultan Selim placed David ibn Abi-Zimra as the head of the Jewish community in Cairo.

- The French Invasion of Egypt by Napoleon Bonaparte (1798-1801). The French expedition discovered the *Rosetta Stone* and published the *Description of Egypt.* On 1801, British Admiral Nelson captured Napoleon's ships.

- A series of civil wars took place between the Ottoman Turks, the Mamelukes, and Albanian mercenaries resulting in the Albanian Muhammad Ali taking control of Egypt as the Ottoman viceroy in 1805.

- Mohammed Ali Dynasty Rule 1801-1952.

- In 1811, Mohammed Ali invited a number of his opponents to the Citadel for a feast, then trapped them within the gates and slaughtered them. He conquered the Arabian Peninsula and invaded Sudan.

- Following the completion of the Suez Canal in 1869, Egypt fell heavily into debt due to Ismail Pasha lavish life style.

- Egypt's inability to pay back its loans led to the appointment of foreign debt commissioners in 1876, and the inclusion of British and French ministers in Egypt's cabinet in 1878. It finally forced the abdication of Ismail in 1879. Under European pressure, the Ottoman sultan installed Ismail's son Tawfik.

- In 1881, an Egyptian colonel named Ahmad Orabi led a mutiny against Tawfik. He demanded an elected legislature. In 1882, nationalists gained control of the cabinet and the army, threatening Tawfik. Riots broke out, and Britain and

France sent warships to Alexandria harbor.

- On July 11, 1882, British battleships bombarded Alexandria. Tawfik, siding with Britain, declared Orabi a rebel. British invasion and occupation took place. Orabi's troops were defeated. Orabi and his followers were jailed, tried, and exiled to Ceylon. Tawfik was restored to power.

- United Kingdom seized control of Egypt's government in 1882 and declared Egypt a protectorate. Egyptian nationalism grew.

- Official census in 1898, mentioned that there were 25,000 Jews in a total population of 9,734,405. Under King Fuad, Jews played important roles in the economy, and the Jewish population climbed to nearly 100,000. Fuad died in 1936, his Son Farouk became king.

- Egyptian nationalism was aided by the French and the Ottomans, who resented the substantial British role in Egyptian affairs. The nationalists gained strength under the leadership of Mustafa Kamil, who died in 1908.

- In 1914, World War I led to the fall of the Ottoman Empire. Nationalist sentiments became more prominent. Anti-Turkish feelings grew; the Sharif of Mecca launched the Arab Revolt. The Ottomans were defeated and the Sharif's son Faisal entered Damascus in 1918.

- 1917, the Balfour Declaration, and the secret Sykes-Picot Agreement between Britain and France were revealed.

- Sadat was born on December 25, 1918, in the village of Mit Abu al-Kum, el-Munufia.

- After World War I, the British exiled several nationalists among them Saad Zaghlul to Malta. In March 1919, a nationwide revolt broke out. Egyptian Parliament drafted and implemented a new constitution in 1923.

- Egypt granted independence from Britain on February 28, 1922 and declared an independent monarchy under king Fuad I.

- Mubarak was born on May 4, 1928, at Kafr el-Meselha, el-Munufia. In the same year, the Muslim Brotherhood was founded by Hassan al-Banna.

- 1924-1936, Egypt's Liberal Experiment.

- World War II. Germans led by Rommel invaded Egypt and made their way to within 70 miles of Alexandria to be defeated by the British.

- In 1942, Sadat was arrested and charged of spying for the Nazis. In January 6, 1946, Sadat was also accused of plotting to assassinate Egyptian minister Amin Osman. Sadat escaped prison in April 1948 to join King Farouk's Iron Guard and later attempting to assassinate Egyptian Prime Minster Nahas Pasha.

- In 1945 Egypt became a leading member of the Arab League.

- In 1948 Arab armies invaded Palestine and were defeated. The State of Israel was declared by David Ben-Gurion on May and recognized by the UN.

- On December 28, 1948, a member of the Muslim Brotherhood assassinated Prime Minister al-Nuqrashi. Muslim

Brotherhood's leader al-Banna was killed later by government agents in Cairo in February, 1949.

- In 1949, Mubarak joined the Egyptian Military Academy.
- January 27, 1952, an angry mob set the Cairo Fire.
- In July 23· 1952, a military coup led by Nasser, Sadat and other *Free Officers*, forced King Farouk to abdicate. Farouk left Egypt into exile in Italy where he was poisoned.
- In August 1952, two activist workers Mostafa Khamis and Mohamed el-Baqri were arrested, tried by a military court and executed.
- Egypt declared a republic in June 18, 1953. General Naguib became the first President.
- General Naguib was forced to resign and go under house arrest in 1954 by Nasser.
- Nasser became president in 1954. He forced the British out of Egypt on June 18, 1956.
- The Muslim Brotherhood became an illegal organization since 1954 when some of its members attempted to assassinate Nasser.
- In July 1954, several Egyptian Jews were apprehended and brought to trial in December 1954.
- Nasser nationalized the Suez Canal on July 26, 1956, leading to the takeover of the Canal and Sinai by Britain, France and Israel.
- On November 23, 1956, a proclamation by Nasser's

government was issued stating that all Jews are Zionists and enemies of the state.

- In 1956, Nasser expelled almost 25,000 Jews and confiscated their property. As a result of the Sinai campaign, 1,000 more Jews were imprisoned. The Jewish population of Egypt was reduced to 100 people, from 100,000 before 1952.

- Nasser managed to contain and control the trade unions under a tamed entity loyal to his regime in 1957.

- Between 1958 and 1961, Nasser undertook to form a union between Egypt and Syria known as the United Arab Republic.

- Nasser and his successors; Sadat and Mubarak, established a strong presidential political system largely dependent on a pervasive security apparatus maintaining a firm grip on all aspects of civil society.

- On June 5, 1967, the Six Days War erupted, in which Egypt lost Sinai to Israel.

- From 1967 to 1972, the War of Attrition continued between Egypt and Israel.

- On 28 September 1970, Nasser died of a heart attack and succeeded by Sadat.

- Sadat switched Egypt's Cold War allegiance from the Soviet Union to the United States. He expelled Soviet advisors in 1972. Sadat clamped down on religious and secular opposition alike.

- In October 6, 1973, Egypt, along with Syria, launched a surprise attack on Israel in the Yom Kippur War. The United States and the USSR intervened.
- In October 1973, following the Yom Kippur War, Mubarak was promoted to the rank of Air Chief Marshal.
- In April 1975, Mubarak was appointed Vice-President of Egypt. In 1978, he was selected Vice-Chairman of the National Democratic Party (NDP).
- In 1977, Sadat made a historical visit to Israel leading to the 1978 peace treaty. Camp David Accords signed between President Carter, Sadat, and Israeli Prime Minister Begin on September 17, 1978. Sadat and Begin received the 1978 Nobel Peace Prize.
- Sadat's peace initiative with Israel led to Egypt's expulsion from the Arab League to be re-admitted in 1989.
- Egypt has been receiving U.S. foreign aid since 1979, with an average of $2.2 billion per year after Camp David.
- The mysterious deaths of popular Defense Minister Ahmed Badawi and 13 senior Egyptian Army officers in a helicopter crash on March 6, 1981 increased the public anger on Sadat and his policies.
- In September 1981, Sadat cracked down on intellectuals and activists of all ideological stripes, His police imprisoned socialists, Nasserites, feminists, Islamists, Coptic Christian clergy, university professors, journalists, and members of student groups. The arrests totalled nearly 16,000, receiving worldwide condemnation.

- Sadat was assassinated in Cairo by fundamentalists in October 6, 1981. He was succeeded by Mubarak in 14 October 1981. Mubarak became President and declared a state of emergency ever since.

- In 1986, 17,000 workers at the Esco textile plant in Shobra el-Khima, Cairo, initiated a sit-in asking for a one-day per week holiday. The Mubarak government responded by storming the plant beating and arresting hundreds of workers.

- In 1986, thousands of the Central Security Forces recruits took to the streets looting and burning tourist businesses. Mubarak declared martial law and called in the military to restore order.

- Workers opposition for the Mubarak regime at the Helwan Iron and Steel factory in the summer of 1989. The steel plant was stormed by the Central Security Forces resulting in the death and injury of many workers.

- In the early 1990s Islamic militant groups attempted to overthrow the Mubarak government conducting a wave of terrorist attacks against the police, top government officials, Christian Copts, and foreign tourists. The Luxor Massacre took place on November 17, 1997. Sixty-two people were killed.

- On June 8, 1992, liberal writer Farag Foda was assassinated in Cairo by extremists.

- On June 26, 1995, fundamentalist attempted to assassinate Mubarak in Addis Ababa, Ethiopia.

- On May 2001, Egyptian-American, Professor Saad Eddin

Ibrahim, was arrested and brought to trial on charges of *defaming Egypt abroad.*

- September 11, 2001, terrorist crashed two planes into the WTC twin towers and the Pentagon resulting in the death of thousands of innocent Americans. The War on Terrorism was declared.

- Two years later, Saddam's regime is overthrown and Iraqis liberated by American forces. Saddam was excuted in December 2006.

- In 2002 Mubarak appointed his son, Gamal as General Secretary of the Policy Committee.

- After three years and two heavily flawed trials Saad Eddin Ibrahim was sentenced to seven years imprisonment. In March 2003, Egypt's Court of Cassation exonerated him of all charges.

- On April 8, 2004, on the eve of Mubarak's meeting with President George Bush in Crawford, Texas, the Anti-Defamation League (ADL) issued a report exposing the use of anti-Semitic caricatures, stereotypes and images in Mubarak's state media.

- Kifaya, the Egyptian National Movement for Change made its first public protest on 12 December 2004, in front of the High Court in downtown Cairo.

- Mubarak re-elected for a fifth term in September 2005 amidst cries of intimidation of voters and rigging.

- On September 8, 2005, Ayman Nour, a dissident and

presidential candidate from *Al-Ghad* party, contested the election results and demanded a recount.

- On September 9, Nour, the runner-up in Egypt's 2005 presidential elections was given a five year jail sentence. On the day of Nour's sentencing, the White House Press Secretary denounced the Mubarak government's action questioning its commitment to democracy, freedom, and the rule of law.

- In 2005, Transparency International Corruption report ranked Mubarak's regime 115th out of 159 countries.

- On July 4, 2006, Kifaya released a report alleging that corruption has infiltrated all aspects of Egyptian society and stands in the way of further social and economic development.

- Several terrorist bombings took place in tourist sites in Sinai in 2005-2006. The bombings were quickly blamed by the Egyptian and Arab media on the Israelis.

- On November 2008, Barack Hussein Obama was elected President of the United States of America promising change in America's foreign policy towards the Middle East.

- Under pressure from the Obama administration, the Mubarak regime released opposition leader Ayman Nour in March 2009.

- Human rights groups claim that about 15 thousand political prisoners are still in Mubarak's jails without a charge or a trial.

[illegible]

[illegible]

[illegible]

[illegible]

[illegible]

[illegible]

[illegible]

[illegible]

[illegible]

[illegible]

ACKNOWLEDGEMENT

I am eternally indebted to numerous people who played a major role in my life at different stages by providing me with valuable insight into many complex subjects. One of those people was my late grandmother, Fatima Elaasar, a tall, strongly built, illiterate country woman, whose wisdom, struggle and amazing stories were unmatched. As a young child, I used to sit on her prayer carpet surrounded by my many cousins listening to her words of wisdom and fascinating stories. She was a widowed at an early age, lost two of her eldest sons, as well as her husband following the birth of my mother. Nevertheless, she built her own large house, raised her children, and insisted that my mother, her only daughter, receive the best education available at the time, so that she could later become a school teacher. My grandmother was a true matriarch.

I am also indebted beyond words to my parents, who were my earliest teachers, and who instilled in me the love of learning foreign languages early on. They insisted that I would learn English and French and spent many hours and nights teaching me. Their hard work for forty years, and sacrifices made it possible for me to attain the best education available, me and my four other siblings.

I was quite fortunate to have had so many great teachers during my twenty five years of study in Egypt. One teacher with considerable impact on me was Ustaz Mahmoud Sultan, who taught us Egyptian history. He made me love history as a compelling story that needs to be told. During my graduate and postgraduate years, I was also fortunate to have been taught by some of the best intellectual minds in Egypt.

During the writing and research for this book, I received encouragement and support from many people. My special thanks go first and foremost to the librarians at public libraries, my second home, who have always been helpful in assisting me in research and finding me the books and documentaries I sought. So, to those librarians, the unknown soldiers and unsung heroes of our society, at such places as the Library of Congress, the Chicago public libraries, the libraries in Schaumburg and Palatine, Illinois, the public libraries in San Jose, Santa Clara, Cupertino, and Monterey, California, I offer you my deepest gratitude.

My special thanks also go to many of my colleagues in academia; namely Professor Tate Miller, Senior Lecturer at the Monterey Institute of International Studies. As an expert on international negotiations, conflict management, government relations and diplomacy, cross-cultural communication, he read the early draft of my book giving me insights which had definitely improved it. My thanks also go to my friend Catherine Haldorson for providing an index to the book.

I am also deeply grateful to a number of friends, students,

research assistants and colleagues for their help, ideas and inspirational work on that topic, such as: Professor Mohamed Abed al-Jabri, recently awarded by the UNESCO, Niven al-Kabbani of the Human Rights Center for the Assistance of Prisoners, Professor Nazih Ayubi, Professor Amy Chua, Professor Saad Eddine Ibrahim, AUC professor of Political Science Maye Kassem, Professor Bernard Lewis, Professor David Pryce-Jones, AMIDEAST President Ambassador William Rugh, Ambassador Edward S. Walker, Jr., President and Chief Executive Officer of the Middle East Institute, former Assistant Secretary of State for Near Eastern Affairs, and Ambassador to Egypt.

My book has been ispired also by the works, ideas and writings of the following people; Dr. Robert Satloff, the Executive Director of the Washington Institute for Near East Policy, Mr. Joseph Stork, the Advocacy Director of Human Rights Watch, Retired Colonel Muhammad al-Ghanam, former Director of Legal Research at the Egyptian Interior Ministry, Ayman Nour, leader of the opposition Al-Ghad Party, Ahmad Nagi Qamha, researcher at the Al-Ahram Center for Political and Strategic Studies, Menahem Milson, Professor of Arabic Literature at the Hebrew University of Jerusalem, Professor Joel Gordon, Professor Bryan Spellman for his editorial suggestions and keen eye for details. My thanks also to former intelligence analyst at the Defense Intelligence Agency and Professor of Arab Studies Owen Sirrs for his important books on Nasser's missile program and security apparatus, and for his review of the manuscript.

My special thanks also to Professor Joel Beinin for his

ensyclopediac writings on the Jews of Egypt, Professor Yahya Sadowski at the Johns Hopkins School of Advanced International Studies, Satirist writers Ali Salem and *al-Akhbar* columnist Ahmad Rageb, Professor Thomas Barnett, Egyptian writers Tarek Heggy and Magdi Michael, and last - but not least, *Newsweek* columnist and editor, Fareed Zakaria.

Many organizations indirectly contributed to this book and to my better understanding of Egyptian politics through their important work for many years. Some of these organizations are the Ibn-Khaldun Center for Development Studies, the Anti-Defamation League (ADL), the Egyptian Organization for Human Rights (EOHR), and the Kifaya movement.

FOREWORD

By
Professor Tate Miller,
Monterey Institute of International Studies

For many, Egypt stands alone in its historical and cultural mystic. Yet, we sometimes ignore the harsh reality of an Egypt whose iron-fisted government may well be the antithesis of our most fundamental values and beliefs. Like millions of others, my thoughts and opinions of Egypt were largely shaped from the armchair of Western civilization. Although immensely alluring as a place of cultural and historical interest, the Egyptian political landscape left me with a sense of unease I never fully understood.

Perhaps this lack of understanding resulted from the over simplified and passing views of Western media, too often pressured to simply report on the immediacy of human drama rather than the potentially cataclysmic events of Egypt's long term power struggles. Or, perhaps it is the daunting complexity of Egyptian politics, which themselves serve as a deterrent to understanding and dialogue.

Combining an uncanny sense of clarity and understatement, Aladdin Elaasar weaves Egypt's historical grandeur with an unnerving cascade of political intrigue that reveal a side of Mubarak the world cannot long ignore. In one fell swoop, my admiration for Egypt is both strengthened, and the source of my unease revealed, as the author sheds light on the darkness of Egyptian politics that could one day turn catastrophic.

History has shown us that man is only as free as his culture permits. When the freedom of the Egyptian people is measured by this same standard, a dismal and dangerous picture begins to emerge. Ruling with the pervasive clout of a modern Pharaoh, Mubarak's hold on the Egyptian people smothers every aspect of personal freedom.

Perhaps no nation has greater potential to influence the destiny of the Middle East, and hence the world, than Egypt. Yet, like a lingering and unrecognized apparition, Egypt's influence in regional and global affairs seems always just out of sight, and never fully understood. That is, until now. In this remarkably frank and revealing portrayal of Mubarak's Egypt, no reader of this book could ever again think of Egypt as anything less than the potential tipping point of Middle Eastern society.

Even in societies with a free press, where people are able to gather and glean information from virtually limitless sources, they are still susceptible to harboring uninformed opinions, and inadvertently supporting causes contrary to their own self interests. Such is the case with how Americans generally misunderstand the importance of Egypt. That is, we have taken the avenue of least resistance; and hence we make ourselves vulnerable to those with designs on our thinking and support. Our views, perceptions, and prejudices of the Middle East and Egypt have been shaped almost entirely by well-placed sound bites and staged media events.

With so much at stake, the West is slowly coming to grips with a new reality; a reality which no single book or author could possibly address. But the views expressed by Aladdin Elasar should be indispensable to anyone hoping to understand Egypt's role, not only the Middle East, but the potential for Mubarak's Egypt to impact the destiny of global events.

"Whoever follows the news coming from Egypt – and the positions of most of Egypt's intellectuals, journalists, and politicians – begins to think that the world wakes up every morning, rubs its eyes, and exclaims: Oh my Goodness, it's seven, I'm late, I have to start immediately to conspire against Egypt. "

- Arab intellectual, Hazem Saghiya

AUTHOR'S FOREWORD

EGYPT: WHAT WENT WRONG?

In an article in the widely circulated London-based *al-Hayat* newspaper, journalist Hazem Saghiya attempted to explain the reasons for a long list of scandals and other phenomena in recent Egyptain headlines. This thought-provoking article analyzes the ailments of Egyptian society under the Mubarak regime. Here are some excerpts of that article that eloquently touches the pulse of today's Egyptian society.

"Whoever follows the news coming from Egypt – and the positions of most of Egypt's intellectuals, journalists, and politicians – begins to think that the world wakes up every morning, rubs its eyes, and exclaims: *Oh my Goodness, it's seven, I'm late, I have to start immediately to conspire against Egypt.* This, however, is not the case. The world loves Egypt, its people, its Nile, its pyramids, and the *al-Azhar* University. Napoleon's story of Egypt; Champollion and the deciphering of the secrets of Egypt's ancient writings; the exhibitions of ancient Egyptian culture in European museums; Laurence Darrell and even Agatha Christie in her own way– they have all loved Egypt. Awarding the Nobel Prize for literature to

Naguib Mahfouz and the Noble Prize for science to Egyptian-American physicist Ahmad Zueil is an honor for Egypt as well. Five million tourists each year is not evidence of hatred. They were not discouraged by the Luxor massacre, although their numbers would have been higher without it," Saghiya explains.

"Why, then, is the news coming from Egypt so bizarre? Why is the world perceived by Egypt this way? For years now, alligators fly in Egypt's skies, elephants pass through a needle's eye, and treasures grow beneath pillows. For years now, *mystical realism* develops in Egypt as a way of life, rather than as a literature genre. Yet worse: the *Inquisition Courts* of the days of Nasser and Sadat have become popular again in Egypt. They break into research and universities, knock on the doors of houses, and interrogate the body and soul." Saghiya's claims caused a political storm and put the Egyptian state media on the defensive.

"How can a conspiracy be found beneath each stone?"

"How can one understand the repetitive events of which was the arrest of the *Satan Worshipers* and the *New Clan of Lot* [the nickname for a group of homosexuals arrested and tried recently]? How can one understand the fuss about translating Arab literature to Hebrew? The separation of husbands, who were accused of *apostasy* from their wives, and wives from their husbands? The fear of bubble gum that causes sterility [that was claimed to be spread in Egypt by Israel]; the assassination attempt on Nobel Prize laureate Naguib Mahfouz; the indictment of democracy activist Saad al-Din Ibrahim; the banning of films and books; and emergency courts. How can a column by Thomas Friedman about Egypt cause such conflagration? How can the Copts living abroad be described as if they plan to invade Egypt? How can a conference about minority rights be considered a threat? And a conference about women's rights an even bigger threat?" Saghiya exclaimed.

Challenging the Mubarak regime' state of denial, Saghiya gave his panoramic view of the ailments of Egyptian society by stating: "Let's portray some of the characteristics of this surrealistic picture: Egypt's Islamists operate between two poles: executing people on the one hand, and controlling the cultural, social and public space, on the other hand. Egypt's intellectuals swing between Emanuel Kant on the one hand, and Saladin, on the other. The popular desire is war. But Egypt was the first Arab country to accept peace! An overwhelming majority of Egyptians prefer the severing of relations with the United States. But American aid to Egypt has reached $50 billion since Camp David in 1979. Let's talk statistics: The number of Copts, for example, is a secret. But what about the number of graduates from universities who are unemployed? The opposition says four million, the government says only one. When the facts do not reach the public, rumors, exaggerations, fantasies, and fears develop. We must remember that in Egypt, a ministry of information still exists, and there is a *national press* that does not have competition, and lacks any innovations. Last year, for example, several independent journals were shut down. History is not debated. The existence of a *Copt problem* is denied. Denial has become part of both the popular and official ideology. Most of the criticism of Nasser or Sadat is sensational."

The main issues are not subject to serious discussion. Peace and openness can be the way to salvation, Saghiya explains: "When it turned out that, apparently, they were not, they were ridiculed. The beginning of relative political life in the days of Sadat was done in the same way political life was terminated by Nasser: the father always decides, and the children always obey. A man who thinks and elects independently is not allowed to appear. The state continues to be the boss, as it always has been. In view of this old heritage - from where would a free man appear? *From the Civil Society?* The Civil Society makes the news only when it deals with pan-Arab issues by burning flags".

Political life has no meaning. *Elections?* Yes, Saghiya exclaims, "but the results are known in advance. In a way, these are Iranian elections. They do not touch the president of the republic and the governing party. *Political parties?* Yes, but let us examine the age of their leaders: Numan Guma, the leader of the *al-Wafd* party, is the youngest among other leaders. He was born in 1934. Had Allah given longer life to the late Pasha Fuad [the leader of the Wafd Party], he would still be sitting on his chair. Mustafa Mashour of the Muslim Brotherhood was born in 1921. Ibrahim Shukri of the Labor Party was born in 1916. Khaled Muhyi al-Din of the Tagamu Party was born in 1922. Dhiyaa al-Din Dawoud of the Nasserist Party was born in 1926. And President Mubarak, as the head of the ruling party, was born in 1928."

The youth, who are three quarters of the population, do not participate in the decision-making process. Saghiya warned of excluding Egypt's youth and others from the political process. "More than half of them [youth] do not know anything about it. Politics are alien to the people. The younger forces that could have infused new blood to the elite do not get licenses to form new parties. In twenty years they may get the license, if they mature, by Egyptian standards! Some of the problems were bequeathed. They are accumulated. Others are newly-born. Egypt's transformation is very slow. The dead are sitting on the chests of the living".

What will become of Egypt? Saghiya stated that: "Egypt is no longer what it used to be in the first half of the twentieth century. Then, an Arab who was looking for celebrities in the press, literature, cinema, or poetry, went to Cairo. A visit by Egyptian writers Muhammad Abdu or Taha Hussein in any Arab country was an event by itself. Today, the number one export product of Egypt is televangelist al-Qaradawi, spiritual leader of the Muslim Brotherhood movement. Egypt was once the center of progress and enlightenment in the Arab world. Now we are witnessing Egypt's cultural deterioration".

Today, in our confusion and stress, we look like the *Weimar Republic* [pre-Nazi Germany], only without the joy, the freedom, and the creativity." Saghiya decried.

CONSPIRATORS AND DOGS WHO BARK WHILE THE CONVOY MOVES ON.

Will technology and globalization help bridge the gap and build bridges between Egypt and its neighbors? Saghiya stated few conditions in order for that to happen:

"There was progress in Hi-Tec: The internet and cellular phones. The government encourages this trend, but the internet has not reached the schools and the libraries. More important, the internet is the aim and not the goal. The goal is to establish a strong and modern middle strata whose control of knowledge would make people free *vis-à-vis* the government. This requires changes in the social system, participation in political rule, the liberation of economic initiatives, and the establishment of institutions. The regression in the role of people in society increases paranoia, rather than stimulating minds to think independently and freely. The cohesion between the homeland and the regime is a disaster. The sensitivity to any little criticism directed at Egypt is not helpful. Criticism should be listened to and encouraged. Expressions such as *conspirators and dogs who bark while the convoy moves on* do not help anyone. The political culture has become an idle-duality: greatness versus treason; nationalism versus normalization; fundamentalism versus globalization... these express the intelligence of a simple mind. Egypt is too great to be limited to such a simplistic duality. The Egyptian culture and history should give Egyptians confidence in a realistic initiative. The challenge proposed emphasizes the need that Egypt renews its role in the rationalization of the region in a more effective way. *Wake up Egypt. Indeed, wake up.*"

"Let me give you the four scariest words I can't pronounce in Arabic: Egypt after Mubarak. Mubarak's emergency rule dictatorship is deep into its third decade, making him one of Egypt's most durable pharaohs. His succession plan is clear: Son Gamal tries to replicate Beijing's model of economic reform, forestalling political reform..."

- Thomas P. M. Barnett
In his *Esquire* article titled: *The Country to Watch: Egypt*

PREFACE

FROM A GLORIOUS PAST TO AN UNCERTAIN FUTURE!

Throughout history, Egypt has held a special place in the hearts of many people. Given its unique location at the crossroads of Africa and Asia, Egypt has played an important role in human history.

It is no wonder then that many prophets tread the land of Egypt and received their messages on its land. Abraham, the Patriarch was said to have visited Egypt. Moses was born and raised in Egypt, defied the pharaoh and delivered the Israelites from his tyranny. Joseph and his brothers, Christ and his mother the Virgin Mary - all took refuge in Egypt. Egypt embraced Christianity early on and welcomed early Christian Saints.

The *Age of Martyrs* marked a defining era in the history of Christianity, as early Egyptian Christians defied the Roman persecution and went literally underground. To this date, many underground caves adorned with Christian icons and symbols are being discovered in Egypt, where early Christians hid from their Roman persecutors and worshipped.

Egyptian Christians, also known as Copts, helped the conquering Arabs in order to free themselves from the Romans, more than fourteen centuries ago. Egypt gradually became an Arab and Muslim state playing an important role in both the Arab and Muslim worlds.

Throughout the centuries, the Egyptians wrote their history as a great story of struggle against foreign invaders; the Hyksos, the Hittites, the Romans, the Greeks, the Mamlukes, the Turks, the British, and even against their own homegrown tyrants and pharaohs.

The whole world still watches with amazement the touring exhibitions of the treasures of King Tut, Queen Cleopatra and other Ancient Egyptian pharaohs. Egypt has been home to many wonders of the ancient world like the great pyramids of Giza, the Sphinx, and the old library of Alexandria and its lighthouse. Ancient Egyptian monuments and religious sites still drive millions of tourists every year to have a glimpse of the burial sites at the Valley of Kings in Luxor, the Aswan Philae temples, Saint Catherine Abbey on Mount Sinai and the hanging church of the Holy Family in Cairo.

Egyptologists and the faithful around the world regard Egypt as a fascinating, exotic, and a romantic place inspiring imagination and adventure. But to many Egyptians nowadays, the fascination and the love of their country is still there; except for the fact that their daily life has been a struggle just to make a living and get by from one day to another! *Why is this the case?* How could the people of one of the earliest civilization on earth become so trapped in a hopeless future and so consumed with their mere subsistence? What went wrong?

Many people consider that the Pharaonic era in Egyptian history had ended thousands of years ago. But to the Egyptians, the memories of their pharaohs are still fresh. The word pharaoh is still used in Egyptian daily language, Arabic, meaning tyranny, arrogance, haughtiness and unjust power. Throughout their history, Egyptians have learned how to live with their oppressors and pharaohs.

They developed a unique sense of humor coated with sarcasm and symbolic jokes. It has been their safety valve to vent their anger and frustration against their rulers who have been unjust and overbearing. Egyptians are known, especially through the Arab world, as tellers of jokes and people of great skill and resourcefulness. It is the outcome of mixing throughout the ages with people of many cultures. They are the most mixed amongst Arabs, most educated, and their Egyptian Arabic is the most understood of Arabic dialects.

Yet, Egyptians remain nowadays very pessimistic about the future of their country. The future seems to be very bleak and uncertain. Egypt has the highest rates of unemployment, young unmarried people, pollution, corruption, and the highest rate of educated people who see no light at the end of the tunnel. The Egyptian economy is in shambles with a very high rate of inflation and a great gap between the super-rich and the millions who live under the poverty line. Egypt also has one of the highest rates of child labor, infant mortality, female illiteracy, corruption and abuses of human rights.

The 81 years old President Mubarak of Egypt has been in power since 1981. He was elected for six more years in 2005, in one of the most controversial and rigged elections in Egypt in fifty years, following the military takeover in 1952. Concerns about Mubarak's health draw much greater attention to the question of who will next rule the nation of Egypt.

Rumor has it that he has been preparing his son Gamal Mubarak to be his successor or inheritor - in a country which is supposed to be a republic with elected officials! Mubarak vehemently denies these allegations. Unlike Sadat and Nasser, Mubarak has persistently refused to appoint a vice-president. Mubarak is the continuation of the military rulers who staged a military coup in July of 1952 toppling King Farouk.

Farouk was deposed and lived in exile in Italy until he was poisoned during his last meal in a restaurant where one member of the military junta which deposed him was working undercover on the same night as a waiter. He was Colonel Ibrahim Baghdady [Source: *Baghdady: How I Killed Farouk*, by Egyptian journalist Mahmoud Fawzi].

Since 1952, the military institution in Egypt has taken over every aspect of Egyptian life. Mubarak, a former commander of the Air Force during the Yom Kippur War came to power right after the assassination of late president Sadat. This occurred on October 6, 1981, the very day Sadat was celebrating a personal victory. Mubarak was then Sadat's Vice President. Sadat was assassinated by members of his army who considered him a *pharaoh, a tyrant and a sellout.* The assassins, who were religious fundamentalists, were enraged at Sadat for signing the Camp David treaty with Israel and starting his controversial economic open-door policy.

Mubarak was sitting next to Sadat when the later was assassinated while viewing the military parade in his *victory day* over Israel. Sadat was surrounded by his top brass, foreign diplomats and dignitaries. It was so ironic and tragic that the first Arab leader to sign a peace agreement with Israel was assassinated on the same day he was keen to celebrate as his so-called *military victory*, showing off his military troops and weapons. Ever since that day, Mubarak has been considered the luckiest man in Egypt, and a survivor.

The assassins were a group of military officers with a religious zeal, masterminded by a former military intelligence officer, Colonel Aboud el-Zumor. Their spiritual leader was none other than the infamous blind cleric, Sheikh Omar abdel-Rahman. After being acquitted in Egypt, abdel-Rahman headed to the United States to be arrested and charged with giving another *fatwa* (religious ruling) to the conspirators behind attempting to blow up the World Trade Center towers in New York, years later.

During the trial of the assassins of Sadat, the first defendant, Khalid al-Islambouli, boasted about killing the *Pharaoh* and fully admitted his guilt considering himself a martyr. He was to be sentenced by a military tribunal and later executed. El-Zumor was given a life sentence.

Sadat, Mubarak's predecessor, was also a survivor. By a similar amazing stroke of luck, he came to power after the death of late President Nasser who died of heart failure in 1970. Nasser was considered eternal; a larger than life figure and a true pharaoh.

During his funeral, more than two million wailing Egyptians took to the streets. With Nasser gone, they could not imagine where their nation was going. Sadat was appointed vice-president by Nasser shortly before the latter's death.

Sadat's regime began with rivalries by former *Free Officers* and members of the Revolutionary Council who thought Sadat was unfit and unworthy to rule Egypt, and conspired to overthrow him. Sadat the survivor, managed to outmaneuver them, round them up, and throw them in jail, instead.

Every year in May, Sadat celebrated, among the other things that he celebrated, his victory over his political rivals - what he called the *Corrective Revolution, to correct the course of the Mother Revolution.* Those conspirators believed that Sadat, a former Free Officer and member of the Revolutionary Council, was not trustworthy to carry the banner of Nasserism. They also considered him someone with a checkered past, dubious leanings and loyalties. In fact, Sadat did not make it a secret about his past. In his quasi-confessional tell-all autobiography, *In Search of Identity,* Sadat stated that he plotted the assassination of Amin Osman, a former finance minister during the monarchy whom Sadat considered as a traitor and a collaborator with the British. Osman was killed and Sadat arrested, stripped of his military rank, tried and jailed.

Sadat also admitted that he attempted to assassinate another political figure, Nahas Pasha, the former Egyptian Prime Minister and arch enemy of late King Farouk. Sadat was recruited in King Farouk's *Iron Guard* by Dr.Yussef Rashad, Farouk's physician.

During the World War II, Sadat played another subversive

role. He was a member of a Nazi German spying ring in Cairo, who operated from the houseboat of a famous belly dancer, Hekmat Fahmy. The goal of that ring, which was supplied with a large amount of counterfeit Sterling pounds, was to subvert the Allied Forces' efforts during the war. They were supplied with a wireless transmitting device by the S.S. to contact and aid an Egyptian military general called Aziz al-Masry. The whole ring was busted by the British military police and Sadat was again sent to jail. In an attempt to escape, al-Masry took off from Egypt in a military plane towards Libya to crash shortly after.

For that checkered past, Sadat was looked down upon with mistrust by some of the Free Officers. This is why he was met with hostilities and conspiracies in his early years as president of Egypt.

Sadat also inherited from Nasser the heavy burden of the devastating military defeat of 1967, known as the Six Days War. And the biggest challenge to his regime was what Sadat called the *Power Centers*, or what Nasser referred to, in his final days, as the *State of Intelligence.*

What Sadat referred to as *Power Centers*, was what Nasser woke up one day to discover after his military defeat in 1967. In an attempt to justify that humiliating defeat by Israel to the Arab armies, Nasser declared in his speeches that the country was being ruled by a *State of Intelligence.* What Nasser meant was that Egypt was being run by a group of high-powered individuals, which he himself handpicked, and who controlled and ran the country behind his back. These individuals were mainly former military officers who served in intelligence capacities and applied their military skills to running the state's affairs. One of them was Field Marshal Amer. Amer was in charge of the armed forces during the 1967 war, and had a power struggle and a show down with Nasser himself till his last days before committing suicide.

The same circle continued to operate in the same fashion even after the death of Nasser and considered Sadat to be an obstacle on their way to total control of the country. This prompted Sadat to initiate what he called the *Corrective Revolution* and purge those elements left from the Nasser's regime.

In his final years, Nasser came to the conclusion that he helped create a monster beyond control. He had appointed military officers and former military colleagues in almost every position in government. Military officers ran banks and became chairmen on boards of newly nationalized companies. They were chosen to confiscate the wealth of members of the former royal family and the super-rich class and the aristocracy during the monarchy. They did that with a vengeance. They even took to themselves some of the jewelry and properties of those deemed to be *enemies of the revolution*. They became the new arbiters of Egyptian society and the new bourgeoisie.

Military officers headed kangaroo courts and summary military tribunals, or what was known as the *People's Courts.* They also presided over the *Confiscation Committees* that targeted the thriving European communities in Egypt and the rich Muslim, Coptic and Jewish families that resulted in scaring them and to their ultimate flight off Egypt.

During Nasser's reign, and later continued by both Sadat

and Mubarak, the military assumed power and command over almost every facet of Egyptian life. They were ministers of education, information and national guidance, editors-in-chief of newspapers, military censors over the media, ministers of foreign affairs and diplomats, heads of the intelligence and the security apparatus, mayors and governors of cities and provinces, and ministers of the interior. The minster of the interior in Egypt has unmatched exceptional powers: he runs the internal security services, civil registry, the whole police departments, all law-enforcement agencies, and security across the country.

In addition, Nasser's solution to abolish the political parties that existed before his coup, introduced what he called the *Arab Socialist Union,* which was ceremoniously replaced by Sadat as the *National Democratic Party, NDP.* The *Arab Socialist Union* was a one-man-party that loosely consisted of spiderweb-like cells around the country. It was run mainly by former intelligence officers to report back and be able to mobilize and marshal the masses on demand. The *Socialist Union'* cells penetrated almost every street, factory, military unit, school and government in Egypt. The result was the eradication of the political life that existed before 1952.

Before 1952, political life in Egypt consisted of a myriad of parties like al-Wafd, al-Ikhwan (the Muslim Brothers), Misr al-Fatah, and a communist party. Eradicating these parties led to the concentration of power in the hands of the military institution, and especially the president's. Egypt has been run by a centralized government with exceptional powers in the hands of the leaders that followed, thereby reducing the masses to mere cheerleaders.

In his early days as president, Nasser embarked on a more damaging unprecedented practice by nationalizing all the media outlets - that enjoyed a considerable margin of freedom even during the British mandate. Following the military coup, all Egyptian media became owned and run by the state [even Sadat was once appointed by Nasser as an editor-in-chief of a newspaper]. At times, the media fell under the supervision and the administration of the Ministry of Information and the Ministry of Culture and National Guidance. Both ministries were headed by former military officers, a practice that made Egypt fit the profile of an Orwellian police state.

Except for few tabloids, Egyptian media to this day is still controlled and run by the state. The TV and Radio services are a part of the Ministry of Information. There is not a single independent or private TV or radio network in Egypt owned by individuals. The state assumes strict control over what the Egyptians see, hear, or read through several censoring agencies.

In spite of the fact that many Egyptians do have access to the internet and satellite TV broadcasts, their main source of news and information comes from the state-run media. Thus it makes it almost impossible for any political candidate, other than those handpicked by the regime, to reach his/her constituencies. The Egyptian state media has the upper hand promulgating and perpetuating the official government propaganda and even conspiracy theories. The result is that it has become a common practice to idolize the head of the state and praise his every decision or move.

Egyptian presidents have turned into bigger than life figures, demi-gods; a reminder of the ancient Egyptian practice of worshipping the God-Kings of Egypt, whose temples and pyramids were erected to immortalize their image. Today, in Egyptian cities, building-size murals and statutes of Mubarak are common sights everywhere.

But what is it about Egypt that makes it so important and special? Why do we have to worry, care about who rules Egypt, or who comes next? Let me give you the four scariest words I can't pronounce in Arabic: Egypt after Hosni Mubarak, says Thomas Barnett in his article in *Esquire* titled *The Country to Watch: Egypt*. "Mubarak's emergency rule dictatorship is deep into its third decade, making him one of Egypt's most durable pharaohs. His succession plan is clear: Son Gamal tries to replicate Beijing's model of economic reform, forestalling political reform", Barnett explains.

The problem? Another political force is connecting to the restive Egyptian people, and this force is the Muslim Brotherhood, known otherwise as *al-Qaeda 1.0.* By hardwiring themselves into the goodwill of the masses through highly effective social welfare nets, the Brotherhood is retracing the electoral pathway to power blazed by Hamas in Palestine and Hezbollah in Lebanon: hearts and minds first, blood and guts later.

It is now basically a race: Gamal's quest for foreign direct investment and the jobs it generates versus the Brotherhood's quest for the political support of average Egyptians tired of lives led in quiet desperation. *Who will win?* Using Thomas

Friedman's terminology, Barnett is betting another *olive tree fight* breaks out long before any Egyptian *Lexus* goes to market. Gamal's economic reforms are not working, but it's likely a case of too little too late. "If the Muslim Brotherhood were to achieve power in Egypt, Israel's demise would once again become the overt unifying principle for governments in the region. *The difference this time?* It still may be our blood, but it's mostly Asia's oil and gas now. You pit East versus West in a flat world, and you've just made Osama the fulcrum for a new cold war", Barnett warns.

Barnett goes on to explain: "*Sounds incredible*? It isn't, because the more likely scenario is that *Mubarak the Elder* dies before *Mubarak the Younger* can turn himself into Egypt's Deng Xiaoping, yielding a *Tiananmen Souk* that lights up the country pronto with the Brotherhood's prodding. And since these students will be hoisting pictures of Osama instead of a makeshift Goddess of Democracy, President Obama is likely to find himself facing an unbelievably bad choice in the largest Arab country. Would America intervene militarily to preserve Gamal's faltering rule, making good on all the strategic promises implied by the $50 billion in aid to Egyptian regimes since 1975? Or would we throw up our hands at that point, write Tel Aviv a blank check, and hope that this twenty-first-century Masada can hold out in a Middle East where Iran has the bomb?"

"Let me tell you something you don't want to hear: The smart money inside the Pentagon is betting any future president will choose to draw the next line in the sand at the Nile's banks rather than alongside Israel's security fences going up in Gaza and the

West Bank. And once we cross that rubicon into Africa...buddy, there ain't no turning back in this *Long War*. And success in the *Long War* (so named by the generals) will not be signaled by less violence but by a geographic shift in its center of gravity. Drive *al-Qaeda & Co.* out of the Middle East and it will be forced into its current strategic rear of choice—Africa. Africa is where *al-Qaeda* hides its money, guns, recruits, training camps—and its future. Africa will be the last great stand in this *Long War*, where all those impossibly straight borders once drawn by colonial masters will inevitably be made squiggly again by globalization's cultural reformatting process. Now this fight heads south...and yes, the *Long War* will be even uglier there", says Barnett.

If that scenario is not frightening enough, there are few others that are even scarier. A scenario where an ambitious general from the same military institution and with some popularity would stage another coup, which is common in Africa, the Arab World and Third World countries, turning Egypt into a *God-knows-what* regime. Would that general follow the steps of Sudanese generals and ally himself with the Muslim radical groups e.g. the Muslim Brothers, Gama'a Islamia, Hamas, Hizbollah, etc? Would Egypt witness another Khomeini-style revolution with the usual anti-American and anti-Semitic rhetoric? Taking into consideration the recent rise of Hamas in Palestinian territories and Muslim Brothers in Egypt, this is not a farfetched scenario.

Considering the alarming rising poverty figures in Egypt and the disparities between the classes, could Egypt be overrun by an angry and hungry mob, i.e. *French- revolution style*? Egypt would then erupt into lawlessness, chaos, or perhaps civil war, with the dissolving of the central government, its head figures and upper class already preparing for such a turn of events. Their money is secured in Western capitals. Rats do indeed leave a sinking ship.

Whatever the scenario would be, spillover from what could occur in Egypt in the near future would impact the sum of Arab, Muslim and Mid-Eastern nations. With America already engaged in an Iraqi quagmire, and another foot in Afghanistan, the Palestinian territories boiling with rage, Hezbollah backed by the Baathists in Damascus and the Mullahs in Tehran, who all agree on one thing: hatred for America and wiping the state of Israel off the map; the un-certaininty and anxiety grows among people of the region.

Just south of Egypt lies another unfriendly neighbor. Sudan's government with its generals, clerics, and fundamentalists, plus pirates taking over in Somalia, brings more bad news to policymakers in Western capitals. Stockholders in major global corporations, and the average citizens and consumers have to pay the price with every Middle East crisis.

Western capitals and observers in the region are keeping tabs on the situation in Egypt, fearing a domino effect in case of a trigger event occurring in Egypt. But none could give an answer to what would be the way out of that bottleneck? Inspired by their fatalism, Egyptians have developed an attitude of *coping with the situation,* leading to more apathy and a state of hopelessness waiting for a divine intervention. Their government continues to give promises of reform knowing that giving up absolute power and opening the door for free speech and elections would hasten its demise. The military institution in Egypt is on the guard and waiting to intervene. The banned Muslim Brothers movement has been gaining momentum amid its claim that *Islam is the solution*. Nevertheless, America continues to bet on Mubarak.

No one has offered a vision of hope for the Egyptians. The average Egyptian citizen finds himself/herself in a *we're-stuck* situation. This situation manifested itself in an angry, restless, anxious and irrational behavior that reflected on Egyptian society witnessing a high wave of violent crimes such as: rape, murder of spouses, a high rate of divorce, drug use, white collar crimes, road rage, embezzlement, military service desertion, domestic violence, and countless other crimes. This is why whatever unfolds on the Egyptian landscape will be a story of monumental proportions.

- Aladdin Elaasar, 2009
Chicago, USA.

"In recent years, visible signs of discord between the United States and Egypt over a wide array of issues appeared. Over the past few years, public disputes, disagreements, and divergences between the U.S. and Egypt have increased. Today, we have sadly reached the point where the foundation of bilateral relationship has eroded. Divergences are in a wide array of issues... from Egypt's role in the peace process, both bilateral and multi-lateral tracks, to the lack of warmth in Egypt's own relationship with Israel, to Egypt's relationship with terrorist supporting states on its borders."

- Dr. Robert Satloff, Executive Director of the Washington Institute for Near East Policy in his testimony before the Senate

INTRODUCTION

Nothing is more disturbing to political analysts, policymakers and stockowners in the U.S. and Western capitals than waking up one day to the breaking news coming from the Middle East that one of the long assumed allies have been toppled by a coup or a popular uprising of angry masses creating chaos, panic and uncertainty in international markets.

Average citizens and consumers worldwide have been paying the price for conflicts in the Middle East in terms of jacked up oil prices; consequently increasing the prices of gasoline, heat and energy bills and other commodities. Political stability means economic growth, less spending on military conflicts, more cash to social programs, happy voters, and hence high ratings for politicians. It is all one big picture, a cycle of connected events, inevitably and inextricably linked in our ever-shrinking *Global Village*. Given this equation, any near term trigger event in Egypt would garner at least the same global attention as any other Middle East regional conflict.

U.S. policymakers are still haunted by the memories of the overnight fall of the Shah of Iran to the Ayatollahs. The Shah, thought to be a strong U.S. ally lost his grip over power to the fanatical clergy, turning Iran from an open society into a closed door medieval ultra-zealous, nationalistic, anti-Semitic and anti-American society sabotaging every American effort for peace and stability in the region. America bet on the Shah with his lavish life- style, who turned brutal on his people in his final days. The Ayatollahs took this as an excuse to turn on America in return.

Similar scenarios took place in several parts of the world, namely in South East Asia in the Philippines and Indonesia. Two old military dictators considered strong U.S. allies fell to the angry and hungry mobs. The Marcos and the Suharto families oppressed their people, looted the national treasury, and established a highly corrupt and ruthless system, where only the elite benefited. Their end was inevitable. Anti-American sentiments were promoted by the regimes that followed these two dictators. In the case of the Philippines, America had to close one of its biggest bases in the world. In Indonesia, ethnic violence directed against Chinese and Christian minorities - thought to be the beneficiaries of Suharto's cronyism - erupted throughout the country. Killing, burning, looting and raping were carried out by angry mobs.

THE RIFT IN U.S. - EGYPTIAN RELATIONS

American-Egyptian relations strike a similar cord. After the state of Israel, Egypt is the second largest recipient of U.S. foreign aid. U.S. aid has been provided to Egypt since the signing of the Camp David Accords between Sadat, Begin and Carter. Over the past 10 years, the United States has provided $12.99 billion in military grants and $10.2 million in International Military Education and Training funds, an average of just over $1.3 billion per year. Some Members of Congress believe U.S. aid to Egypt ensures U.S. access to the region's oil reserves, trade opportunities, or military bases.

Congress members opposed to U.S. aid to Egypt often base their opposition on the belief that Egypt has failed to establish the close economic, political, and cultural relations with Israel expected after the 1979 peace treaty. Or *because they believe that the U.S. is financing the wrong kinds of projects.* (1)

In June 1997, a subcommittee of the Senate appropriations committee dropped the earmark for Egypt because in the subcommittee's judgment, Egypt was hindering the peace process and Egypt was improving its relations with Libya, thereby *encouraging the Libyan quest for chemical weapons and the Libyan programs to assist terrorists.* (2)

In March 2001, Members of Congress reportedly considered legislation to cut military assistance to Egypt. An amendment offered on July 15, 2004, to the FY2005 foreign operations bill (H.R. 4818) to reduce U.S. military aid to Egypt by $570 million. From 1993 through 1998, Egypt received from the United States $815 million in Economic Support Funds (ESF) annually, $200 million of which was designated for the Commodity Import Program, and an equal amount was direct transfer not associated with any specific program. In the past, Egypt also received food aid. Economic aid has dropped in annual $40 million increments from $815 million in FY1998 to $535 million requested for FY2005.

This was not the first time that Congress considered legislation to cut assistance to Egypt. On Thursday, April 10, 1997 the Mubarak government was *on its nerves* - as the Egyptian saying goes - panicky and desperate. The cause of panic and nervousness was due to the recent rift in the relations between the U.S. and Egypt. The U.S. government has had its doubts about the stability and the future of the Mubarak regime.

On that very same Thursday, the U.S. House of Representatives decided to hold a hearing about the Mubarak regime recommending a decrease in the U.S. foreign aid to his government. That explained the frantic efforts and nervousness of Mubarak's government to maintain the American political support it did enjoy for several years.

The committee on International Relations in the U.S. House of Representatives met that morning at 10.04 a.m., presided by Congressman Benjamin Gilman as Chairman. Chairman Gilman stated the purpose of that hearing as "to take stock of one of our more important bilateral relationships, if not the most important, that between the United States and Egypt, and to assess the current status of American-Egyptian cooperation, where it stands, and where we should like to see it go. Since the 1970's, our relations with Egypt have been a key element in the American policy in the Middle East. The United States and Egypt appear to be moving further apart on a range of critical issues. The latest example of discord occurred most recently when, under Egyptian leadership, the Arab League recommended that its member states ceased normalizing relations with Israel and restore the old economic boycott. Egypt's leadership role in that vote puzzles and dismays many of its friends in the United States. Both Egypt and the Arab League appear to have taken an unfortunate step backward with the failed politics of confrontation with Israel," Chairman Gilman explained.

"But the Arab League vote is only the latest in a series of other moves by Egypt in recent years, which indicated a pattern in its foreign relations that has been distressing. For example, Egypt has repeatedly called for easing sanctions against Libya and has refused to support even a mild anti-terrorism resolution against Sudan. Egypt has opposed U.S. initiatives to compel Iraqi compliance with UN resolutions and advocated the re-integration of Iraq into the Arab fold. Egypt has also derailed regional arms reduction talks by insisting on discussing Israel's purported nuclear arsenal, a move that has prevented progress on the more urgent issue of conventional arms in the region. Egypt has abdicated its role for peace, and is gradually adopting a more hostile posture towards Israel. Egypt's friends are puzzled by the prevalence of a number of anti-Semitic themes in the Egyptian press and in academia!" Chairman Gilman added.

Then came into the scene in that heated morning session, Dr. Robert Satloff, the Executive Director of the Washington Institute for Near East policy. Mr. Satloff was introduced as a distinguished expert on Arab and Islamic politics and on U.S. policy in the Middle East. Mr. Satloff began his testimony by stating that: "In recent years, as visible signs of discord between the United States and Egypt over a wide array of issues have appeared. Over the past few years, public disputes, disagreements, and divergences between the U.S. and Egypt have increased. Today, we have sadly reached the point where the foundation of bilateral relationship has eroded. Divergences are in a wide array of issues... from

Egypt's role in the peace process, both bilateral and multi-lateral tracks, to the lack of warmth in Egypt's own relationship with Israel, to Egypt's relationship with terrorist supporting states on its borders". Satloff explained.

"I think there are a number of pieces of evidence that support this contention... I will just list a few briefly. Egypt relationship with Israel, having turned from what was characterized as cold peace in the 1970's and the 1980's to what I think is cold war today. I was saddened that in a recent issue of the *Jerusalem Post*, President Mubarak in a cover story interview was asked about cold peace and replied, *believe me, it will stay cold for a very long time to come.* In this context, it is imperative that Egypt's leaders cease making public statements or taking action, such as military maneuvers, which characterizes Israel as a threat to Egyptian national security." Satloff continued.

"The U.S.-Egyptian relation is broken and it needs fixing.... Given the great strides Egypt has taken, now is the time for us to reshape the $815 million economic assistance package, to bolster reform, cut back the aid bureaucracy, and places the economic relationship on a healthier footing. President Mubarak understands this and has admitted so in public." Satloff ended his testimony.

Then the Chairman called upon the next expert witness, Joseph Stork. Mr. Stork is the Advocacy Director of Human Rights watch, an independent human rights watch based in New York and in Washingtonand former Chief Editor of the *Middle East Report* in Washington.

Mr. Stork started his testimony by stating: "U.S. policymakers have long viewed Egypt as a key military and political ally. The status however, in our view, has far too long exempted the Egyptian government from the kind of human rights scrutiny and criticism warranted by the serious and recurrent nature of human rights abuses there. Although U.S. officials have assured us human rights concerns are raised privately by embassy officials in Cairo, we see no signs that it is at this level in this fashion producing results".

"One State Department official recently acknowledged to me, for instance, that when President Mubarak visited Washington in 1996, staffers at the Bureau of Democracy, Rights and Labor were essentially told by the White House not to bother forwarding the briefings they prepared because the subject of human rights would not be raised in his meetings with President Mubarak. As far as we know, the only U.S. rebuke to Egypt's human rights record is the chapter in the annual State Department Country Reports, and that appears to have no policy consequences. There is no evidence, furthermore that the Clinton administration has used the leverage provided by the annual $2.1 billion aid package to insist for instance, the Mubarak government lift the state of emergency under which it has ruled since 1981, or that Egypt takes specific steps to approve other aspects of its human rights record. And by urging the government of Egypt to increase the space for non-violent political association, to end the impunity of the security forces and to implement legislative reforms that would encourage broader participation in the political process, the United States can contribute to a more durable stability in Egypt, one of which pluralism and respect for the law would help to marginalize militant extremism." Stork added.

"Under the Emergency Law, the government has the power to restrict freedom of assembly and conduct searches and detain subjects without following the criminal procedure code, to censor publications, and to try accused persons, even those not accused of committing or advocating acts of violence before security courts. The need for a speedy trial, however, does not permit a government to circumvent internationally guaranteed rights, including the right to a fair trial and the right to appeal a conviction to a higher tribunal, especially when conviction can mean a death sentence." Stork further explained.

The concerns in the U.S. over the hostility and instability of the Mubarak's government have increased intensely especially after the tragic events of 9/11. U.S. policymakers have been reviewing traditional stands about old allies and their effectiveness. American public opinion has been infuriated knowing that 19 of the hijackers were Arab and Muslim young men mainly from Saudi Arabia with their leader, Mohammad Atta, who was Egyptian. All of these hijackers came from countries thought to be strong U.S. allies. To make things worse, the response that came from the Arab media, especially in Egypt, added insult to injury. Arab state media, especially in Egypt, did not try to at least send direct apology to the American people already hurt by these tragic events. On the contrary, Egyptian state media teemed with bizarre conspiracy theories that were spread through the Arab and Muslim worlds and found some audience that believed in them. Some of these conspiracy theories claimed that "the Israeli Mossad and CIA were behind 9/11".

The topic of anti-American incitement coming from the Egyptian state media has been brought to the attention of the American public. The Egyptian newspaper, *al-Ahram Weekly*, received hundreds of emails from Americans responding to those flagrant conspiracy theories regarding the tragic events 9/11. One American reader wrote: "Whatever policies we followed with regard to Israel, bin- Laden would still have wished to engage in the mass murder of Jewish and Christian civilians ... The U.S. could increase foreign aid a hundred times over and he would still seek our blood... He wants the restoration of the universal caliphate, the recovery of all lands ever ruled by Muslims, and the mass murder of those who stand in the way of this restoration – including women and children..."(3)

Another American reader wrote: "If Americans knew more about the response of the Arab and Islamic worlds to the acts of terror against the U.S., they would be vastly more upset... If they read your newspaper, they would be furious... Americans have no idea that the leading theory among Egyptians is that Jews did it and that tens, perhaps hundreds, of millions of Muslims believe this grotesque lie. Americans have no idea that one of your frequent columnists alleges that U.S. security services crashed the planes into the buildings... Your columnists rant about purported anti-Arab columnists in the U.S., but their vituperation and lack of concern for the facts vastly exceeds U.S. columnists..."(4)

Lt. Col. Michael Kaiser, SYNCOMPAC, Operation Enduring Freedom, wrote: "I was immediately reminded that I have always respected the honest and forthright, even if I disagree with them, and find despicable the too slick, the propagandist, the hypocrite, and the liar masquerading as a wise one. Even the *Jihad, American is Satan crowd* are at least honest in their presentation. Your produced-in-Egypt English-language paper is a pseudo-intellectual pretense, trying to imitate a journal of free thought. Your contributors are well written, in the technical sense, but only your probably unsophisticated readers are fooled by your presentation…"

Sara Welsh of Los Angeles wrote: "It came as a shock to many of us in the U.S. to see Egypt's weak response in regard to the WTC attack. After talking to several people I know in diplomatic circles I was told that it was typical – you take what you can get from us ($2.2 billion a year) and have neither the courage nor the ethics to show friendship at a time when we are facing one of the biggest crises in our history."

In its September 20-26 edition, *Al-Ahram Weekly* published a letter by Tom Knox of Tallahassee, Florida, who wrote, "Several things become very evident. There is very little tolerance in your society… No wonder so many of us here in the States feel that we are talking to people still living in the 11th century!"

The American reader added, "I noticed with a wry disdain that many Arab countries do not treat dissidents with the open arms of inclusiveness. Indeed, they are rather brutal in their intolerance of dissent and punishment of dissenters. Isn't that interesting? Yet the U.S. is castigated for *rushing to judgment* and *lack of caution*. You make me laugh… If it is truly believed that terrorism is wrong, why then the leaders of Islam haven't not demanded that the acts cease and that the perpetrators be dealt with? They did not. America will. Your readers can join us, stand aside, or be part of the problem we will deal with. It's all about choices." (5)

Another angry reader expressed her disappointment towards the Mubarak government's attitude and its reaction towards the tragic events of September 11, 2001, she wrote: "Dictatorship – interesting concept of government... Oh yeah, that's the kind of government you have in Egypt – a dictatorship with one third of the population illiterate and getting a $2.2 billion a year handout from the U.S.A. Do your readers know that? Even before September 11, the majority of the food aid for Afghanistan came from the U.S.A. The bags of wheat in those Red Cross warehouses all say U.S.A. on them. I swear I did not see even one that said Egypt... I don't care that your country hates us, but I do care that we give money to people that hate us. There is a movement now to stop such foolishness. I am writing my congressmen and senators tonight and providing links to your articles as I have already done with Fox News Network." The reader added (6)

On April 6, 2006, the U.S. Department of State's International Information Programs in Washington D.C., the Public Affairs Office at the U.S. Embassy in Israel, and the Global Research in International Affairs (GLORIA) Center jointly held an international videoconference seminar focusing on the current political and economic state of Egypt, the regime and opposition, and Egyptian foreign policy.

Ambassador Edward S. Walker, Jr., who has served as President and Chief Executive Officer of the Middle East Institute since 2001, following a distinguished diplomatic career which included Assistant Secretary of State for Near Eastern Affairs (1999-2001), and Ambassador to Egypt (1994-97), criticized "the duality of

Egyptian policy written broadly, which can be called having its cake and eating it too. Egypt has a generally good relationship with the United States and gets benefits from that relationship. But at the same time it plays to its domestic audience through the media, officially sponsored clerics, and the educational system. The regime blames all its shortcomings on imperialism, Zionism, the West, and the United States and uses that to build domestic support. Egyptian textbooks still claim that the American Air Force attacked Egypt in 1967. Egypt plays this game very well. They really get away with it with virtually no cost in terms of U.S. or Western relations and to a large extent their audience still accepts it. It is a brilliant, well-handled maneuver. But in practical terms, therefore in policy in the Middle East is just not very important, it is not going to have a big impact."

Dr. Elad-Altman, Director of Studies at the Institute for Policy and Strategy, also raised concerns about the future of American-Egyptian relations by stating: "One aspect of foreign policy is public diplomacy, mainly how you try to influence populations. The American ambassador travels around Egypt giving money to open up small businesses, and America invests a lot in the Egyptian economy, but what the grassroots get about America is not what the ambassador says to the governor of the province, but what they get in the meetings and writings of the Muslim Brotherhood and their like. This is what is going to mold Egyptian public opinion for the coming generation. If you follow the Muslim Brotherhood's attitude towards the United States and what it stands for, it is clear that the Muslim Brotherhood tries to be a leading anti-American, anti-globalization Third-World movement worldwide, not only in the Muslim and Arab world. They are opposed to *the American project*, claiming America is trying to dominate the Muslim world and the entire world, and they claim to seek to stop it".

In her last visit to Egypt, Secretary Condoleezza Rice at the American University in Cairo June 20, 2005, demanded that "the Egyptian Government must fulfill the promise it has made to its people and to the entire world by giving its citizens the freedom to choose. Egypt's elections, including the Parliamentary elections, must meet objective standards that define every free election".

The anger, the miscommunication and the anxiety about the future of American-Egyptian relations continue. The relation seems to heading into an unknown territory, a dark tunnel that hardly anyone on both sides has presented a clear understanding or a vision to as where it should go!

"Years of declining funding for public diplomacy and the marginalization of public diplomacy specialists at the U.S. State Department have hampered American outreach efforts in the Middle East", said AMIDEAST President William Rugh in a presentation at the Georgetown University 2003 symposium titled the *U.S. in the Middle East.*

Ambassador Rugh feels strongly about the need to explain American foreign policy to the region's public. Any effective public diplomacy campaign requires that U.S. Foreign policy be addressed and explained in an honest and open manner, no matter how unpopular that policy may be.

The U.S. Government, said Ambassador Rugh, should also increase its monitoring and analysis of foreign opinion.

Public policy specialists, he argued, need to be organized into their own autonomous department. These public diplomacy specialists should be charged with designing statements issued by government officials on foreign policy matters. Cultural exchange should be increased, as should overseas broadcasting by U.S. Government media agencies like the *Voice of America.* Most important, said Ambassador Rugh, *effective public diplomacy requires good use of empathy and listening.*

"In order to help to maintain their charismatic authority, such regimes will often establish a vast personality cult, which can be seen as an attempt to gain legitimacy by an appeal to other forms of authority. When the leader of such a state dies or leaves office and a new charismatic leader does not appear; such a regime is likely to fall shortly thereafter unless it has become fully reutilized. Charismatic authority is resting on devotion to the exceptional sanctity, heroism or exemplary character of an individual person, and of the normative patterns or order revealed or ordained by him."

- Sociologist Max Weber

"Listen kid...Whoever rules Egypt, has to be a Pharaoh. God, in order to bring the Pharaoh down, sent two prophets to him; Moses and Aaron. The age of prophets ended, but the age of Pharaohs has not."

- Sadat

As told to and narrated by Abdul-Moneim Umara,
former Governor of Ismailia province to Mona Makram Ebeid
Al-Majalla, December 2006.

PART ONE:

THE LEGACY OF THE PHARAOH CONTINUES

1. From Nasser to Mubarak; A One-Man Show

President Mubarak's regime has been described as an authoritarian, autocratic, and a neo-sultanistic. It is an equivalent to what the Egyptians have been using for millennia to describe their rulers, especially in the last fifty years, as Pharaohs. A neo-sultanistic regime is a form of personal rule. The system's underlying structure is that "loyalty to the ruler is motivated not by his embodying or articulating an ideology, nor by a unique personal mission, nor by any charismatic qualities, but by a mixture of fear and rewards to his collaborators. In other words the ruler exercises his power without restraint, at his own discretion...Unencumbered by rules and without any commitment to ideology or a value system". (1)

THE "TWO LAST GREAT PHARAOHS OF EGYPT"!

No Egyptian president since the 1952 could resist the allure of connecting to Egypt's Pharaonic past. Mubarak and his predecessors, Sadat and Nasser, have referred to themselves as the only native pharaohs in modern Egyptian history. They held a fascination with one pharaoh in particular, Ramses II.

In August 2006 Mubarak's government spent millions on restoring and relocating the colossal statute of Ramses II from its place at *Ramses' Square* in Cairo since 1955 to a more suitable spot in Egypt's new museum. Egyptian presidents' special fascination with Ramses II fits perfectly in their nationalistic policies and the image that they tried to build after Ramses II.

Ramses II was an Egyptian pharaoh of the Nineteenth Dynasty who was born ca. 1302 BC. At age fourteen, Ramses II was appointed Prince Regent.

Ramses II is believed to have taken the throne in his early 20s and to have ruled Egypt from 1279 BC to 1213, for a total of 66 years and said to have lived to be 99 years old. He attained many titles such as *Powerful one of Ma'at*, the *Justice of Ra the Powerful, Chosen of Ra, Ra bore Him*, and *Beloved of Amun*. Ramses is said to have had fathered around 100 children; 48-50 sons and 40-53 daughters, some of them from his beautiful wife, Queen Nefertari. Merneptah, Ramses' first born son, would eventually succeed him (Similar to Gamal Mubarak's succession plan).

To establish his credentials as a successful warrior like his predecessors, Ramses II decided to attack territory in the Levant which belonged to a more substantial enemy: the Hittite Empire. At the Battle of Kadesh in May 1274 BC, towards the end of the Fourth year of his reign, Egyptian forces under his leadership marched through the coastal road through Canaan (nowadays Israel) and south Syria through the Bekaa Valley and approached Kadesh from the south. Ramses planned to seize the citadel of Kadesh which belonged to king Muwatallis of the Hittite Empire.

The battle almost turned into a disaster. Ramses had fallen into a well-laid trap by Muwatallis whose thousands of infantry and chariotry were hidden well behind the eastern bank of the Orontes River (Jordan River) under the command of the king's brother, Hattusili III. The Egyptian army itself had been divided into two main forces – the Re and Amun brigades with Ramses and the Ptah and Seth brigades – separated from each other by forests and the far side of the Orontes River. The Re brigade was almost totally destroyed by the surprise initial Hittite chariot attack effectively winning the war. Ramses was compelled to retreat south with the Hittite commander Hattusili III relentlessly harrying the Egyptian forces through the Bekaa Valley; the Egyptian province of Upi was also captured (Nasser's defeat at the Six Day War).

In the twenty-first year of his reign (1258 BC), Ramses decided to conclude an agreement with the new Hittite king at Kadesh, Hattusili III, to end the conflict. He signed the earliest known peace treaty in world history (Sadat's Camp David treaty).

In spite of his defeat, upon his arrival in Egypt, Ramses gave a different account of the battle of Kadesh. He turned his humiliating defeat into a glorious victory. He was depicted on the walls of his temples as single-handedly smiting, decimating and decapitating the Hittites. He was the first spin doctor in history. Hittites archives revealed that *a humiliated Ramses was forced to retreat from Kadesh in ignominious defeat* and abandoned the border provinces of Amurru and Upi to the control of his Hittite rival without the benefit of a formal truce. (2)

By contrast, in Ramses II's version of events, the Pharaoh fictitiously states just a day after his narrow escape from death in battle that *the cowardly Hittite king sent a letter to the Egyptian camp pleading for peace*. Ramses, still claiming an Egyptian victory refused to sign a formal treaty. Ramses returned home to enjoy his personal triumph, which was to be retold many times as an epic poem. (3)

Nasser, Sadat, and Mubarak, later followed suit. Disastrous military adventures were turned into epic sagas only comparable to Homer's Odyssey and the Lliad. In 1986, Mubarak gave orders to an elite group of Special Forces to storm the *Egypt Air* hijacked plane by Palestinian terrorists risking the lives of Egyptian passengers and crew members. The result was the massacre of more than a hundred people on board. Egyptian state media turned it into a heroic deed and a wise decision on part of Mubarak.

Ramses II was identified as the pharaoh from whom Moses demanded his people be released from slavery. Ramses II is believed not to have drowned in the Sea and the biblical account makes no specific claim that the pharaoh was with his army when they were swept into the sea. Jewish records indicate that Pharaoh was the only Egyptian to survive the Red Sea, and later became the King of Nineveh (Assyria) in the Book of Jonah. (4)

The Bible states that the Israelites toiled in slavery and built for the Pharaoh's supply cities, Pithom in the Egyptian Delta. (5)

The latter is probably a reference to the city of Pi-Ramesse.(6) Ramses II greatly enlarged this city both as his principal northern capital and as an important forward base for his military campaigns into the Levant and his control over Canaan (modern day Israel).

Egyptologist Kenneth Kitchen believes that Pi-Ramess was largely abandoned from 1130 BC onwards. (7) Therefore, Ramses II could have been the Pharaoh who reigned Egypt during the time of Moses. His son and successor Merneptah mentioned in the Merneptah Stele that the Ancient Israelites already lived in Canaan during his reign. Ramses boasted about the utter destruction of the Israelites.

Ramses II constructed many impressive monuments, including the renowned archeological complex of Abu- Simbel, and the mortuary temple known as the Ramesseum. He was buried in the Valley of the Kings, Luxor where his mummy was found in 1881 at Deir el-Bahri.

No other Egyptian pharaoh had ever had that number of statutes and temples built for him; a tradition that was kept by the three presidents that came after 1952 claiming to be the only natives to rule Egypt after centuries of foreign domination. Nasser, Sadat ad Mubarak had almost every public project, building, park, street, named after them, in addition to a countless number of statutes, building-size murals and posters displayed everywhere in Egypt.

THE PERSONALITY CULT

Ramses II had stretched the personality cult culture that existed in Ancient Egypt to an unprecedented sphere. Egyptians were used to having a mighty God-King, who was not only obeyed, but worshipped as well. Questioning the decisions and demands of that king (or sometimes queen) was deemed sacrilegious, literally.

This practice was predominant in the Ancient World and even in Medieval Europe. Through the principle of the *Divine Right of Kings*, rulers held office by the *Will of God*. Imperial China, Ancient Egypt, the Incas, the Aztecs and the Roman Empire elevated monarchs to the status of god-kings. Foreign Greek, Romans and Muslim rulers, mindful of that notion, were keen to give the Egyptians the holy status expected of a ruler. Whether practicing Moslems or astute secularists, Muslim Sultans, Caliphs, and Kings who ruled Egypt meticulously presented their public image and persona as *god-fearing servants-of-Allah*. State and Church have never been separated in Egyptian politics.

Recent Egyptian presidents were mindful of that practice. In addition to their personal admiration of Ramses II, Nasser, Sadat and Mubarak exerted keen efforts to build their public images upon the model of Ramses II. In its modern history, Egypt has witnessed the making and breaking of similar political cults. Egyptians were introduced to the Nasser's cult that was challenged by his humiliating military defeat in 1967. Then came Sadat who started building his own cult on the ruins of Nasser's allowing public criticism of the Nasser's era for the first time.

After Sadat's assassination, Egyptians started to hear about the corruption in the Sadat's era. Mubarak's cult was being built upon the same principle of charismatic rule of his successors. "In order to help to maintain their charismatic authority, such regimes will often establish a vast personality cult, which can be seen as an attempt to gain legitimacy by an appeal to other forms of authority. When the leader of such a state dies or leaves office and a new charismatic leader does not appear, such a regime is likely to fall shortly thereafter unless it has become fully routinized," as defined by sociologist Max Weber.

Weber defined charismatic authority as "resting on devotion to the exceptional sanctity, heroism or exemplary character of an individual person, and of the normative patterns or order revealed or ordained by him."

Nasser, Sadat and Mubarak became un-accountable to any authorities. They created a cult-of-personality, striving for a position of authority free from oversight. For more than half a century, Egyptian society has been transformed from a multi-party system to a monolithic regime where all the power is concentrated in the hands of one person, the president. The Mubarak regime that started in 1981 has not been an invention of his, but rather a continuation of the legacy of his two predecessors, Nasser and Sadat, and the dynamic of regional politics.

The image of the Pharaoh has consistently haunted Egyptians and their rulers to come. As the late president Sadat liked to portray himself as another pharaoh, he once said: "*Nasser and I are the two Last Great Pharaohs of Egypt*". (8)

"To look on himself simply as a successor to Nasser- his real predecessor was Ramses II. His manner certainly began to be increasingly autocratic, even Pharaonic", columnist Heikal described Sadat in his book *The Autumn of Fury.* Sadat once said to Heikal, who was a close confidant to him and a speech writer of Nasser's and held few ministerial cabinet positions: "Nasser and I always wanted the same things. The difference is that he tried to get them through dictatorship; I try to get them by democratic methods" (9)

Heikal was to be thrown in jail later by Sadat along with many other journalists, Muslim and Christian religious leaders, and university professors and students. It was estimated that Sadat ordered the rounding up and arrest of about 15,000 dissidents who remained in jail till after his assassination in October 6, 1981. Before Sadat's rounding up of opponents to his policies, the Nasser's regime made Sadat's look like a democratic one, indeed.

Author David Price-Jones describes the Nasser era as follows: "Nasser's opponents were cast into Nasser's Gulag, only a secondhand replica of the Soviet original application of mass terror in the Arab World. Tura and Abu-Za'abal, the Cairo Citadel, Dakhla Oasis in the Western Desert, Khargah Oasis [concentration camps], where prisoners and camps were spoken of with horror".

The conditions of these concentration camps were described by Swiss journalist Hans Tutsch as "the shocking tortures inflicted on the prisoners surpassing everything yet seen in the Middle East". (10)

Fear has been an effective tool used as needed by the consecutive regimes that ruled Egypt since 1952. It has been deemed as a *necessary evil* to silence political opponents and keep the rest of population in line, and maintain the unchallenged grasp of power by the regime.

The fear factor has also been proven convenient to the three last rulers of Egypt; fear of the outside enemy, in this case, the *Zionists and their backers, the Imperialist Americans.* Since the establishment of the state of Israel in 1948, no regional conflict has gained such reference into Arab politics more than the *Palestinian Cause.* The Palestinian cause has been excessively exploited and politicized by Arab leaders over the years.

No Arab government has resisted the allure of middling with the Palestinian issue since 1948. It had occupied headline news around Arab capitals and Arab League summit conferences ever since. It has proved to be a convenient and a highly emotional cause to marshal and mobilize Arab masses behind a military or an autocratic regime with a free hand at the financial resources of a country.

The result has been the concentration of power in the hands of few military officers in Egypt and in other parts of the Arab world, and the skyrocketing of military expenditure. It resulted into the delay of many development plans throughout the Middle East, as explained by Amin Houaidy. (11)

Houaidy held many high ranking positions in the Egyptian government, but unlike many of his colleagues and ex-servicemen, he decided to speak out. Houaidy was a military officer who rose to the rank of Minister of Defense, a National Security Advisor to Nasser, Minister of Information and National Guidance, Director of the General Intelligence Agency, and Ambassador to Morocco and Iraq.

In his book *Militarization and Security in the Middle East: Its Impact on Development and Democracy*, Houaidy appealed to Mubarak since the mid-eighties to rationalize military expenditure, but with no avail.

Egypt spends about 10 billion dollars annually on defense and security while the basic services of the citizens are hardly met. Arab countries have spent hundreds of billions in the last decades on defense and security. The state of war does benefit authoritarian regimes by drawing attention to the outside enemy. This gives the regimes a free hand in dealing with arms deals (thought to be the best and quickest way to negotiators of military contracts to pocket lucrative commissions that can reach up to 40% of the deal).

The state of war gives the ruler an absolute power deeming opponents *un-patriotic*. Militarism has been in full gear in Egypt since 1952. The *Free Officers* adopted a militaristic view that discipline is the highest social priority, and claimed that the development and maintenance of the military ensures that discipline. They expanded military culture to areas outside of the military structure; most notably in areas of private business, government policy, education, and entertainment. The result was the spread of a mixture of many slogans such as extremism, loyalism, and warmongering.

Therefore, it was not surprising to hear the late president Sadat to declare before his last war with Israel that *no voice should be heard over the sound of battle.* With that said; Sadat guaranteed to silence the voices of any opposition to his policies as he was preparing for his *historically dictated final battle with the Israelis.* Any voice of dissent was considered not as an opposition to Sadat's policies, but was an *act of treason to Egyptian and Arab causes in a critical moment of the nation's history.* In that sense, Sadat represented his image as a full-fledged pharaoh, an embodiment of Egypt. Egypt was Sadat and Sadat was Egypt! He accepted nothing less.

Moreover, with that logic, Sadat expected a status bigger than a ruler of Egypt. Sadat's media depicted him as the *Arab warrior against the Jews who usurped Palestinian and Arab land with Muslim holy places, the hero of war and peace.* Sadat also expected and solicited unlimited support from other fellow Arab and Muslim nations for his war effort. He instigated the *Arab Oil Embargo* prior to his Yom Kippur War in October 1973. This also explains Sadat's fascination with Ramses II, who fought the Israelites at the time of Moses.

The politics of demonizing and dehumanizing the Israelis and the Jews have been prevalent in the Arab world since the inception of the state of Israel to the present day. Arab state controlled media, from Egypt and throughout the Arab world, are teeming with anti-Semitic images that wholly reminiscent of Nazi Germany. The images have been perpetuated and given a green light by most Arab governments to deflect public attention from the other nagging domestic issues and to unify the public against a common enemy. "*As a result…an intense Arab ethno-nationalism, along with tremendous hostility against Israelis, Jews …exists throughout the region*", says Professor Bernard Lewis. (12)

Arab Nationalist politics and pan-Arabism have occupied center stage in Egypt and in the rest of the Arab world. On his death, Nasser was lamented as *the hero of the Arab nation and the father of pan-Arabism.* Pan-Arabism has failed to bring the Arabs together, nor to unify them. On the contrary, it caused many rifts, conflicts, internal Arab wars and the deterioration of relations amongst Arabs.

Arabs are not the homogeneous group of people as some might think. Arabs are not all Muslims, and Muslims are not all Arabs. Most Arabs nowadays would laugh at the idea of Arabism and they have grown weary toward the politicization of the Palestinian issue that most Arab governments have tried to make them believe was the core of Arab issues.

Mubarak's government still tries to draw and build its legitimacy on being an active player and mediator in the negotiations between the Palestinians and the Israelis. A typical example of a career politician and diplomat in Mubarak's regime, who echoes the old tones of Arab nationalism and the exploitation of the Palestinian cause for popularity, is former Minister of Foreign Affairs, Amr Mousa.

Mousa was appointed minister for foreign affairs in May 1991, on a personal recommendation of Osama el-Baz, Senior Political Advisor to President Mubarak. Mousa gained popularity in Egypt, the Arab media and in the so-called *Arab street* due to his controversial views in regard to the Palestinian-Israeli conflict.

His popularity peaked in 2000 when rapper Shaaban Abdel-Rahim released a highly popular song titled: *I hate Israel and I love Amr Mousa.* (13) Fearful of Mousa's rising popularity, Mubarak relieved Mousa of his post in March 2001. Mousa later became the head of the Arab League.

How to remain a Pharaoh? Lessons Learned

President Mubarak, a survivor of the assassination attempt on Sadat and other assassination attempts, learned the lessons very well. The hard learned lessons from his predecessors are; for starters, *never ever trust your generals.* Since the days of Nasser, it seemed that Egypt has embarked on a popularity contest, so fierce that there is no second place for contestants. There is only one place; first place, which is reserved for the president, and the president only. The pharaohs of Egypt contested among themselves for images; who would get the biggest, more tantalizing and everlasting memory? The proof of that theory lies in the Giza Plateau where the three great pyramids and the Sphinx are.

It all started with the Saqqara step-pyramid built for King Zoser as a burial place where he would ascend to heaven after his demise. Thus began the competition. A bigger, then another even larger pyramid was ordered, until the competition reached the top of the Chephos pyramid.

The pharaohs not only competed to build bigger images, but as soon as the late pharaoh's body was put to rest, his name would be effaced from temples and monuments, his tomb looted and body dismembered and spread around the country, in order for that pharaoh never to come back again, even as a spirit.

The practice has continued to modern day Egypt. Huge monuments have been ordered to be built in the name of Mubarak, Sadat and Nasser. Every new project has to be dedicated and inaugurated by the president. The cliché goes like this; *based upon the directions and guidance of his Excellency President Mubarak, this project has been his gift of love to his people.* The President has to claim credit for every major and minor project done in his era. The president's photo is a fixture on major newspapers, magazine, and daily TV news across the country.

Even senior ministers and prime-ministers in several governments appointed by Mubarak, Sadat and Nasser, would not dare take credit for themselves for projects done by their ministries. The same above cliché has to be repeated, or otherwise, it would be doomed almost-sacrilegious, or at least an act of disloyalty that would result in serious consequences.

The first lesson that Mubarak learned as *never ever trust your generals*, proved to be true over and over again. As a continuation of the rule of the jumta of the 1952 coup, Mubarak does not distinguish between what belongs to Caesar and what belongs to the Pharaoh. In his case, there's not a clear distinction between the pharaoh and Caesar, or Egypt and himself. He is the Supreme Commander of the Armed Forces and no other general should even aspire to compete with him. He must always remain at the top of Egypt!

Mubarak has seen internal military conflicts turn ugly since 1952. Although Mubarak was not a member of the original military junta, yet he celebrates the coup anniversary every year.

The coup has produced many ambitious young officers who see in themselves the qualifications to be another Nasser. After the military defeat of the Arab armies of Egypt, Syria and Jordan by the Israeli military that led to the loss of the Golan Height, Gaza Strip, the West Bank and the Sinai Peninsula, Egypt witnessed a melodramatic conflict between President Nasser and Marshal Amer.

Amer was to blame for the military defeat of 1967. He was Nasser's former colleague at the military academy. Nasser and Amer plotted the military coup together along with others. They also came from the same province in Upper Egypt and their families inter-married.

Yet, Nasser became threatened by Amer's popularity within the Egyptian armed forces and a showdown after the 1976 defeat culminated into Amer's controversial suicide and surrounding conspiracy theories. One conspiracy theory alleges that Marshal Amer *was suicided* by the ruthless General Salah Nasr, Nasser's chief of intelligence. Nasr was tried and sentenced to jail after Nasser's death.

Fearful of similar power struggles within his regime, Mubarak removed his long serving Minister of Defense and ever popular, Marshal abdul-Halim abu-Ghazala. Abu-Ghazala was appointed by Sadat as minister of defense after the helicopter crash of Marshal Ahmed Badawi in 1980. Abu-Ghazala had similar qualifications to Mubarak; he was the chief of the Artillery Corps during the Yom Kippur war. Mubarak rose to popularity as chief of the Air Force during that war, as well. Both Mubarak and Abu-Ghazala survived the assassination of Sadat: they were sitting next to Sadat the day he was killed.

"As a popular and charismatic leader who managed to establish a sprawling patronage system within the armed forces, abu-Ghazala posed a threat to Mubarak from the beginning of his presidency", wrote Egyptian professor of political science at the American university in Cairo, May Kassem. (14) "Furthermore, a former military attaché to Washington, abu-Ghazala's political connections and his public anti-communist position, further elevated his status within the inner circles of U.S. policy-makers", explains Kassem. Abu-Ghazal reached a position during Mubarak's rule that "made it very difficult for anyone to undermine his authority". (15)

The abrupt removal from office of popular and potentially challenging individuals remains a dominant feature of Mubarak's rule. (16) Hiring and firing of key cabinet positions, depended mainly on loyalty and personal trust; a word of mouth, not necessarily on one's professional capacities.

Thus, key cabinet positions during the Mubarak era, a practice and tradition also maintained by his predecessors, were hired, kept and fired, based on the trust factor. The trusted elite came mainly from the ranks of the armed forces and the National Democratic Party, NDP, Mubarak's party. In a pure military tradition, all nominees in the government have to report to Mubarak, personally, as the Commander-in-Chief of the Armed Forces and head of the NDP.

The smaller circle and elite within the Egyptian government has been reserved to those clansmen from Mubarak's province of Munufia. Like his predecessor Sadat, Mubarak came from the humble countryside area of Munufia. They are two successive

Munufi presidents in Egyptian history. Sadat used to make reference to his roots from Munufia and was usually interviewed on TV on every special occasion from his favorite countryside home in Meit-Abulkom, Munufia. Mubarak followed suit and his hometown of Kafr el-Messelha, Munufia, became some sort of a national spiritual capital.

It is a *good-enough-credential* just to be from that province to ascend to power due to tribal and clannish ties with two successive presidents. Many leading political figures in the Mubarak era had their links to Munufia; such as Zachariah Azmi, chief of the office of the president (a post similar to the White House Chief of Staff - except with more power), Kamal el-Shazli, the speaker of the People's Assembly (a position similar to the Speaker of the House with the exception of no claim to succession, or a chain of command), and former Prime Ministers Atef Sidqqi and kamal el-Ganzouri. That practice of choosing key government elements from one's tribe might raise some eyebrows in the West, but definitely not in the Arab world. Tribalism has infested the whole Middle East.

Former Iraqi dictator Saddam Hussein kept most key and important government positions to his brothers, half brothers, sons, cousins, sons-in-law (that he later executed), and men from his hometown of Tikrit.

The result was the downfall of his regime after surrounding himself with *Yes-Men* who would nod their heads in approval to his every whim and decision. Hence, Saddam was expected to run every aspect of life in Iraq; an impossible task. None of his ministers or generals dared to take a decision without the personal approval of Saddam even during battle. In that sense, Saddam created the environment of his eventual downfall by politically emasculating his people and government.

It was a self-destructive regime similar to those in the former Soviet Union and Eastern Europe. Thus, with the disappearance of Saddam from Baghdad by the moment American troops entered, everything dissolved with him; the whole government and party. It seemed that the whole system was created to serve and cater to Saddam. By his disappearance, the system was of no use after the loss of its head.

Saddam was thought to be the last to fight after all the belligerence he was quoted saying about the *mother of all battles*, and the *new Mongols will suicide on the walls of Baghdad* - that found some audience in the *Arab Street.* His capture in a dirty hole, unshaven and looking more like a vagabond, exposed many lies and brought down the myths of many Arab dictators who have showed a similar attitude and bravado.

The fate of Saddam, his sons and his Baathist regime, sent shock waves through the spines of Arab dictators. Many Arabs do believe that without the Americans entering Bagdad, Saddam would be still in power over Iraq maneuvering his way, as usual, and grooming his sons for his succession. The Iraqi people would not have had any hope for change without the American intervention.

Mubarak's and Saddam's practices of hiring *men-of-trust* from their clan and creating a culture of cronyism, is a common practice throughout the Arab world. It has become the norm and almost accepted by the Arab masses as the status quo.

Among other Arab countries, Syria is a flagrant example of the same practice repeated over and over again. After thirty years of ruthless rule over Syria, President Assad (1970-2000) who came to power by a military coup - after a series of military coups - made sure that his son Bashar would inherit him as president of Syria through the support of the only political party in Syria, Baath, and the support of his trusted Alawite kinsmen. (17)

Nevertheless, the Assad regime was plagued by several uprising attempts in 1973, 1980, and 1982, that were brutally suppressed by his military. For instance the popular uprising of the people of Humms and Hamat were suppressed by the Syrian military which bombarded those cities and resulting into the deaths of almost 20,000 people.

President Assad was even threatened by his own brother, General Rifaat al-Assad who finally defected and lived in exile in Paris, where allegations of corruptions, drug and arms dealings followed him. Son Bashar Assad is under similar heat after the defection of his former Foreign Minister Abdel-Halim Khaddam, who declared a unified opposition front against Assad from London.

Recently, Colonel Ali Abdallah Saleh of Yemen, after decades of autocratic rule since coming to power by another coup, has been elected for another term as the *Necessity Leader,* in an election described as orchestrated and rigged, to say the least. He is also rumored to be grooming his son as the next president of Yemen.

Similar speculations are circulating around the Arab world about the fate of other Arab regimes after the demise of their old leaders. Speculations are centered on Libya and its dictator Muammar Gaddafi. Gaddafi has been in power since 1969 after a military coup that he staged with few officers from his tribe.

Gaddafi is in his mid-seventies and is rumored to have been grooming his son Seif el-Islam to inherit him as the next president of Libya. Why not, since Assad did it and Mubarak is going to do it? Such practices prompted Abdel-Barie Atwan, editor-in-chief of the London daily Arabic newspaper, *al-Quds al-Arabi,* to sarcastically ask the question: *"Do we live in the Arab world under monarchical republics, or republican monarchies?"*

"I am filled with wonder by his ideas, his moral standards, his deeds, his vision, his penetrating gaze, his love of good, of development, and of the progress of his sons and the entire people. He is a prophet of peace, an angel in the form of a president, who was sent to us from the heavens to propagate good.... He is a ray of light that breathes hope into a dismal world. He draws his strength from his genuine belief in Allah and in his message, which calls for love, good, and development, with determined will, great patience, and wisdom and understanding of the needs of the nation. Mubarak forever, on us and on all Egypt."

- Coptic Priest Giorgios Al-Sumaili describing Mubarak

2. Cheerleaders, Star-Makers, and Yes-Men: Mubarak's Political Machine

The High Priests of the "Mubarak Cult"

Many Westerners would have difficulty making sense of the Egyptian political system. Monitoring Egyptian media would give a false impression that Egyptian people under Mubarak are leading a life of eternal bliss with hardly any problems at all.

In Western democracies, the media is the watchdog which exposes political scandals, cronyism, and scrutinizes the private lives of politicians and even celebrities. Nobody is above criticism, or above the law. But in the case of Egypt and many other Arab countries, the story is different.

The president is literally sacred and is above the law. He is the law. The presidency in Egypt means absolute power. The president rises to a status bigger than his people and the country. The rhetoric of the Egyptian media is self-evident of that.

In Western democracies, politicians and law-enforcement

officers pride themselves on their role as public servants. But, being a servant in the Arabic language still bears negative connotations. Taking a closer look at the rhetoric generated and recycled by the Egyptian media during the Mubarak era and in the last fifty years, is a case study of the making of a pharaoh.

Pharaohs are thought to be made not born. Mubarak is a classic case of a pharaoh made by his own people. There's a famous saying in Egypt about the making of the pharaoh. The Pharaoh was once asked: *Oh mighty Pharaoh, how did you become a feared mighty one?* The answer came simple: *I have not found anyone who dared to stop me."*

The Egyptians very well know that by their own un-involvement in their own ruling and lack of defiance to the authoritarian rule of their pharaohs, they have created them. Egyptians are so fatalistic. Their pharaohs have taken advantage of their fatalism and submissiveness. The Pharaohs have skillfully mixed religion with politics, contrary to Western democracies, where the lines are clearly drawn between the state and the church.

In Arab and Muslim countries, the ruler claims the highest religious role. He has to be the *Prince of the Believers*. He claims his divine right to lead. He holds all the powers and all the noble titles. Nothing has changed much in the political life of Egypt since pharaonic times, or in the Egyptians' attitude towards their rulers. They curse them in the dark and cheer for them in broad daylight. For the Egyptians; a pharaoh seems to be a necessary evil.

This is why the pharaoh-making machine has never ceased to work. It is always in full gear and every new pharaoh has to pay homage to the preservers of his throne; the clergy, the media, the military and the social elite. Mubarak has not invented that machine; it was in place a long time before. But he has not bothered or tried to undertake any changes. It seems that he actually enjoyed and defended his role as the *Pharaoh of Egypt*.

Names change, pharaohs come and go, but the pharaoh-making machine stays, ready to create a new pharaoh to the Egyptians and perpetuate the status quo where the high priests of that order are the major beneficiaries.

One of those beneficiaries indeed, is the Mubarak's propaganda machine. As most of the media outlets in the Arab and Muslim countries are owned and run by the state, most of what Egyptians hear, read or watch is dictated by the government of Mubarak. Journalists, editors, and newscasters are government employees who are beneficiaries of that system. They have clear guidelines and red lines that they cannot cross. Heads of these institutions are handpicked based on their absolute loyalty to the regime. They are being censored by censoring agencies in addition to their own implemented self-censorship. Loyalty and membership in the president's party is the only guarantee to their promotion and maintaining their privileged status. For them, the regime has to stay. Without it there is uncertainty and loss of everything they have had. In their quest to preserve and polish the regime, they are actually preserving their own survival.

In that regard, the Mubarak regime does have an eerie resemblance to the systems in the former Soviet Union, Iron Curtain countries, many other Arab countries; like Saddam's Iraq, Gaddafi's Libya, Assad's Syria, Castro's Cuba, North Korea, and many other totalitarian regimes.

To give an example, one has to read through Egyptian state-owned press to find the simplistic, shameless and laughable idolization and glorification of Mubarak by his media.

For instance, on October 14, 2001, Egypt marked the 20th anniversary of Mubarak's presidency. The government papers held a month-long celebration, interviewing practically all members of Egypt's political, military, economic, and social elite.

Live for Egypt, and Egypt will live through you!

The most obvious manifestation of the link between the government press and the government itself is the editors' and columnists' declarations of loyalty to Mubarak. *Al-Gumhuriya* editor-in-chief Samir Ragab presented his own hand-written letter on the front page of his paper. In the letter, he pledged loyalty to Mubarak on behalf of the Egyptian people: "Your Excellency the President, the people that gives you back love in exchange for your love, and gives you its loyalty in exchange for your loyalty, pledges its support to you on the occasion of the 20th anniversary of your rise to power… Live for Egypt, and Egypt will live through you." (1)

He will live with us and we will live with him also in the years to come, Allah willing, for the good of dear Egypt

Al-Akhbar editor Galal Dweidar also wrote a celebratory article in honor of the occasion, titled *Mubarak: Sacrifice without Limits*, where he said: "Although 20 years have passed since he took power, the river of sacrifice has never stopped flowing, and the stream of achievements continues endlessly, with every step he takes...He will live with us and we will live with him also in the years to come, Allah willing, for the good of dear Egypt." (2)

Al-Gumhuriya newspaper featured another article where it said: "the commander and leader Hosni Mubarak begins, together with the Egyptian people, a new year of serious work and ongoing sacrifice. Since he, with the consensus of the nation, accepted responsibility into his hands under difficult circumstances on October 14, 1981, Mubarak has succeeded in navigating the ship of the homeland to a safe shore, a shore of stability of regional and international change. Mubarak's Egypt advances every day, from achievement to achievement, in all areas: political, economic, social, and cultural... The phenomenal achievements are the best testimonial to the love and faith that the commander and leader and his people place in each other. " (3)

Allah has permitted you to write pages full of sacrifice and anyone who is beloved by Allah is also beloved by the people!

The weekly *October* magazine jumped onto the bandwagon with a similar rhetoric: "Dear reader, today Egypt begins a new year of Mubarak's leadership, in which it will continue the voyage of development and peace... Every old man, every youth, child, man, and woman says today to Mubarak: Thank you. You gave your life and your best years for your homeland. You have made countless sacrifices. Allah has permitted you to write pages full of sacrifice, and anyone who is beloved by Allah is also beloved by the people; victory will remain at the right hand of anyone whom Allah supports. Long live the leader of the nation; long live the Egyptian people, who are at your side…' (4)

THE ART OF LEADERSHIP, THE ART OF PRESIDENCY OVER PEOPLES!

As for the weekly *Roz Al-Youssuf,* it published a special supplement titled: *20 Years President and 52 Years in the Service of Egypt; the Art of Leadership, the Art of Presidency over Peoples.* The introduction of the special supplement, 210 pages long read "we at *Roz Al-Youssuf* celebrate the 20th anniversary of the rule of the president Mubarak. This event merits more than a special issue. Every one of the many aspects in which the president has accomplished achievement after achievement deserves a special issue, so that we can give him the appreciation he deserves… Our celebratory words come from the heart, and express the conscience and emotions of the people and their support of their monumental and exceptional president Mubarak." (5)

ALL THAT IS LEFT FOR ME TO DO IS TO CALL FROM THE DEPTHS OF MY HEART ON ALLAH TO PROTECT HIM FOR THE SAKE OF EGYPT AND FOR THE SAKE OF ALL EGYPTIANS!

Al-Akhbar columnist Ahmad al-Gendi wrote: "What can I write about in his fourth term, which is based on the absolute support of the masses and their love for him, and on their devotion to his leadership in every one of his terms of office? In his first term of office, it was Mubarak the president; in his second, Mubarak the president and the commander; in his third, Mubarak the president, the commander, and the leader; in his fourth term of office, it is Mubarak, about whom no one disagrees that he has more experience, wisdom, determination, and faith in Egypt than any of those titles. What shall I write about Mubarak, after all those who have preceded me over the course of 20 years? All that is left for me to do is to call from the depths of my heart on Allah to protect him for the sake of Egypt and for the sake of all Egyptians." (6)

Twenty Years of Love!

Al-Ahram journalist Izzat Al-Saadani, and fellow clansman of Mubarak from his province of Munufia, undertook a special project. In a full-page article, entitled *Twenty Years of Love*, he interviewed three youths born October 14, 1981, the day Mubarak became president. The story ran as follows: "The three told me in unison, as if singing the national anthem in school: Throughout our lives, we have known, seen, felt, and been influenced by only one president and that is Mubarak. We were born and live with Papa Mubarak, and with no one else. We love to call him Papa Mubarak, because we feel that he is the father of us al. Al-Saadani concluded his article with the following: President Mubarak, who is starting his 21st year on the throne of responsibility, does not have Moses's staff with which to strike Egypt's troubles and pain, and to produce an eruption of solutions, gold, and silver, of rivers of pure honey with flowers on its banks. But he has something more powerful than Moses's staff: He has the love of the people." (7)

In *al-Akhbar*, Mumtaz al-Qott wrote another article on the same subject, in which he described how Mubarak addresses the problems of the common folk: "President Mubarak has, from his first day in power, managed to make himself a melting pot which has collected all hopes, aspirations, and problems. Mubarak is the symbol and the truth embodying 66 million Egyptians, and he bears upon his shoulders all their concerns. My problem is his problem; my dreams are his dreams…"

The Egyptian press was also full of letters and paid announcements from governmental and non-governmental organizations pledging support for Mubarak. One example was the *Love Letter* by Muhamad abul-Yazid Abdallah, chairman of the board of directors of an insurance company: "This letter of love and gratitude from the bottom of my heart I send to the leader and president Hosni Mubarak… My tongue cannot express, just as my mind cannot grasp, President Mubarak's achievements… Blessings, and complete admiration to the leader of Egypt, Hosni Mubarak. May he live for us in good health always, *Allah Willing*. May Allah give him long life for us, as president and as leader for us and for all the Arabs." (8)

Some newspapers also extended their flattery to Mubarak's family. *Al-Akhbar*, for example, wrote that Mubarak's family was *a wonderful picture of the ideal Egyptian family, enjoying love and harmony*. Egyptian-American Professor Dr. Mamoon Fendi wrote: "We must not forget the role played by family stability. Here she is, the First Lady, working night and day on the education project; she makes the books available to the Egyptian family at a negligible price, and handles the affairs of the Egyptian and Arab woman. May Allah protect her and may she continue to be the glowing face of Egypt. And here he is, Gamal Mubarak, spending most of his time in public activity and also trying to construct an education project based on youth. *Blessings to him.*"

When President Mubarak came to the throne of power in Egypt…

Fendy continued his unashamed praise of Mubarak, reminiscent of odes to Ancient God-Kings of Egypt saying, "When President Mubarak came to the throne of power in Egypt and took command of the ship; the Middle East was a stormy sea, whose waves were raging. Many were blinded by this, but the man's eye was always as clear as the eye of Horus, the son of Isis and Osiris, half man and half falcon, who traditionally protects Egypt. Egypt was wrapped in a mantle of sorrow when the powers of terror assassinated the late president Sadat… And behold, the army gives the Egyptian nation the bravest and most faithful of its men, the first-strike man in the 1973 war and the hawk of the Egyptian air force. On this stormy sea Mubarak appeared, to lead the ship…"

Mubarak and His Poets: "A bouquet of love from the depths of the heart of the homeland"

Under the headline *Mubarak in the Eyes of the Poets, al-Ahram* published several works by Egyptian poets, presenting them to Mubarak as *a bouquet of love from the depths of the heart of the homeland.* Dr. Samir Sarhan, head of the Writers' Association, head of the Egyptian Book Organization, professor of English

Literature at the College of Belles Letters at Cairo University and holder of many other official titles, is a classic example of an intellectual turned opportunist, he wrote: "Just as the president became one with the Nile and with the pyramids, and they became one with him, thus the hearts of the poets became one exquisite national melody of love and loyalty. The harp of the poets of Egypt has begun to play the sweetest and most beautiful of tunes, out of love for Mubarak and out of loyalty to his historic leadership. The poets do not speak with one tongue. Some wrote in literary Arabic; some wrote in popular Arabic; but the music of love was always the same. The sweetness of the sublime melody, the melody of tremendous loyalty to the commander and leader resonated, and will continue to resonate across the homeland, and it will fill the air with the perfumes of love… When the poets express Mubarak-love, the hearts tremble and yearn for the creator of good, truth, and beauty in the homeland of good, truth, and beauty." (9)

MUBARAK AND HIS GOVERNMENT

The Egyptian press also presented the views of government officials and members of parliament regarding Mubarak's 20 years in office. Egypt's Foreign Minister Ahmad Maher, a former army officer, used the recurring motif of a ship at sea: "Despite the storms and gales of the past 20 years, which damaged the region and the world… the captain of the ship, President Mubarak, has not only managed to protect Egypt and her people, but also to turn challenges into opportunities…"(10)

BEHOLD, THE ENTIRE WORLD LOOKS UP TO HIM AS IF HE HELD THE KEY TO SALVATION IN HIS HANDS…

Dr. Rabah Rathib, a lawyer and a member of the Egyptian Shura Council, wrote, "Out of loyalty to our dear homeland, Egypt, I found myself compelled, with complete pride, love, and appreciation, to direct a blessing of honor and magnificence and offerings of thanks to the man who elevated our affairs throughout the world and who proved to the entire world that Egypt is, truly, the mother of the world. Here he is, liaising with the strongest power in the world [the U.S.], with reason and rationality. He treats the U.S. calmly and in a balanced manner, with wise and serene policy, as if he was the leader of the entire world. He gives it counsel after counsel, and America follows all his advice… Behold, the entire world looks up to him as if he held the key to salvation in his hands… Because of all this, and because of many other things, I say again, and with me all Egypt, and even the entire world, says: Thank you, Your Excellency, President Mubarak…" (11)

Others wrote praising Mubarak's foreign policy and referred to America's war-on-terror following the attacks of September 11, 2001 in an inflammatory way. Wahid Hamed wrote an article in *Roz al-Youssef* titled: "The President – Solid as a Mountain, Because He Supports Truth and Justice: When a blaze breaks out, the men appear, and the heat of the fire soon reveals which of them are genuine and which are bogus. Some are consumed by the fire; some cannot stand the heat and run far away, seeking a pool of cold water in which to disappear until the fire is out; others settle for screaming and shouting that a destructive blaze has broken out, and think that they have thus done their job; in contrast, only those who break through to the heart of the blaze can put it out and prevent it from spreading."

Hamed further said: "The attacks were severe blows that completely toppled the American arrogance and made the patronizing American conceit bow its head… America's strength is no longer capable of defending itself, and one can apply to it the saying, 'We remembered the snakes but forgot about the scorpions,' until the fatal sting of the scorpion came… Following this, President Bush declared: 'Either you are with us or you are with terrorism' – a declaration that in and of itself is a terrorist statement. From most of the countries in the world, the cry arose: 'We are with you, oh master of the wounded America; oh cowboy who has fallen from his horse.' But in Egypt the situation was different, reasoned, and wise… Mubarak, because of his military past and his political and human experience, chose to stand with justice". (12)

Egypt's top officials expressed their extolling of Mubarak. Minister for the People's Assembly and the Shura Council Affairs Kamal el-Shazli wrote, in an article titled, *Twenty Enlightening Years in the Life of Egypt*, that "Egypt's achievements under its president and leader, Mubarak, over the past 20 years must be documented and compiled into volume." (13)

LONG LIVE MUBARAK THE GOOD… THE SYMBOL OF SACRIFICE.

In a full-page ad in *al-Ahram,* Minister for Environment Affairs, Nadia Makram Ebeid wrote of Mubarak, "as we have always been accustomed, he attaches importance to the problems of the nation and is ahead of his time. We all unite around such a commander and leader, who has earned respect and appreciation from all peoples of the planet Earth, so that he will continue the campaign… Long live Mubarak the good… the symbol of sacrifice. Every day we draw from him inspiration for a new idea and for unceasing sacrifice for our sons, our present, and our future…" (14)

Many members of the Egyptian parliament also used the press to show their loyalty to Mubarak. Parliamentarian Housing Committee head Muhammad abul-Einin stating that "the president's experience must be a lesson to all those wishing to learn how to deal with terrorism. Will the world learn from the experience of President Mubarak and go in the correct path to eliminate terrorism in all its forms?" (15)

Mubarak and the Clergy

Even the sheikh of *al-Azhar* University Tantawi, gave interviews to several papers assuring that Mubarak observes the commandments of Islam. In his *Roz al-Youssef* interview, Sheikh Tantawi said:

"I remember that when I was mufti, he would call me on the night of seeing the moon before the month of Ramadan and tell me, 'Oh so and so, tomorrow do we eat or do we fast? I would answer His Excellency, 'Tomorrow we eat' or 'Tomorrow we fast,' and he would say, 'Happy New Year. ..President Mubarak respects the religion and respects Islamic religious law. He respects religious values and does not violate them; on the contrary, he fully supports them… We call from the depths of our hearts to Allah to give him everlasting health."

I AM FILLED WITH WONDER BY THIS PHENOMENAL MAN... MUBARAK FOREVER, ON US AND ON ALL EGYPT.

Christian clerics felt that they had to join the line of Mubarak's loyalists. Coptic priest Giorgios al-Sumaili wrote, "I am filled with wonder by this phenomenal man. I am filled with wonder by President Mubarak, who is good, noble, and broadminded. I am filled with wonder by his ideas, his moral standards, his deeds, his vision, his penetrating gaze, his love of good, of development, and of the progress of his sons and the entire people."

Al-Sumaili also added: "While the entire world is in conflict and uses destructive means to sow ruin – behold, he builds and calls for peace and brotherhood. Behold, he inaugurates the Mubarak Bridge, the fruit of the love and recognition by the international community of the ability of this giant of a man... He is a prophet of peace, an angel in the form of a president, who was sent to us from the heavens to propagate good in an age in which many moral standards have been destroyed and evil, selfishness, and self-interest have taken root. He is a ray of light that breathes hope into a dismal world. He draws his strength from his genuine belief in Allah and in his message, which calls for love, good, and development, with determined will, great patience, and wisdom and understanding of the needs of the nation. Mubarak forever, on us, and on all Egypt." (16)

ALL THE PEACE-LOVING PEOPLES OF THE WORLD CELEBRATE THE DAY ON WHICH THE HEAVENS SENT US THE PRESIDENT..

Another prominent Christian Copt, Gergis Hilmi Azer, wrote in a similar vein: "Egypt and all the peace-loving peoples of the world celebrate the day on which the heavens sent us the president, the commander, and the heroic leader Hosni Mubarak, so that he could navigate the ship of peace, of good, and of blessing in Egypt and in the Middle East. Furthermore, I state in complete faith that Allah chose him to bear the message of peace to the entire world. Anyone tracing the course of this man's life senses that his appointment to the position that he fills is a blessing for the Egyptian people... I, like the others, hope that Allah may grant him health, so that he can actualize our hopes and so that every year Egypt will celebrate the holiday of his glorious presidency with him." (17)

Ikram Lami, head of the Anglican Church in Egypt, was obliged to follow suit as his Coptic colleagues:

"When we look at the land of Egypt today, we say that on this land has walked a man who has succeeded in changing the place and enriching the time. When we look around us at the world full of violence, terrorism, and wars, when we see the peoples of the world who do not know their way and do not look towards their future, we find that Mubarak is [the one who] tips the scales in the Middle East, and he is the judge to whom all the leaders, and all the press, turn to find out what he thinks ..." (18)

A religious tone was also dominant in articles by several columnists in the government-sponsored press. *Al-Ahram* columnist Said Abdel-Khallaq wrote: "I would not be exaggerating if I were to say that providence chose Mubarak to lead Egypt out of this dark tunnel. Providence chose him at a difficult hour, in which we stood on the brink of an abyss! The question should be asked: Was there anyone suited to take up the reins of government at that time besides President Mubarak? In truth, the answer is no. There was no one else. It was fate that chose President Mubarak for the task. There were, of course, several relics remaining from the Revolutionary Council of 1952, but political life had not elevated any personages capable of sailing a ship on the verge of sinking, except for Mubarak, who saved the ship from sinking and with it crossed the breaking waves and the winds of the gale, and brought it back to a safe shore!" (19)

Many high level Egyptian officials were interviewed by the press on that occasion, the twentieth anniversary of Mubarak's ascension, and emphasized the role of Mubarak as an uncontested ruler. Ismat abdel-Maguid, former secretary-general of the Arab League and who held several ministerial positions, recounted his first meeting with Mubarak.

Abdel-Maguid was present at the December 1977 Egyptian-Israeli meeting between President Sadat and Israeli Prime Minister Begin at Mena House Hotel in Giza. Mubarak, who was vice-president at the time, was also there. At that meeting, abdel-Maguid claims that he had won an argument with Begin over whether Begin's roots were in Palestine or Poland. After that, Sadat told the journalist Anis Mansour, Ismat proved himself to be a *real he-man*, and Mubarak told me, *Bravo*. Abd el-Maguid explained that… 'at the meeting, President Mubarak noticed my performance, and added that what increased my honor in his eyes was that the Israeli media labeled me the *Bad Guy*' " (20)

Democracy Already Exists?

Dr. Madhkour Thabet, another intellectual, ironically turned *Big Brother*, as he held the official title of *General Superintendent of the Supreme Council on Art Censorship*, in a twisted logic, wrote, "Like every creative person who engages in art and culture, I am always in the opposition, as this is characteristic of the artist, whether he likes it or not. But a surprise awaited me when I began to bear responsibility [i.e. when he was appointed censor]... I discovered that I alone was the one who made the decisions and that I had to implement all the principles of freedom and democracy in which I believe. It became clear to me that the matter was much simpler than we think: Democracy already exists, and all that is left for us to do is to believe in its existence. " (21)

Nobel Prize laureate Naguib Mahfouz was the only honest and reasonable sound who spoke critically of Mubarak's policies: "I hope that President Mubarak will change all the laws restricting freedom, and amend the constitution – which establishes that Parliament must comprise at least 50% of farmers and laborers, something which is completely unjustified and which harms democracy. The election process must change such that there is more than one candidate – even if we are certain that the republic will elect Mubarak. With regard to the problem of terrorism, I think that the only solution is having a true democracy, something that requires much courage in changing the constitution and in abolishing the laws restricting freedoms." (22)

"Mubarak has encouraged the Interior Ministry and the Intelligence Services to loot public money through forming companies that offer construction services and, contrary to the law, are given deals by the state for huge sums, in some cases 20 times the amount offered to other companies. These funds are distributed among the top people at the ministry and in intelligence agencies. The Mubarak era will be known in the history of Egypt as the era of thieves". (1)

- Retired Colonel Muhammad al-Ghanam,
Former director of legal research
At the Egyptian Interior Ministry
Geneva, Switzerland

3. THE BENEFICIARIES: WHO REALLY RULES EGYPT?

Retired Colonel Muhammad al-Ghanam, Former director of legal research at the Egyptian Interior Ministry defected and joined the ranks of the Egyptian opposition to the Mubarak regime and resided in Switzerland as a political asylee, like many Egyptian expatriates around the world.

Al-Ghanam claims that "the government has sold the great part of the public sector companies for less than a quarter of their value to businessmen working for Mubarak's sons, or to foreign companies in return for huge commissions for Mubarak and his sons or other top officials. To get a high position in the Interior Ministry or Intelligence it is necessary to be involved in corruption for corruption is an asset. Through corruption, Mubarak secures the loyalty of the heads of the security departments, making sure they will execute his policies and oppress his political adversaries."

Al-Ghanam also alleges that "Mubarak has encouraged the interior ministry and the intelligence apparatus to loot public money through forming companies that offer construction services and, contrary to the law, are given deals by the state for huge sums, in some cases 20 times the amount offered to other companies. These funds are distributed among the top people at the ministry and in intelligence agencies. The Mubarak era will be known in the history of Egypt as the era of thieves."

In his public speeches and online interviews, al-Ghanam calls on "the United States and Europe to insist not to support this corrupt regime, and then at least they should provide financial aid on condition that the regime accepts international procedures to secure democracy, human rights and anti-corruption measures. Such procedures should include forming an international committee to evaluate the fortune amassed by Mubarak, his sons and the heads of his regime, an international committee to supervise the elections, and a committee to promote human rights."

Al-Ghanam warns that *the absence of a connection between aid and these procedures means that American and European taxpayers are accomplices in the crimes of murder and torture committed by the Mubarak regime. We implore you not to participate in the killing and torture of our people.* (2)

On a similar note, Kifaya, the Egyptian National Movement for Change, that seeks to establish democratic reform in Egypt, opposes the Mubarak regime, the largely rubber-stamp parliament, and the practices of his ruling party and government. The movement is mostly composed of leftists, Islamists, liberals and nationalists, as well. Kifaya made its first public protest on December 12, 2004, in front of the High Court in downtown Cairo.

Kifaya is an Arabic word which means *enough.* On June 6, 2005, Kifaya called for a vigil in Cairo streets. Three thousand protestors showed up and demonstrated for two hours for two consecutive Tuesdays. Kifaya's main activities began as a protest against a fifth term for Mubarak in 2005. Although Mubarak was re-elected, Kifaya continues to protest his rule and the possible inheritance of power by his son Gamal.

On July 4, 2006, Kifaya released a report saying that *corruption has infiltrated all aspects of Egyptian society and stands in the way of further social and economic development.* (4) "This report deals with corruption in the inclusive sense," says George Ishaq, Kifaya spokesman and coordinator. "It is diverse and includes the political and the cultural, as well as the economic and the social. Corruption has become a social law." The extensive 249 page report, titled *Corruption in Egypt: the Black Cloud is Not Disappearing*, was compiled by Kifaya members with information from local and international reports, Transparency International and the UNDP, court and legal records and Egyptian media sources.

The report takes a broad view of corruption in Egypt's privatization program, corruption in the Ministries of Health, Agriculture, Petroleum, Finance and Antiquities, and a section on the interference of security forces in public life. It also discusses the use of political influence to gain government contracts and the rampant system of bribes which citizens must pay to navigate governmental bureaucracy.

Ishaq considers addressing the issue of corruption a primary step in political change in Egypt. "We are looking at the issue from the perspective that all political change must start from the top. This country's corruption started from the top and all possibilities for fighting corruption are doomed to failure until we can assure the end of this regime. Corruption, as the report shows, is the primary reason for the loss of so many development opportunities and for the destruction of public associations. It is impossible for the nation to rise up without putting an end to it," says Ishaq.

Egypt's Ministry of Interior declined to comment on Kifaya's damning report and the ruling NDP conceded that corruption is a problem in the country. "We admit that corruption is an issue and that it has to be addressed," said Investment Minister Mahmoud Mohieddin, at the NDP's annual conference in October 2006. "We want to be frank about the problem. We also want to be frank about how we are dealing with it." He also added that the NDP was in the process of drafting a comprehensive program to eliminate corruption. (5)

Egypt earned a score of 3.4 out 10 in the Berlin-based Transparency International's 2005 Corruption Perceptions Index, which is compiled through surveys from 10 institutions. This puts the country at the rank of 115 out of 158 nations surveyed. Egypt still falls below the 5-point mark, above which a country is said not to have a serious problem with corruption.

Ahmad el-Sayed el-Naggar, an economic analyst with the governmental Al-Ahram Centre for Political and Strategic Studies, also believes that the money siphoned off by corruption hampers development. "Quite simply, the funds that are stolen from the public domain should be put into the public budget to be spent on social programs that will benefit the poor, and spent on public health and education." El-Naggar also noted that money lost through corruption is not re-invested in the economy in ways that will help create jobs for Egypt's unemployed.

"If this money were not being stolen, it could be used for new investments that could create jobs for the unemployed and help them help themselves. It could give them a constant source of income through honest employment instead of creating a breeding ground for violence, crime and political extremism and leading to a tragically impoverished human existence," said George Ishaq. (6)

In its extensive report, Kifaya analyzed the political climate in Egypt and pointed fingers at prominent figures in the Mubarak regime, and even at Mubarak himself and his family, revealing who benefits from the continuation of that regime. "Corruption has actually become a social law and a hidden behavior that rules the different aspects of the Egyptian life".

"Political corruption is the basis of the political crime that has continued for more than 25 years, violating freedoms, practiced torture, constructed detention camps and destroyed civil institutions, by enforcing a state of emergency", Ishaq added. (7)

In Egypt during the last 25 years, economic corruption has been the cause of wasting several development opportunities. Corruption became a ruling social law that corrupted tastes, ambitions and the spiritual value of justice, equality and equal opportunities among the Egyptian citizenry. It was natural in this era that favoritism spread with a negative influence on the economic and social development.

Development rate dropped to 2% currently compared to a 4.6% years ago. Depression dominated the Egyptian market while citizens purchasing ability decreased. The increase in the interest rate led to the devaluation of the Egyptian pound against the dollar. Competition increased between local products and those imported ones, in addition to the lagging few foreign investments in the country. (8)

The UNCTAD report on the international investment revealed that foreign investment decreased in Egypt from $600 million to only $200 millions. Egypt was one of the most aspiring developing countries able to attract investment in the 1980s. Egypt also suffers from a rising rate of unemployment and poverty. Official statistics said that the number of the unemployed in Egypt rose from 112.535 in 1950 to 5 millions in early 2004, meaning that the number of the unemployed increased at a rate of
4000 % in the last 54 years. The World Bank report in 2003 indicated that 52% of the Egyptians were living with less than two dollars daily and that about 23% were living under the poverty line.

In the last two decades, Egyptians have been accustomed to hearing of a new corruption crime or the arrest of a big corrupt figure, cheating, bribery, and fraud. A foreign observer once said that, *living in Egypt is living under corruption*. Satirist Ahmad Ragab suggested a new name for Egypt under Mubarak; *Fasadistan* or *Corruptionistan* [the Land of corruption]".

Corruption became the daily crime headline. The consequences of the political monopoly appeared obviously in the economic performance. *Parasite capitalism appeared suddenly with no work or effort, and it became obvious in seizing bank money and smuggling it abroad,* says Kifaya. Amid an increasing monopoly of power, economic activities decreased, which destroyed the new producers and small enterprisers as people of power and influence. A corrupt class appeared consisting of parasite capitalism, in addition to the inflated profits by a few. (9)

One of the most outrageous cases exposed by the media and led to a public outcry was the *Air Oil* case. Amir Riyad Chairman of *Air Oil* services ordered a plane to carry an entourage of 50 persons. The cost was deducted from the public money. The plane was to carry the Minister of Oil, his family, the Deputy Prime-Minister, his family and two Asian maids to a resort in Marsa Matrouh, a northern resort on the Mediterranean west of Alexandria.

Shortly after taking off, the Minister's wife found out that she forgot her purse and ordered that another 52-passenger plane fly to Matrouh to bring back her purse! (10)

The Egyptian public started to hear about corruption in higher places at the end of the Sadat era. Allegations of corruption of his wife Jehan, their relatives, misuse of power and influence, drew many speculations about several illegal activities through which they attained a great deal of wealth.

Investigations of Esmat Sadat, the late president's brother, revealed that he turned from a junior employee to a millionaire to gain more than $250 millions, through monopolizing the distribution of some products in the black market, imposing taxes on merchants, seizure of state lands, smuggling of goods and even alleged drug trafficking.

In his recent book, *Corruption Use*, Egyptian writer Badr Okal, says that the former Egyptian Socialist Attorney General, Abdel-Kader Ali was himself facing criminal charges after his wealth surprisingly increased to about three million Egyptian pounds (E£). Investigating him unveiled charges against 25 political figures, including seven prime ministers and former ministers, twelve of the People's Assembly members, and a number of former governors.

Okal indicated that those people misused their power in illegal practices and and benfited from dealing with some currency exchange companies. He also indicated that some of these figures already participated in some activities of these companies as subscribers or depositors either with their names or their relatives'. Among those who were incriminated was Kamal Hassan Ali, former Prime- Minister, Minister of Defense and Chief of the General Intelligence Agency.

The writer claimed that Ali rendered these companies a great service through ousting the Minister of Economy in his cabinet, Mosataf al-Said for the sake of the black market currency traffickers who became later the owners of these companies.

Another high public figure indicated in these investigations was conglomerate Osman Ahmad Osman, the former Chairman of the Popular Development Committee in the National Democratic Party, NDP, father-in-law of one of Sadat's daughters, and owner of the Arab Contractors construction company.

The *Arab Contractors* reaped billions in government contracts in Egypt and other Arab Gulf countries. Osman was considered the *spiritual father* of some of these currency and investment companies. He was a partner with Ashraf al-Saad with a share of 40% in a clothes factory. Al-Saad collected billions of dollars from Egyptians working in the Arab Gulf countries promising a return on their investment up to 25 %.

Al-Saad claimed that he invested the money in an all *Halal* way (adhering to Islamic Sharia law). It turned out that he squandered most of it in stock market biddings (forbidden by Sharia), currency trafficking, and shares for bribes to several high-level government officials.

The collapse of his company and other similar ones had a catastrophic impact on hundreds of thousands of Egyptians families who worked during the seventies and the eighties in oil rich Gulf States. Enticed by the prospect of a highly unusual return on their savings and encouraged by many religious figures that al-Saad managed to recruit for publicity- like the late preacher and televangelist Sheikh Metwally el-Shaaraway - drove those families to entrust these companies with their life savings.

Exploiting the new Wahabi tide that crept into Egyptian society in the seventies, eighties, and the nineties - due to the petrodollar economic boom - which forbade a good Muslim from dealing with banks for the suspicion of usury, TV Star personalities like el-Shaaraway gave their blessings to these companies in return for a disguised tax-free commission called *Kushoof Elbaraka*, or the Blessings Accounts.

In reality, it was hush money. The *Blessings Accounts* were exposed and some of the founders of these companies ended up in jail, or fled Egypt. The Mubarak government froze what was left of their assets in a desperate attempt to retrieve some of the money and pay back the defrauded investors.

The list of those given the *Blessings Accounts* also included former Giza governor, Abdel-Hamid Hassan. Hassan left his post to work in another *Islamic Investment* company, *Al-Rayyan*. The former Interior Minister, police General el-Nabawi Ismail, and former governor of el-Sharkiya province, General Amin Mitikis, also worked for these companies.

Al-Rayan company was reported as saying that "we represent a state inside a state...we are paying to all". The deposit interest was determined according to the depositor's post and influence as it reached, sometimes, 100%. Even the weekly magazine *Roz al-Youseif* concluded a printing contract at the value of more than two million pounds in fall 1987 with *al-Rayyan* Company. Hence, its editor-in-chief Abdel-Aziz Khamis joined the prompters of these companies. (11)

In May 1988, after a loss of 350 million dollars as they speculated on gold and currencies, *al-Rayyan* and *al-Saad* companies decided to merge.

Criminal Case no. 19 in 1981 stated that an investigation unveiled that the owners of the two biggest companies al-Rayyan and al-Saad, traded in foreign currency and seized from one of the investment banks, E£ 1.850.000. The cousin of al-Saad and his brother-in-law were defendants in the case no. 364- 082, for illegal financial imports. They were accused of smuggling E£ 340,000,000 owned by al-Saad to offshore banks.

The owner of *Al-Helal Investment Company*, Mohammed Abdel-Hady, a former basketball player who worked in Arab Gulf states, started his his own investment company in 1980. In a very short period of time, his company's assets reached E£ 250 million after its intial public offering. A report prepared by the Egyptian Anti Money Laundering Administration in January 26, 1983, listed the following among 55 currency traffickers, who had close ties with these Islamic Investment companies. The suspects manipulated the black market of foreign currency in Egypt.

The list included among others, Sami Ali Hassan, Ahmad Tawfeek Abdel-Fatah, Mohammed Tawfeek Abdel-Fatah and Ashraf al-Saad. In August of 1984, the bank accounts of currency dealers were frozen and travel bans were ordered on them by the office of Egypt's Socialist Attorney General. (12)

LOAN MPs

Between the years 1994-1996, it was unveiled that a number of officials in Mubarak's National Democratic Party suddenly became big millionaires by seizing from private banks more than E£ 1,200 billion. By the end of 2001, another high profile corruption case came to the public attention. Another businessman who failed to pay back his huge debts fled the country. Some members of the Egyptian Parliament, the People's Assembly and the Shura Council, were involved. Thus many of these cases and the Memebers of Parliments behind them were dubbed as the *Loan MP's Cases.*

In the People's Assembly session on January 28, 1996, the Minister of Justice demanded the Assembly lift the immunity off its members Tawfeek Abdu Ismail, and Khaled Mohamed Mahmoud. These members allegedly looted huge amounts of money from the Nile Bank. Another MP, Yassin Abdel-Fatah Aglan, was accused of looting huge sums of money from the same bank, as well. The People's Assembly refused to lift the immunity. It later approved it on October 2, 1998 after the Minister of

Justice demanded again, to lift the immunity off member Khaled Mahmoud.

The trial of these defendants at the Supreme State Security Court in the case no. 390-1997, revealed many surprising facts. The four members formed a network of 18 individuals of rich businessmen and bank officials that succeeded in defrauding eight banks: Nile Bank, National Dakahilia Bank, Mohandes Bank, Crédit Lyonnais, Alexandria Trade and Marine Bank, Cairo Bank, Faisal Islamic Bank, and Cairo-Barclays Bank. (13)

The prosecution referred 12 officials to the Supreme State Security Court for bribery and forgery. They were prominent officials in the Drainage Department, Egyptian Dodge Company, Arab Trade Company and other government offices. In September 26, 2002, the Supreme State Security Court sentenced seven senior officials in the *Port Said Free Zones.* They were tried in the so-called *Big Customs Case* for evading paying customs in millions. Their sentences varied from ten years imprisonments, life sentences, to paying a fine of 21 million pounds.

A number of bribed judges were also arrested in the same month. On May 25, 2002, the Egyptian Socialist Attorney General investigated 19 suspects including two of the People's Assembly members in Al-Fayoum province. Parlimentary members Bahaa el-Meligi and Sobhi Ewes were accused of forming and the heading a gang to seize the state properties, documents forgery, and wasting about E£ 164 million of public money.

The case of *Nasr Metal Company*, where the chairman and a number of officials were accused of wasting about E£ 2.1 billion, made headlines in the Egyptian opposition press. By the beginning of summer, officials at the Department of Mechanics and Electricity at that company were accused of squandering more than E£ 43 million.

In August of the same year, another big corruption case made headlines. This time it was at the *Radio and TV Union* at the Ministry of Information. Mohammed al-Wakil, head of the news sector, was accused of bribery and public money squandering. Also accused of similar charges was Yousef abdel-Rahman, chairman of Development and Agricultural Credit Bank, who held more than 20 positions in the Ministry of Agriculture and its different departments.

Within nine months, parliamentary immunity was lifted off more than 20 of the N. D. P. members due to accusations such as uncovered checks, desertion of military service, and unguaranteed credit facilitations. (14)

In August, 2002, the press reported a *wide-range scandal* involving senior members of the Ministry of Education. The defendants allegedly conspired with some teachers to assist dozens of secondary school students to cheat on their exams. According to press reports, several of the cheating students came from prominent families whose fathers were members of Mubarak's party. Minister of Education, Ahmed Gamaleddin Moussa referred the case to the administrative and public prosecutors. By the year's end, no action was taken. Moreover, Minister Moussa lost his cabinet portfolio in the December reshuffle of minsters.

The Ministry of Agriculture witnessed several corruption cases, as well. It included the bribery case of Judge Ahmad abdel-

Fattah with the owner of the *European Country Farms.* In 1996, Abdel-Fattah was allegedly facilitating selling state-owned lands for low prices. The lands then were sold in return for millions pocketed as a price difference. The actual price of a piece of land in the bribery case was up to E£ 5,000 per acre. Nevertheless, was offered for sale at only E£ 200 per acre.

Dr. Yousef Wali, former Minister of Agriculture for 24 years and Deputy Chairman of the National Democratic Party was also beleaguered with scandals. His name was repeated 2,638 times in the *Ministry of Agriculture Bribery Case* investigations while the case papers reached 3000 pages. The case shocked Egyptian society as the main defendant was none but Yousef abdel-Rahman, one of the pillars in the Ministry of Agriculture. Abdel-Rahman was accused *of leading a gang that...spread cancer among Egyptians.* Abdel-Rahman was still facing charges of bribery, ill-gotten money, abuse of power, and importing and using banned insecticides.

The opposition press also criticized Wali's agricultural policy claiming that he replaced key crops with crops for export, destroying the crop structure, thus increasing the food gap and reducing the cotton plantation region from 1.5 million to only 600,000 acres. Surprisingly, Egypt imports vegetable oils at a value of $1.5 billion every year despite its agricultural resources and wealth.

The corruption case also alleged that cattle wheat was imported to make bread for the Egyptians. A foreign company exported 31,500,000 tons of wheat, deemed unfit for human consumption, for bread for Egyptians, was being investigated. High level

Agriculture Ministry officials were tried. The Cairo Criminal Court sentenced Ahmad Abdel-Fattah, the legal adviser to the Minister of Agriculture Yousef Wali, to ten years in jail with a fine of E£ 1000,000. (16)

In the case of the *Agricultural Stocks*, Wali was investigated for allegedly importing cancerous insecticides. *"For* E£ *19 million, Dr. Yousef Wali approved of using the cancerous insecticides and sacrificed the citizens' health,"* was the headline of an Egyptian newspaper. (17) Another Wali's employee, Randa al-Shami, was sentenced to seven years in jail and cleared from the sexual bribery charges that she was initially accused of. (18)

Looting Public Money and Bank Loans

According to the Egyptian Ministry of Economy report in 2000, bank loans in recent years reached $207 billion, including E£ 200 billion loans whose recipients failed to pay back, even with the favorable rate of 6%. This led the public sector banks to increase their financial assets to meet the questioned debts at $27 billion. The questionable loans were given to businessmen with links to some People's Assembly members, with no actual or enough loan guarantees.

A study of Dr. Salwa al-Antari, the research director at the Egyptian National Bank, found out that Egyptian private sector banks gave 52% of their loans with no guarantees. The report mentioned the biggest 20 clients who got 20% of the total facilitations and bank loans. The study also added that 250 businessmen received 36% of the total facilitations for loans, and that the total amount of the defaulted and uncollectible loans reached a rate of 20% of the total loans.

Another study revealed that *dead debts* in the Egyptian banking system reached E£ five billion by that year only. Some of businessmen who received these loans disappeared, or simply fled Egypt. Dr. Hamdy Abdel-Azeem, Professor of Economics at Sadat's Academy for Administrative Sciences estimated that $36 billion were smuggled out of Egypt in 1998 only, through a variety of ways such as bank transfers, international deposits and importation operations, including $25 billion in secret dealings.

The phenomenon of businessmen - with connections to politicians - looting public money has plagued Egypt over the last 25 years. Businessmen obtaining unreasonable loans from Egyptian banks with hardly any guarantees, and then fleeing the country, have become the norm.

Businessman Tawfeek abdel-Hai was one of the first who fled the country after a scandal concerning the importation and selling of 1,426 tons of rotten chicken deemed unfit for human consumption and selling it to the Egyptian public as food. After receiving $45 million from three banks without guarantees or enough documents, he fled the country. He allegedly also received E£ 11 million from the Suez Canal Bank, using the influence of Osman Ahmad Osman.

In 1987, Hoda Abdel-Moneim, known in Egyptian press as the *Iron Lady*, defaulted on her loans and fled the country. She established *Hedico Egypt Co.*, for construction and contracting in 1986, with a huge publicity campaign in the Egyptian media. Egyptians flocked to buy shares in her company. She was able to collect E£ 45 million in few days. One of her enterprises was the purchase of large lots of land near Cairo airport. Despite a ban on construction in that area, she managed to construct a limited number of buildings there.

The Attorney General later issued a travel ban and a sequestration order against her for debts that reached E£ 30 million. The Administrative Censorship Authority, an investigative agency that deals with corruption cases, reported that Abdel-Moneim received several loans from the Cairo Bank and the African Arab Bank without sufficient loan guarantees.

Yet, surprisingly, she fled Egypt under mysterious conditions, while investigations continued for 17 years. She was sentenced in absentia to 10 years in jail.

Ashraf al-Saad head of *Al-Saad Islamic Investment Group* managed to collect about E£ one billion from loans and deposits of shareholders. In February 1991, he traveled to Paris for medical treatment. Three months later, he was listed among those under travel ban and was sentenced to two years in jail for unpaid debts. In January 1993, Al-Saad suddenly returned to Egypt where he was referred to the Criminal Court for seizing E£ 188 million in addition to other eight charges. By late December 1993, he was released on E£ 50,000 bail. While still on a travel ban, he managed to flee to Paris on June 4, 1995, and has since failed to return.

George Ishaac Hakim, owner of a chain of auto tires and batteries stores, also fled Egypt in June 1994, after seizing E£ 60 million from Dakahliya, Gulf and Cairo banks. Abdel Ghani Atta, head of the National Cement Company, fled Egypt, as well, after embezzling $70 million during his post in that company. Businessman Mohammed Anwar el-Garhi, owner of Mega

Investment Company, also fled Egypt after receiving E£ 456 million from banks. Mark Adel Fahmy Dawarf, known as the *King of Tuna*, fled to London in February 1999. The Minister of Economy, Yousef Boutros Ghali later declared that the debts of fleeing-buinessmen to banks reached E£ 200 billion.

Egyptian-American Mahmoud Wahba, also known as the *King of Cotton*, fled Egypt to the U.S.A. after his debts reached more than E£ 380 million. Egyt's Attorney General issued an order to seize his financial assets. Wahba failed to make a settlement with the Egyptian National Bank over an amount of E£ 380 million, which he received through credit facilitations and bank loans.

The case of flamboyant French-Egyptian businessman, Ramy Lakah made headlines in the Egyptian opposition media and tabloids. Lakah, a former member of the Egyptian Parliament, was a fixture on gossip columns for his affairs with several Egyptian movie actresses, fled to London after his companies stumbled and was unable to pay his debts. He owed ten banks more than E£ two billion including E£ 1.1 billion to Cairo Bank and the rest to 16 other banks.

In 2000, the Attorney General banned businessman Mostafa el-Belidei, his wife and his sons, from using their money. El-Belidei was not an ordinary businessman. He established several companies and headed the Chamber of Commerce in Cairo. El-Belidei fled Egypt in July 2000, after he sold half of his properties in el-Sharkiya province, Cairo and Alexandria.

The Cairo Bank filed a claim against el-Belidei of a total sum that reached E£ 555 million. *Al-Ahram Al-Arabi* magazine reported on his business dealings saying that, in May 8, 1995, he bought real estate property in the U.S., consisting of tourist resorts overlooking California's coast for $83 million which he paid in cash.

El-Belidei's extravagant life style was most evident when he held an engagement party for his son and the daughter of businessman Omar el-Marzouki in the Cairo Sheraton, followed by a lavish reception in his palace in Aagamy, Alexandra. More than one thousand guests were catered by food brought from London on a special plane. El-Beilidei's line-of-business was in cosmetics and ready-made clothes, in addition to dealing in a number of other products used in manufacturing cars, food and cigarettes. He headed a business empire, known as *El-Belidei Group* that consisted of nine companies, the most prominent of which was *Hiotech Cosmetics.* He obtained franchises from German companies like; Buyers Drove, Lancôme, Shelton, and Swiss brands like; Tseer Probonds, Wrangler, Mark & Spencer, Jual Van, and Vanhowzen.

Al-Arabi newspaper reported extensively on el-Belidei's fast life and romantic escapades with famous actresses. It mentioned that he had relations with several well-known actresses like Mervat Ameen, Hoda Ramzy and others. He once paid a dowry of E£ 10 million to one of his wives. After divorcing her, he paid her a deferred sum that reached E£ five million and left her jewelry worth E£ ten million.

The list of the businessmen who fled Egypt included many well-known figures such as; Ahmad Khafaga with a debt of E£ 350 million, Mahmoud Hayen a.k.a. *Alexandria's King of Wood* with a debt of E£ 40 million, Amer Nashartti owed banks E£ 600 million and the Al-Hawarri family which owed E£ two billion.

Reporting on this wave of unprecedented corruption and looting, *al-Ahram* newspaper declared that: *It was clear that those figures prepared their lives abroad after smuggling the billions which they got through false feasibility studies, plans with some bank officials, apparent declaration of bankruptcy or imaginary debt scheduling* .

Experts in Egypt confirm that 5% of the total loans granted to businessmen reached the sum of E£ 15 billion and became *dead debts.* The International Monetary Fund estimates that the figure reached not less than E£ 25 billion, while latest figures from Egypt's authorities say it has reached E£ 247 billion.

Dr. Faieka el-Refaei, former deputy chairman of the Central Bank of Egypt, said that *this crisis resulted from the non-application of law and the use of bribery.* By late 2001, the number of cases which the banks filed against businessmen who fled Egypt reached 853.

According to a UN developmental program report, "most banking scandals in Egypt since 2001 are related to un-guaranteed loans presented to businessmen and governmental officials. Beginning in 2003, all these cases were referred to the courts that issued tough sentences against those condemned. Deficit in loans completion between 1999 and 2003, reached about 8 to 10 billion dollars, or 10% of the yearly total gross income. Cairo Bank was the most harmed since 2003, trying to recover from the looted sum of 1.3 billion dollars of stumbled loans".

Entrenched Corruption is a *Roadblock to Reform*, said the authors of the *Arab Human Development Report*, published in Amman, Jordan, on April 5, 2005, that stated that: "Corruption must be confronted and uprooted in Arab countries if the region is to develop free institutions and implement the rule of law".

Political and economic corruption is so commonplace in the region that surveys conducted in five Arab countries for the AHDR 2004, the *Freedom Survey*, showed that 90 percent of the people believe that corruption pervades their societies. Another international survey also shows that nearly 70 percent of the public in five Arab countries believe that "the country is run for the benefit of the influential few."

Corruption takes on many forms, both large and petty, the authors say. The majority of respondents to the *Freedom Survey* said that they were aware of bribes paid or favors rendered through personal contacts during the year preceding the survey to either obtain services that are legitimate and to which they are entitled, or to avert a punishment by the authorities, the report states. "Aspects of corruption are also clearly visible to citizens, particularly those in the business sector who complain that the people in power monopolize the main areas of the economy, either directly or as partners of successful businessmen," the authors reported.

"Moreover, persons in power and their close circle receive huge commissions for contracts concluded between the state and international or local companies, including armament contracts. Corruption exists—the governments themselves admit as much, by periodically launching their anti-corruption campaigns," the authors said.

THE VICIOUS CYCLE

"Those in our region who demand freedom, and who struggle

for it, may be in the majority; however, those who stifle it are stronger and more powerful," says Rima Khalaf Hunaidi, United Nations Assistant Secretary-General and Director of UNDP's Regional Bureau for Arab States. "They [Arab regimes] not only possess the means to oppress, marginalize and impoverish, but they also control key forums and are able to recruit those adept at twisting various texts to perpetuate their interests and at bending intellectual norms and theories in order to prohibit freedom and permit its confiscation."

By controlling all the levers of power, Khalaf said that, "country leaders can use the judiciary to eliminate and tame opponents, rivals and even supporters who step out of line. This is linked with what is known as *unspoken corruption*, which is hushed up, where close supporters are allowed to exploit their positions for unlawful gain, while *enforcement of the law* against them remains a weapon to ensure that their total loyalty will continue. Manipulation of the law also opens the way for economic corruption, the natural result of political corruption," Khalaf contends.

Structural and Systematic corruption

Structural corruption, as the authors of the aforementioned report contend, is *part of a systematic state policy* in the Arab world. In this type of corruption, "personal abuse of public office and misuse of public finances are considered normal according to prevailing custom, or even necessary for the regime to endure. It is distinct from conventional corruption where the perpetrator acts behind the back of officialdom, in fear of the law."

The report authors maintain that *structural corruption* is one of the biggest obstacles to reform since it is systematically used to sabotage political and civil activity and create classes with vested interests in the status quo. The report further indicates that political and legal structures in some Arab states make it is difficult to differentiate between corruption in its conventional form—abuse of public office for personal gain—and inherent failings in the system itself. "In some States, law and custom decree that the land and its natural resources belong to the ruler, and fail to distinguish at this level between the private and public natures of the ruler, while the private property of the ordinary citizen becomes a grant from the ruler. In such a situation, it is difficult to talk of corruption in governance, for whatever the ruler does, he is disposing of his own property."

Dependency on oil sales in many Arab countries has also contributed to corruption in many countries, the authors claim. In oil-dependent economies, "the government can act as a generous provider that demands no taxes or duties in return," say the authors. These regimes perpetuate themselves in power "through generous financing of agencies of organized repression and the mass media."

The authors argue that nothing short of sweeping political, institutional, administrative and societal reforms that establish representative government, accountability, transparency and disclosure at all levels of society, will effectively root out corruption. "If ending corruption entails, among other measures, deep economic reform, active laws and mechanisms of accountability and transparent governance, *structural corruption* can be overcome only by radical reform of the political architecture," the authors concluded.

The Group of Eight-Broader Middle East and North Africa (G8 BMENA) civil society dialogue on Transparency and Anti-Corruption is one of four civil society dialogues undertaken as part of the Forum for the Future 2005 held in Bahrain. This dialogue has been attended by representatives from both civil society and the private sector in G8 countries, 16 BMENA countries and Turkey. It produced a concrete and practical *Platform for Action* including three recommendations: to ratify and implement the *UN Convention against Corruption*, to implement policies and practical measures to ensure transparency in public financial management, and to take anti-corruption action to address the social deficit.

The *Platform for Action* focused on the overall status of the *UN Convention against Corruption* in the region and examined concrete steps to promote its ratification and effective implementation. The conference was attended by government ministers, MPs, diplomatic missions, the private sector and the media.

Egypt, according to the World Bank, is *one of the most corrupt countries in the MENA region.* Egypt ratified the UN Convention against Corruption in February 2005. It has not signed the African Union Convention on preventing and combating corruption and still faces severe problems through ongoing scandals linked to the ruling party.

"I don't believe that the 1952 coup had any positive features, since democracy is still missing. Even its social reforms led to the failure of our economy. The greatest failure of the revolution is the lack of democracy. Egypt has never experienced a democratic government from 1952 up till now. The press is not free in reality; otherwise article 809 of the penal code would never exist. This article criminalizing harming Egypt's image in effect means no one can criticize the government, as in the old days when it was a crime to dishonor the person of the king. It is this article that is disgraceful to Egypt and taints its status within the family of nations. The revolution embraced the slogan raise your head, my brother, for the age of oppression is over, but it replaced it with the heavy foot of Nasser that kept people's head down!"

- Reflections by Awad el-Morr,
former chief justice of the Supreme Constitutional Court,
on the fiftieth anniversary of the 1952 coup.

4. CORRUPTISTAN: THE PARTY, THE BUREAUCRACY, BUSINESS MOGULS AND THE MILITARY

A HEAVY BOOT ON THE EGYPTIAN NECK?

One of the most distinguishing aspects of the Mubarak regime is authoritarianism; "an arbitrary use of the law and coercive power of the state to expedite its own purposes of monopolizing power and denies the political rights and opportunities of all other groups for the power" (1)

The Mubarak regime created and maintained a patronage system for the containment and control of the political machine, the party, the bureaucracy, the military and the security apparatus. "It's a system of patron-client ties that bind leaders and followers in relationship not only of mutual assistance and support, but also of recognized and accepted inequality between *big man* and *lesser men*. The ties usually extend from the center of the regime - that is from the ruler to his lieutenants, clients and other followers, and through them, their followers and so on", says Maye Kasem (2)

Mubarak, like his predecessors, came from the military institution and assured the continuation of that institution's rule over Egypt.

From 1952 till present day, the military maintained control over the numerous single-party political organizations. The military has provided a recruiting pool from which all presidents, vice presidents, and most prime ministers originate. Military officers occupied at least a 33.6 per cent of cabinet positions, governorship and many other aspects of life. (3)

During Mubarak's regime, the role of the military, security and political apparatus has been concentrated on preserving and defending the regime and monitoring and containing political activities. Mubarak has used military courts to try political opponents and hand down the most severe sentences in cases that would not be tried in ordinary courts.

According to one study, in the period between 1992 and 2000, 1033 civilians were tried in military courts; 92 received the death penalty, and 644 were sentenced to jail for various periods of time. (4)

Mubarak assumes the titles of Commander-in-Chief of the Armed forces and police, as well. Mubarak has expanded the powers of police and security services to fight against opposition challenges through the use of the Emergency Laws that granted a virtual *Carte Blanche* to arrest and detain political activists. Such practices led to the indefinite detainment of about 15,000 political prisoners from virtually every political spectrum currently lingering in Egyptian jails and concentration camps. (5)

Mubarak's Minister of the Interior assumes a supervisory role over elections in Egypt. Police and security forces play a major role in intimidating political candidates from outside of the president's NDP by counting the votes and reporting the final results to the president. To ensure the loyalty of the military and security services, Mubarak has devised a system of generous patronage in giving away cars, apartments, subsidized medical care and lavish recreational facilities.

This system of patronage includes state-financed training and study abroad programs. Many military and police officers are sent into training courses abroad to Western countries to be trained on techniques of psychological warfare, torture of prisoners and ways of extracting confessions from suspects.

As one author found out in her study of the military in Egypt and the patronage system, she said: "to ensure the loyalty and obedience of the officers, the regime provides opportunities for commission ... so that wealth is spread among a reasonable number of the general officers corps. Military attaché positions in London, Paris, and Washington are the top plums, and hence are rotated on a bi-annual basis, about twice the turnover rate for equivalent foreign ministry positions". (6)

The system of patronage and cronyism has been used to buy loyalty of elements of the regime while turning a blind eye on corruption practices as a policy of a carrot and a stick. As a result, an exclusive elite class has been created where businessmen rub hands with politicians, and often exchange roles, monopolizing and benefiting beyond the realm of the law.

A classic example of that is the case of the Egyptian American Bank. The selling of Alexandria Bank share that reached 24% in the Egyptian-American Bank to the French Calion Bank raised several questions. A quarter of the French Calion Bank shares in Egypt were owned by a company in which the two cousin ministers, Minister of Housing and Construction Ahmad el-Maghrabi owned 3% and Transport Minister Mohammed Lotfi Mansour owned 22%. The selling of the Egyptian-American Bank took place only five days after the formation of the cabinet that included eight businessmen.

The number of Calion shares in Egypt reached about 8.5 million. Its expected profit in 2005 did not exceed E£ 58 million, while its deposits were closer to E£ seven billion. The number of shares in the Egyptian-American Bank reached 64 million. Its profit in the previous year reached E£ 250 million, while its deposits exceeded E£ eight billion. (7) The deal could be least described as insider trading punishable in Western democracies. In a special hearing, People's Assembly members Mostafa Bakri and Jamal Zahran raised the topic saying that selling the Alexandria Bank's shares and the Egyptian American Bank were manipulated by the two ministers; el-Maghrabi and Mansour.

The two minsters owned 25% of the shares in Calion Bank. It was stunning that the stock price was fixed at E£ 45, while it was traded in stock exchanges the day of inking the deal, at E£ 65.5! Crédit Agricole bank held along with El-Maghraby Group about 75% of the shares and both cashed the difference. (8)

For its part, *Al-Ahaly* newspaper announced that the Egyptian government lost about E£ 300 million in the deal of selling the Egyptian American Bank shares to French Calion Bank. (9)

The Cairo's Criminal Court case reviewed on May 4, 2004, and dubbed as *Fuyoum MP's*, is another case of corruption that speaks volumes. The case involved 19 defendants topped by two former members of parliament of the Egyptian People's Assembly:

Bahaa el-Mileegy and Hussein Oueis. In his testimony, Egyptian Deputy Prime Minister Yousof Wali said that the lands which the defendants are accused of taking over are privately-owned, not publicly owned. While the Minister of Water Resources Mahmoud abou-Zeid insisted in his testimony that the encroached lands are state land and not privately owned! The defendants in *Fayoum MP's* case were convicted by the Supreme State Security Court. The judge ruled relieving the defendants of their posts and sentencing them to terms between one and nineteen years, and restoring the lands owned by the state. (10)

In the last few years, the Mubarak government embarked on an ambitious plan to privatize almost all state-owned companies and factories. The policy was decried by the opposition as the *wholesale of Egypt*. Most companies and factories prior to that were owned and run by the state in a Socialist fashion.

For decades, through mismanagement, most of these companies suffered great financial losses due to the practice of placing the wrong people to manage these companies; people whose only qualification consisted of being members of the President's party, i.e. loyal. The Egyptian opposition press has been reporting on a flood of corruption cases involving government ministers, high level officials and MP's who allegedly short sold state companies for less value in return for multi-million dollar commissions. An example of that is the *Case of Omar Effendi Company*.

The *Omar Effendi Company*, with 82 branches throughout Egypt, is a chain of department stores that was founded in 1856, which, in its era, rivaled the greatest stores from around the world. It was the Sears and the Harrods of Egypt. *Omar Effendi* branches are located in affluent neighborhoods. The size of every branch ranges from 3200-9553 cubic meters with all assets including, buildings, a fleet of trucks and trailers, more than 55 buses, in addition to stores, maintenance workshops, and mobile galleries. It has 5870 permanent employees, in addition to more than 3000 contract workers. The *Omar Effendi* scandal started when Yahya Hassanein abdol-Hadi, the chairman of *Ben Zion* Company - another chain of department stores that belonged to Jewish Egyptians - filed a complaint in February 2006 to the Attorney General, against selling *Omar Effendi* branches to Saudi *Anwal Company* for only E£ 540 million.

In his complaint, Abdel-Hadi accused Investment Minister Mahmoud Muhi el-Deen of exercising pressure on the evaluating committee, which included him, among others, to reduce the estimated value of *Omar Effendi Company.* The buyout process, led to the loss of E£ 600 million by the state according to abdel-Hadi. The offer that won the deal was presented by the Saudi businessman Gameel abdol-Rahman al-Qinbit, owner of Saudi Anwal Company. The takeover triggered suspicions of undisclosed backstage agreements, lacking the principle of transparency in the buyout process.

The *Omar Effendi* case was a single episode in a series of high profile corruption cases that involved party and cabinet members.

Ex-Finance Minister, Muhy el-Deen el-Ghareeb, was convicted by the Criminal Court and other officials in the Customs Service and businessmen in the case known as the *Big Customs Case* for bribery and abuse of power. The Supreme State Security Court sentenced el-Ghareeb to eight years in jail.

Another high profile corruption case, that occupied the Egyptian opposition media, is the case of Misr Exterior Bank involving former NDP leader Abdalla Tayil. The defendants in this case were topped by Tayil, the ex-chairman of the bank and former Chairman of the Economic committee in the People's Assembly.

The 18 defendants including businessmen and top officials in Misr Exterior Bank were accused of looting E£ 272 million from the bank money and refusing to pay it back. Some of them escaped the country. The Criminal Court sentenced Tayil to ten years in jail, businessman Tayssir el-Hawari to seven years, and businessman Mahmoud Ali Bedair - the bank's deputy chairman - to three years, and Mohamed abdel-Razeq- the bank's general manager, to two years.

During the wave of corruption cases that swept Egypt in the last two-plus decades the state-owned media kept silent. It failed to fully report on corruption cases; when it did, it would apologetically and unashamedly defend the public figures accused, or raise the topic of a bigger conspiracy theory beyond the comprehension of the average citizen.

This puzzling attitude can only be understood by the fact that since 1952, Nasser, Sadat and Mubarak turned journalists into subservient government employees, who clearly have understood the red lines that they ought not to cross. Right after 1952, the regime confiscated and nationalized all media outlets. Since then, there has not been any privately owned TV or Radio service in Egypt. The only exception is a few opposition newspapers that turned into mouthpieces of the elders of the party. Therefore, in reality, Egypt does not have any independent media outlets that can be the watchdog for the people of Egypt.

A clear example of corruption leaking into the Egyptian media itself is the case of *al-Ahram* newspaper and its former editor-in-chief Ibrahim Nafea. On August 31, 2005, *Elosboa* newspaper accused Ibrahim Nafea, of involvement in corruption. Nafea, who was Chairman of Al-Ahram Press Group, denied the allegations to *Agence France-Press*. According to *Elosboa*, Nafea was receiving an annual salary up to E£ 3 million and huge sums of money as corporate profits bonuses.

Elosboa accused him of receiving also a daily commission up to E£ 83,000 ($14,000) from the revenues of advertising and distribution of Al-Ahram publications, which he headed for 26 years. The newspaper confirmed that Nafea transferred E£ 400 million ($70 million) to his personal accounts before leaving Al-Ahram.

Elosboa published details of the illegal transfer with documents supporting the accusations. According to *Elosboa*, Nafea was celebrating his birthday every year in his Al-Ahram office with expenses that reached E£ 25 million. Nafea responded saying that Al-Ahram refuted these accusations twice in the past, and that it has documents to prove the accusations are groundless.

The state-owned *Al-Ahram* newspaper, which Nafea headed, sells 600,000 issues every day, the best selling in Egypt. It employs 10,000 workers. Nafea was relieved of his post through *a restructural process of state media.*

Referring to Nafae and corruption, *Elosboa* claimed that "the government did not do justice towards the national newspapers by insisting that they become mouthpieces of the government, instead of adopting an approach that can contain all views from different political spectrums. The government also did wrong when it ignored the law and kept the ex-chairman of the board and editor-in-chief of *Al-Ahram* [Nafea] for 11 years, heading the institution with a blatant violation of the law. Nafea should have retired in January 1994. With such violations, the government gave a bad example that encouraged such persons and others to violate the law. Also, the governments wronged when it let Nafea do whatever he wanted regarding financial matters, in return for attacking political opponents of the regime. The regime was satisfied that Nafea devoted the newspaper for propagating and justifying what the government did."

Exposing the financial violations of Nafea, *Elosboa* leaked the official report of the Central Auditing Organization that pointed that "Nafea was paid a sum of E£ 2.73 million and, a total of about E£ 3.56 million in 1994. The salary and benefits he received was E£ 296,000 per month. The newspaper also raised the issue of financial integrity and management at *Al-Ahram*, saying that, "there is a stunning sign of lack of justice and brutality, manifested in the craze for obtaining money at the expense of the *Al-Ahram's* staff, workers and reporters. Nafae's salary was 2000 times more than the salary of a university graduate working in government, and 600 times more than the starting salary of a reporter in *Al-Ahram*. By the way, the U.S. President's annual salary is $400,000 (E£ 2.3 million), E£ 191,000 per month. This means that the President of the United States is poor compared with the former editor-in-chief and chairman of Al-Ahram board who received E£ 296,000 a month. The U.S. President is also poor compared to Hassan Hamdy, the general manager of advertising at Al-Ahram Advertising Agency. Hamdy received E£ 274.400 a month, according to the stated report. The monthly salary of Huda Awadallah, a general manager of advertising during Nafae's era, was E£ 166,000. The salary of the general manager of commercial advertisements, Mohamed Mohammedein, was E£ 105,000 a month."

Elosboa revealed more shady practices during the era of Nafea like the *end-of-year presents* to Al-Ahram board members that reached E£ 106 million, about 265 % of the overall *end-of-year* incentives and profits which were distributed in the same year to all workers in Al-Ahram.

In a column in *al-Arabi al-Nasseri* newspaper, raging over corruption in the state media, columnist Ahmad el-Sayyed el-Naggar, wrote: "There was no transparency regarding these presents [given to board members and high officials]. These presents, with such a stunning size, are blatant corrupting bribes; there'll be no real overhaul in the national press without eliminating such practices. We need to tighten legal punishment against those giving or receiving such gifts, especially workers and officials in the government service and public institutions. The executive, legislative and judicial authorities should work on banning gifts in the financial dealings of the press, public institutions and the economic bodies, and the public sector. What is really bizarre is that these huge give-aways were distributed in a year that Al-Ahram suffered from large losses due to mismanagement. There is no logic, conscience or accountability towards the wasted public money?"

In response to that, Safwat el-Sharif, the Shura Council Speaker and head of the Supreme Press Council, and former Minister of Information, gave in to demands of journalists and fired board chairmen and editors-in-chief who surpassed retirement age. Thereby, he opened their thorny financial files after giving access to some data concerning their financial dealings. Nafea, who was chairman of the Press Syndicate, as well, was condemned by the Central Auditing Organization report that revealed that "he ignored the interests of journalists for the sake of a group of those who received unreasonably huge salaries, allowances, commissions, bonuses and incentives, in a way that violated the law. The vast majority of journalists are paid limited salaries, driving many of them to seek a working opportunity abroad in Arab newspapers or media. Nafea left a heavy burden that paralyzed Al-Ahram and caused grave losses to its workers."

During that year of political scandals, *Elosboa* newspaper broke out another bigger scandal in Egypt's state media. On November 12, 2005, the Supreme Prosecutor of Public Funds ordered the jailing of Abdel-Raman Hafez, the ex-chairman of Egypt's TV and Radio Union at the Ministry of Information. The prosecution accused him of *stealing public money, ill-gotten gain and causing voluntary damages to public money.* The prosecutor included in his investigation businessman Ihab Talaat for involvement in the same case. The complaint was filed against them by the Information Minister Anas el-Fiqi. The charges against Hafez included deception to reduce Ihab Talaat's debts to the TV and Radio Union worth of E£ 48 million, and facilitating the takeover of two companies to re-broadcast the Egyptian satellite channel, and causing damages to public money. A court order was issued to seize the financial assets of Hafez and Talaat.

According to the Administrative Censorship Authority, the violations of Hafez, while he headed the TVRU, included concluding a contract between the union and a company without carrying out the required studies; which led to forcing the union to pay up to $8.18 million during the contracting period. The Information Minister sent another memo to the Attorney General, demanding the investigation of Hafez regarding alleged violations committed while heading the Media Production City.

Hafez conceded that he gave a contract of ad time on local channels to an advertising agency, and giving this agency concessions and facilitations as compliments. He also inked a number of soap-opera co-productions to that agency for E£ 48 million.

Elosboa newspaper further revealed that, after corruption spread in the Media City during Hafez's era, its shares plummeted in the stock exchange from E£ 70 to E£ 7. A government report documented another violation committed by Hafez through his manipulation of the deposits of the Media City to buy shares in the stock exchange for E£ 28 million. He caused grave losses to the Media City whose debts rose to E£ 3 billion. Another violation documented by the official reports of the Central Auditing Organization related to appointing the wife of the City's former chairman as a manager of the international relations body with a huge salary.

The blatant violations documented by the reports included

Hafez and his top aides allocating a luxury *Peugeot* car for every official, and employing two drivers for each vehicle, one for family affairs and the other for the official's public business. His staff reached 2000 employees; some were paid overestimated salaries up to E£ 100,000 per month.

The report of the supervisory services also spotted a blatant violation related to hiring a journalist as a media advisor for the City for E£ 100,000 a month. The report further criticized Hafez for establishing an institution called the *International Cooperation Service, ICS,* for publicity. The *ICS* invited many foreign delegations to Egypt, including the cast of *Cleopatra* movie. The Media City paid E£ 5,000,000 for just bringing them on a private jet.

Hafez founded his production company in the Dubai free zone with a capital of $50 million registered in the name of his son Mohamed Hafez. Later, it was also found that Hafez gave rights of premiership for all works that the City produced to his son's company.

"I am writing to you from the fearful Bastille of Egypt, from that sinful military prison. The whole of Egypt is imprisoned. ..I was arrested despite my immunity as a judge, without an order of arrest... my sole crime being my criticism of the regime".

- An Egyptian judge's letter from a military prison.

5. For God, Pharaoh and Country: Nationalism, Egyptian Style

"Lift your head Brother, the days of humiliation are over"

Shortly after becoming president of Egypt, Nasser set on a campaign of consolidating power into his hands like never before. Whatever freedom of expression and assembly that had survived from the monarchy, was extinguished.

According to author John Waterbury, between 1961 and 1966, 4000 Egyptian families were affected by sequestration measures, and total assets seized in those years may have amounted to E£ 100 million, including 122,000 feddans of land, 700 urban properties, about 1000 businesses and stocks and bonds worth over E£ 30 million. (1)

In 1965, following an attempt on his life, Nasser arrested thousands of members of the Muslim Brothers and executed many including its leader Sayyid Qutb. It was estimated that between 1952 and 1971, a total of 14,499 political prisoners were in Egyptian jails including Muslim Brothers, Christian Copts,

Jews, Communists, journalists and many others. (2)

In December 1969, Nasser himself admitted that 18,000 Muslim Brothers had been arrested. In 1975 an Egyptian newspaper estimated that 27,000 had been swept into Egyptian concentration camps. (3)

Nasser nationalized all media outlets, outlawed all existing political parties that existed before his coup. He confiscated the wealth of prominent Egyptian families; Muslims, Copts and Jews. Egyptian writer and critic, Louis Awad, who was also detained during the Nasser's era, summed up the Nasser's regime by saying: "Nasser first liquidated democracy in Egypt, and later any socialism that may have existed in the country and the Arab world". (4)

Famous Egyptian writer Youssef Idris had his share of imprisonment like most Egyptian intellectuals. Idris described the Nasser's years as *a hell of hunger, disease and war.* The twin brothers and journalists, Mostafa and Ali Amin, nephews of Egyptian Nationalist leader Saad Zaghloul, and founders of *Akhbar Al-Yom* daily newspaper, were accused of plotting with the Muslim Brothers and the United States against the Nasser's regime. They were severely tortured. Mostafa Amin was released by Sadat years later to write his memoirs about Nasser's prisons in a four volume book. Mostafa Amin described that time in the following way: "The Basic rule in those days was that if you were found guilty, you went to prison, and if you were found innocent, you went to a concentration camp". (5)

Ahmad Abul-Fatth, publisher of a former Wafdist newspaper, was arrested and tried before a revolutionary court for the charge of *aiming to destroy the government and spreading hostile propaganda* for which he received a lengthy prison sentence and his property was confiscated. (6)

Nasser who staged his coup under the pretext of liberating the Egyptians from yoke of the monarchy and the British, promising a utopian society, promoted his slogan of *lift your head Brother, the days of humiliation are over* inscribed on banners throughout Egypt.

Louis Awad, a life-long advocate of the need for Egyptians to participate in democracy, described the effect of the Nasser's coup and the legacy that followed through his successors as, "it is more or less the same conservative power and money elite of depoliticized professional deputies, technocrats and administrators whose families have ruled Egypt for more than a hundred years, surviving the quick sands of national and social revolutions and disasters." (7)

Egyptian sociologist, Dr. Sayyid Uways documented the influence of Nasser's coup on Egyptian society by listing the means by which Egyptians managed to cope with oppression as: "indifference, hypocrisy, raillery, and emigration".

Prominent Egyptian intellectual Ghali Shukri warned of the phenomenon of *Cultural collapse* due to autocratic and authoritarian rule throughout the Arab world.

The late outspoken poet Nizar Qabbani described the present-day Arab cultural climate as *nothing but bubbles in washtubs and chamber pots.* Qabbani caused another literary and political storm after writing another poem in 1995 titled: *When will they declare the death of the Arabs?* (8)

Algerian writer Abdel-Wahab Bouhdiba, described the relation between the Arab and his personality in today's world as… *with nature, other people, God; Arabs are in a state of crisis.* In his book *Letters from Hypocrisia*, Egyptian writer Ibrahim Abdu wrote that the encouraging and awarding of flattery by Egyptian and Arab rulers had destroyed the chances of a realistic outlook into the current situation.

In 2005, Egyptian novelist Sanallah Ibrahim caused yet another literary and political storm when in front of hundreds of writers and TV cameras refused to receive a lucrative financial and literary award from Egyptian Minister of Culture, Farouk Hosni, and saying: *I refuse to accept this prize from a regime that lost its credibility.*

FOR EGYPT OR MUBARAK?

The prevailing hyped nationalistic climate in Egypt now is a product of an age-long process that has been boiling down to the concentration of power into the hands of the few and creating a pharaohnic-like regime where criticism directed at Mubarak's regime is considered an attack on Egypt! Egypt has been reduced to the office of the presidency and the voices of millions of Egyptians are not heard or taken into account. Opponents, dissenters and critics of the Mubarak regime are quickly deemed as unpatriotic, and infidels in some cases, by his controlled state media and tamed clergy.

Mubarak cannot claim credit for creating that elaborate system that launched him into a pharaoh-status. The system goes back in history to the earliest pharaonic dynasties and the efforts of Nasser and Sadat to consolidate power into their hands. Nationalism seemed to be a convenient tool and remains so until today.

Arab Politics: the Enemy of My Enemy is My Friend

The French expedition in 1798 led by Napoleon Bonaparte was a rude awakening to the Egyptians who had not have any contact with the West since the seventh and last crusade on Egypt in 1250.

The last crusade was led by French King Louis IX who was taken prisoner in Mansoura, by the Nile Delta, and was not released until a hefty ransom was paid to the Mameluke Queen Shagrat Al-Dorr. Queen Al-Dor, a former slave herself, concealed the news of the death of her husband Sultan Najmeddine Ayub and continued to rule after his demise. She then married her second husband, Ezzedine Aibak, an aid to her late husband. Aibak, however, was already married to Um Ali.

When Aibak refused to divorce Um Ali, Queen Al-Dor decided to have him killed. The queen ordered her slaves to kill Aibak while bathing. They did so by crushing his testicles till he died.

In retaliation, Um Ali directed her slave maids to kill the Queen. Um Ali's maids hacked Shagrat Al-Dor to death in her bathroom with her wooden diamond-studded sandals. Then they threw her naked body off the palace walls. Um Ali revenge was in response to the stealing of her husband and denying her son Ali his right to succeed his father.

Najmeddine Ayub's other son, Turan Shah was shortly thereafter murdered by his deputies who stabbed him, and when he took refuge in a tower, they set it ablaze. Turan Shah then jumped to his death into the sea and was replaced by Sultans Qutoz and Baibars. The sultans managed to stop the flood of the Mongols from the East. Prior to heading for Egypt, the Mongols swept across the Abbasid Caliphate in Baghdad.

The Mameluke sultans continued to rule Egypt till after the French conquest of Egypt. Egypt has always found itself in the middle of crossfire between powers eyeing its strategic location. It seemed to be Egypt's destiny, the gift of its geography that turned out to be both a blessing and a curse.

The French invasion by Napoleon Bonapart contributed to the awakening of Egyptian nationalistic and religious fervor flamed by the remnants of the fleeing incompetent Mamleuks who did not stand against the military might of Napoleon's canons.

Napoleon was confronted by an unexpected source of resistance, the *Al-Azhar Ulama* [learned scholars] and students in what is called *Cairo's Biggest Revolt.* Napoleon responded by storming *Al-Azhar* University and mosque and hanging the rebel leaders; including Sheikh Omar Makram. Makram became an instant martyr. To honor him, a grand Mosque was established in Cairo. Its use is still reserved for state funerals.

In a largely unsuccessful effort to gain the support of the Egyptian populace, Bonaparte also issued proclamations casting himself as a liberator of the people from oppression, and praising the precepts of Islam. Napoleon left Egypt and set out further east in an attempt to build his empire, entrusting his Deputy General Kléber to handle matters in Egypt.

Kléber was assassinated by an *Al-Azhar* student from a remote village in Syria by the name of Suleiman al-Halabi. Al-Halabi knifed the Deputy General through the heart in Cairo on June 14, 1800. The French military made an example of the assassin. His two legs were tied to two different horses running in two different directions at the same time, thus splitting his body into two halves.

Napoleon's dreams of establishing a strong foothold in the Middle East to counter the efforts of the British Empire were short lived. In 1801, Admiral Nelson's warships destroyed the French Navy in Alexandria to secure their access to India, the Jewel of the Crown of the British Empire.

The Mamelukes returned to power as a gift from the two warring empires. A series of civil wars took place between the Ottoman Turks, the Mamelukes, and Albanian mercenaries in Egypt resulting in the Albanian Muhammad Ali taking control of Egypt, where he was appointed as the Ottoman viceroy in 1805.

In an attempt to win them to their side, foreign rulers indirectly stirred the Egyptians' sense of patriotism and religious zeal. Saladin, a Kurdish general, did the same before by calling on the Egyptians to join his army to stop the invading Crusaders. Saladin established the Ayyubid dynasty that ruled Egypt and major parts of the Middle East from 1169-1250, until the Mamelukes (enslaved mercenaries) brought it to an end.

In 1811, Mohammed Ali invited a number of his opponents to the Saladin Citadel in Cairo for a feast, then trapped them within the gates and slaughtered them; thus becoming the sole and uncontested ruler of Egypt setting up a dynasty that ruled

Egypt for more than 200 years. He then conquered the Arabian Peninsula and Sudan. Finally, he placed a number of Egyptians in the highest places in government creating an elite class in Egypt.

The Mohammed Ali dynasty declared itself a rightful Muslim religious one that owed its legitimacy and pledged allegiance to the Sublime Porte, the Ottoman Sultan. The Ottoman Sultan had previously declared himself the Caliph of Muslims; similar to the Pope in the Vatican, as the ultimate religious authority and spiritual leadership to the millions of the Catholic faithful, the High See.

After leaving Egypt, the French pursued their dreams of a foothold in Egypt through the plans of Ferdinand de Lesseps to dig the Suez Canal in order to connect the Mediterranean and the Red Sea. The Canal was finally dug by the mere hands of thousands of Egyptian farmers in 1869.

Ismail Pasha, Egypt's ruler then used the canal's inaugural celebrations to showcase the country's *Westernization*, which included the construction of sumptuous palaces and the Cairo Opera House, which were built using money borrowed from financial institutions in Europe against the proceeds of the Suez Canal. Despite the booming demand for Egyptian cotton, caused by shortfalls of American cotton due to the American Civil War (1861-1865) Egypt fell heavily into debt.

Egypt's inability to pay back its loans led to the appointment of foreign debt commissioners to monitor Egypt's finances in 1876, the inclusion of British and French ministers in Egypt's cabinet in 1878.

Under European pressure, the Ottoman Sultan installed Ismail's son, Tawfik. In 1881, an Egyptian colonel named Ahmad Orabi led a mutiny against Tawfik. Orabi demanded an elected legislature and an increased budget for the army. In early 1882 the nationalists gained control of the cabinet and the army, threatened Tawfik himself.

Riots broke out in the port cities, and Britain and France sent warships to blockade Alexandria harbor. On July 11, 1882, British battleships bombarded Alexandria, setting the city afire. Tawfik, siding with Britain, declared Orabi a rebel, thus setting the stage for a British invasion and occupation after defeating Orabi's troops.

Orabi and his followers were jailed, tried, and exiled to Ceylon, and Tawfik was restored to power. Under the pretext of bringing back order, Britain seized control of Egypt's government in 1882 and declared Egypt a protectorate. Egyptian nationalism continued to grow increasing in the people's desire for independence from British control and Ottoman rule; it was the beginning of the rise of modern day Egyptian nationalism.

Egyptian nationalism was aided by the French and the Ottomans, who resented the substantial British role in Egyptian affairs. The nationalists gained strength under the leadership of Mustafa Kamil, an Egyptian lawyer educated in Paris. He founded the National Party to end the British occupation. Kamil helped Egyptians side with the Ottoman Turks adhering to the Egyptian and Arab adages that: "The enemy of my enemy is my friend, and me and my brother against our cousin, and me and my cousin against the outsider". Kamil died in 1908.

THE RISE OF ARAB NATIONALISM

Arab nationalism grew in the years prior to World War I. Nationalists' demands were of a reformist nature, limited, in general, to autonomy within the Ottoman Empire, greater use of Arabic in education, and reducing compulsory conscription in the Ottoman army. Revolts took place in 1908 within the Ottoman Empire. Turkizisation programs were imposed by the new Committee of Union and Progress (CUP, often known as the Young Turks) government.

Many Arabs gave their primary loyalty to their religion or sect, their tribe, or their own particular governments siding against the Turks. The ideologies of Ottomanism and pan-Islamism exploited by the Turks were strong competitors of Arab Nationalism.

In 1913, Arab intellectuals and some politicians met in Paris at the first Arab Congress. They produced a set of demands for greater autonomy within the Ottoman Empire. They also requested that Arab conscripts to the Ottoman army not be required to serve in other regions except in time of war.

Aziz al-Masri became an inspiring figure to many nationalists during that era. A third generation Egyptian of Turko-Circassian descent, al-Masri graduated from the Ottoman Military College. In 1911, he was in charge of the Ottoman forces in Libya fighting the Italians. His service in Libya earned him the title of the *hero of Cyrenaica*. In 1913, he organized the *al-'ahd*, a secret society of Arab Ottoman Army Officers.

In February1914, al-Masri was arrested and put on trial and sentenced to death. His sentence was later commuted to fifteen years. Al-Masri became a hero and a role model to many Arab *Free Officers* who staged coups in their countries, like Nasser and Sadat.

Ironically, during World War I, the British designed and produced a flag representing Arab nationalism. Mark Sykes, who was one of the two gentlemen behind dividing the Arab world, created the black, white, green, and red banner variations of which can still be seen in the flags of a number of Arab states.

In 1914, war was declared on the Ottoman Empire by European powers eager to divide the inheritance of the *Sick Old Man of Europe*, the Ottoman Sultan. Nationalist sentiments became more prominent during the collapse of Ottoman authority. The brutal repression of the secret societies in Damascus and Beirut by the Turkish ruler, Jamal Pasha, who executed patriotic intellectuals in 1915 and 1916, strengthened anti-Turkish feelings.

The Sharif of Mecca launched the Arab Revolt during the World War I backed by General Allenby, and Bedouin mercenaries led by Lawrence of Arabia. The Ottomans were defeated and the Sharif's son Faisal entered Damascus in 1918.

There was a brief sense of relief and liberation from the Ottoman yoke amongst the Arab masses. But, alas, it was short lived. The Arabs who were used by the British to get rid of the Turks, found themselves under the British and French mandates. Now it was Arab nationalism against the outsiders, the cousins against the non-Muslim Franks [name given to Eurpoean invaders since the Crusades]. It was another reminder of the Crusades.

The Balfour Declaration in 1917 to establish a homeland for the Jewish People in Palestine and the secret *Sykes-Picot* agreement between Britain and France to divide the eastern Arab lands between the two imperial powers were revealed. The Angry Arab masses felt betrayed and doublecrossed by the European powers.

Arab nationalist thinkers in the inter-war period included Christian Lebanese expatriates in America, Amin al-Rihani, Michel Aflaq and Sati al-Husari. Competing ideologies included Islamism and local nationalism. Lebanese nationalism was promoted by predominantly Christian thinkers and politicians in that country. The Greater Syrian nationalism was developed by Antoun Sa'ade. Communism also became a significant ideological force; first and most notably in Iraq, but later also in Syria and to a certain extent in Egypt.

THE UMMA: ISLAMIC NATIONALISM

In March 1928, along with six workers of the Suez Canal Company, Hassan al-Banna founded the Muslim Brotherhood in the city of Isma'ilia. It was both a religious, political and social movement with the credo "God is our objective; the Quran is our constitution, the Prophet is our leader; Struggle is our way; and death for the sake of God is the highest of our aspirations".

Al-Banna called for the return to an original Islam and followed Islamic reformers like Muhammad Abduh and Rashid Rida. According to him, contemporary Islam had lost its social dominance, because most Muslims had been corrupted by Western influences. The Quran and the Sunnah were seen as laws passed down by God that should be applied to all parts of life, including the organization of the government and the handling of everyday problems.

Al-Banna's doctrine of pan-Islamism found its roots in Ibn Taymiya. Ibn Taymiya was born on January 22, 1263 in Harran, located in what is now Turkey, close to the Syrian border. He lived during the troubled times of the Mongol invasions. As a member of the *Pietist* school founded by Ibn Hanbal, Ibn Taymiya is a primary intellectual source of the Wahhabi movement.

Because of Ibn Taymiya's outspokenness, puritanical views, and literalism, he was imprisoned several times for conflicting with the opinions of prominent jurists and theologians of his day. In 1306, Ibn Taymiya was imprisoned in the citadel of Cairo for 18 months on the charge of anthropomorphism. He was incarcerated again in 1308 for several months for having denounced popular worship at the tombs of saints. He is known for this saying: "What can my enemies possibly do to me? My paradise is in my heart; wherever I go it goes with me, inseparable from me. For me, prison is a place of (religious) retreat; execution is my opportunity for martyrdom; and exile from my town is but a chance to travel." This slogan was taken to heart by many militant Islamic groups and individuals such as Muhammad ibn Abd al-Wahhab (founder of Wahhabism in Saudi Arabia, the doctrine of Osama Bin laden), and Sayyid Qutb in Egypt.

Another important individual who played a major role in the development of Arab nationalism was a man named Sati al-Husari. Born in Sanaa, Yemen, to a government official from Aleppo, Syria, in August 1880, he graduated from the Royal Academy in 1900, and worked as a school teacher in a region within the

European territories of the Ottoman Empire. During this period, he began to show an interest in questions of nationality. He took an administrative position in Macedonia, where the officers who would later form the Committee for Union and Progress (CUP) had a strong presence. Later he was appointed director of the Teachers' Institute.

From 1910 to 1912, he visited European countries to examine modern educational methods. Initially a supporter of Ottomanism and the Young Turks, from 1916 onward, he moved towards Arabism. In 1919, after the establishment of an independent Arab state in Syria under Faisal, al-Husari moved to Damascus where he was appointed Director General of Education, and later Minister of Education. In the same year, several nationalists, led by Saad Zaghlul in Egypt, were exiled to Malta. In March 1919, a nationwide revolt broke out in Egypt. Mass demonstrations in the cities, and expressions of national unity between Copts and Muslims took place.

Egypt was finally granted independence from Britain on February 28, 1922 and declared an independent constitutional monarchy under Hussein Kamil's successor, Ahmad Fuad, who became King Fuad I. The Egyptian Parliament drafted and implemented a new constitution in 1923. The Wafd party became the major voice for Egyptian nationalism. From 1924 to 1936, there was a short-lived but successful attempt to model Egypt's constitutional government after the European style of government; known as Egypt's Liberal Experiment.

Al-Husari followed the Hashemite Prince Faisal to Iraq in 1920 after the French imposed their mandate on Syria. From 1921 to

1927, al-Husari held the position of Director of General Education. In addition to other positions, he subsequently held the post of head of the Higher Teachers' Training College until 1937. During these years he played an influential role in promoting Arab nationalism through the educational system, and brought in teachers from Syria and Palestine to teach Arabic history and culture.

In 1941 nationalist army officers, from the first generation to have come under the influence of al-Husari's ideas, carried out a coup d'etat against the pro-British monarchy and government in Iraq, briefly installing a pro-Axis regime under Rashid Ali al-Kailani. When British forces restored the monarchy, al-Husri was deported.

Al-Husari's next major enterprise was the reform of the educational system in Syria. In 1943 the newly-elected Syrian president Shukri al-Quwatli invited him to Damascus, then still under the French mandate, to draw up a new curriculum along Arab nationalist lines for the country's educational system. Al-Husari established a curriculum inspired by his nationalist ideas which considerably reduced the French cultural element and broke away from the French educational model.

In 1947, al-Husari moved to Cairo, taking up a position in the Cultural Directorate of the League of Arab States. He would remain there for 18 years, during which he produced most of his works. He returned to Baghdad in 1965, and died there in 1967, unable to go back to his native Syria that shared with Baghdad a similar Ba'athist nationalist regime partly inspired by his ideas.

While al-Husari was busy promoting his secularist ideas of Arab

Nationalism and spreading them throughout the Arab countries, Hassan al-Banna was busy spreading his ideas of pan-Islamism. By 1936, The Muslim Brotherhood had 800 members. The number increased greatly to up to 200,000 by 1938. By 1948, the Brotherhood had about half a million members. Today, members of the MB are in almost every Arab and Muslim countries, and even in the U.S. and Western Europe.

During World War II, the Germans, led by General Rommel, invaded Egypt and made their way through the desert to within 70 miles of Alexandria. They were defeated by the British. Oddly enough, many Egyptian nationalists hoped that Britain's enemies, the Axis (Nazi Germany and Fascist Italy), would win the war. They were cheering for Rommel to advance into Egypt.

In 1942, Sadat was arrested and charged of spying for the Nazis. On January 6, 1946, he was accused of plotting to assassinate Amin Osman, an Egyptian minister believed to be a collaborator with the British. Sadat escaped prison in April 1948 to join King Farouk's *Iron Guard*, and later attempting to assassinate Egyptian Prime Minster, Nahas Pasha, arch-enemy of Farouk.

The Nazis had no plan of liberating the Arab people. The racist Aryan Supremacist ideas included the Arabs as people they planned to dominate. In August 1939, Hitler called the people of the Middle East as *painted half-apes, who want to feel the whip.* (10) After the French surrender in June 1940, the Nazis were willing to recognize the rule of the Vichy government in both Syria and North Africa.

At a meeting between Hitler and Molotov in November 1940, they accepted the Soviet demand for areas in the Persian Gulf as a center of Soviet aspirations. The Nazis found Arab nationalism useful for their war effort. Their liaison with Arab nationalists was the Mufti [Grand Sheikh] of Jerusalem and leader of the Palestine Arab High Committee, Hajj Amin al-Hussaini. The Mufti appealed to the Nazis due to his seemingly Circassian ancestry, with a red beard and blue eyes, not the average Arab. (11)

The influence of Nazism on Arab nationalism became evident in several Arab parties applying Nazi and Fascist type of politics and rhetoric; paramilitary youth organizations, colored shirts, strict discipline, and more or less populist charismatic leaders. Examples of such are the Syrian Nationalist Socialist Party founded by Christian Antun Sa'ada, and the Lebanese Phalangist Party founded by Christian Maronite Pierre Jemayel. Jemayel fathered two Lebanese presidents, Bachir and Amine Jemayel.

Ahmad Husayn, founder and leader of Young Egypt Party found inspiration in Nazism. In 1936, he went on a visit to Germany and was well received. (12) Nazi sympathizers in Egypt were Prime Minister Ali Maher Pasha, King Farouk, and Aziz al-Masri.

In October 1939, Hajj Amin al-Hussaini helped to set up a pro-German regime in Iraq headed by Rashid Ali al-Kilani. Both staged a coup in April 1940. The British shortly regained control and al-Hussaini fled to Italy with a shaven beard and an Italian passport in October 11, 1941. In Rome, he met with Mussolini who gave him a warm welcome as a head of a secret Arab nationalist organization. To further the Axis plans during the war, al-Hussaini was given an initial grant of one million lire. (13) Al-Hussaini made himself useful to Nazis by playing another role with the German legion based in Greece that consisted of Soviet and Bulkan Muslim prisoners of war. He helped mobilize them for the Nazis.

After the end of the war and Nazism, a request was presented in 1947 to the UN asking for al-Hussaini to be tried as a war criminal at Nuremburg.

Al-Hussaini resided in Egypt after the end of World War II and continued to champion Nazism, inciting the Arab masses from Cairo to end the Jewish presence in his home country of Palestine. During the Nasser's years, al-Hussaini took it upon himself to welcome to Egypt the Nazi war criminals who escaped from Germany after the fall of the Third Reich who were invited by Nasser. One of those guests was Johann von Leers, an expert in anti-Semitic literature, who lived in Cairo till his death in 1965 under the name of Umar Amin. Leers worked as a political advisor to Nasser's information department and believed to have started the *Aryanization* of Egyptians. (14)

In 1948, Arab armies invaded Palestine attempting to stop the expansion of Jewish settlements and immigration to Palestine. Arab armies were defeated and the State of Israel was declared by David Ben-Gurion on May, and was recognized by the United Nations.

Between 1948 and 1949, Muslim Brotherhood members volunteered to fight Israelis in Palestine, while the conflict between the monarchy in Eygpt and the society reached its climax. Concerned with the increasing popularity of the Brotherhood, as well as with rumors that it was plotting a coup, Prime Minister Mahmud Fahmi al-Nuqrashi Pasha disbanded it in December 1948. The organization's assets were impounded and scores of its members sent to jail. On December 28, 1948, a member of the Muslim Brotherhood assassinated Prime Minister Nuqrashi. Shortly after, the Muslim Brotherhood's leader al-Banna was gunned down by government agents in Cairo in February, 1949.

On January 27, 1952, an angry mob set the Cairo Fire, burning down movie theatres and department stores. In July 23, 1952, a military coup d'état led by Nasser, Sadat and other Free Officers, forced King Farouk I to abdicate in support of his baby son King Ahmed Fouad II. Farouk left Egypt to live into exile in Italy where he was later assassinated by poison.

Egypt was declared a republic in June 18, 1953. General Muhammad Naguib became the first President of the Republic. Shortly, General Naguib was forced to resign and go under house arrest in 1954 by Nasser, the architect of the 1952 coup. Nasser assumed power as president in 1954 and forced the British out of Egypt declaring the full independence of Egypt from UK on June 18, 1956. The Muslim Brotherhood has become an illegal organization since 1954 when some of its members allegedly attempted to assassinate Nasser. The remnants of the MB spread throughout the world.

After a relative absence from the political arena during the Nasser years, Islamic militants and extremists came back with a vengeance. Sadat, in order to create for himself a new public persona and generate legitimacy, adopted the title of the *Faithful President*. He encouraged the return of the Muslim Brothers and made sure to be photographed frequenting mosques at religious holidays. His alliance with King Faisal of Saudi Arabia, who helped financed Sadat's war with Israel in 1973; opened the door of Egypt to Wahhabism, through al-Azhar and the Egyptian state media.

Through the influence of Saudi petro-dollars, Egypt- which adopted the more relaxed Hanafi madhab (creed) - has been gradually turning towards the Saudi Wahhabi version of Islam, after centuries of gravitating between Sufi and even Shi'ite beliefs and practices. Thus, a more strict and austere version of Islam was introduced, especially through those tens of thousands of Egyptians who worked and made their wealth in Saudi Arabia and adapted a Saudi life style, introducing what some social critics dubbed as petro-Islam.

Sadat's re-introduction into Saudi circles, after years of boycott during Nasser's socialism and open hostility towards the Saudi monarchy [Sadat was in charge of the Yemen war against loyalists to Saudi Arabia] was initiated by Kamal Adham. Adham, a Syrian national of Turkish origin, rose to power in Saudi Arabia after his sister married King Faisal. Kamal Adham was put in charge of the Saudi intelligence services which his nephew Turki al-Faisal dominated for 24 years after his uncle.

Turki al-Faisal later played a crucial role in assisting the Mujahedden in Afghanistan; including working with Osama bin-Laden, a monster that slipped the leash and turned against his masters. Turki al-Faisal was removed from his powerful position after the September 11th terrorist attacks for his alleged role with the Taliban and al-Qaeda. After his removal, he took posts of Saudi ambassador in Britain and in the U.S. A. consecutively.

Sadat's unleashing of the *Islamists* to counter Nasser's *Old Guard* and the *Left*, released the Jinni out of the bottle. On October 6, 1981, Sadat was assassinated. The assassins were a group of military officers with a religious zeal, masterminded by a former military intelligence officer, Colonel Aboud el-Zumor. Their spiritual leader was Sheikh Omar Abdel-Rahman. The assassins were believed to be members of al-Gamaa al-Islamiyya.

Later, after years of imprisonment and denouncing violence, Karam Zuhdi, leader of al-Gamaa al-Islamiya, expressed regret for his group's terrorist acts. Al-Gamaa al-Islamiyya was believed to have been responsible for the June 8, 1992 assassination of secularist writer Farag Foda, the June 26, 1995 attempt to assassinate President Mubarak in Addis Ababa, Ethiopia. It is also believed to be behind the November 19, 1995 car bomb attack on the Egyptian embassy in Islamabad, Pakistan, where 16 people were killed, the April 28, 1996 Europa Hotel shooting, in Cairo, where 18 Greek tourists were killed, and the November 17, 1997 Luxor massacre at Deir el-Bahri, where 58 foreign tourists and four Egyptians were killed.

"The terror gave Mubarak a splendid alibi and an escape from the demands put forth by segments of the middle class and its organizations in the professional syndicates-the lawyers, engineers and journalists- for a measure of political participation," says Professor Fouad Ajami. (14)

Terror Inc.

During the 1970s, Sheikh Omar Abdel-Rahman developed close ties with two of Egypt's most militant organizations, the Islamic Jihad and al-Gamaa al-Islamiyya. By the 1980s, he had emerged as the leader of al-Gamaa al-Islamiyya, although he was still revered by followers of Egyptian Islamic Jihad, which at the time was being led by future al-Qaeda principal Ayman al-Zawahiri. Rahman spent three years in Egyptian jails as he awaited trial on charges of issuing a fatwa (religious ruling) resulting in the 1981 assassination of Sadat.

Although Rahman was not convicted of conspiracy in the Sadat assassination, he was expelled from Egypt following his acquittal. He made his way to Afghanistan in the mid-1980s where he contacted Palestinian Abdullah Azzam, co-founder of Maktab al-Khadamat (MAK) along with Osama bin-Laden. Rahman built a strong rapport with bin-Laden during the Afghan war against the Soviets and following Azzam's murder in 1989 by a remote controlled roadside bomb, Rahman assumed control of the international jihadists' arm of MAK/al-Qaeda. For five years, Rahman traveled all over the world recruiting new mujaheddin for the Afghan war.

In July 1990, Rahman was sent to New York City to gain control of MAK's financial and organizational infrastructure in the United States. Abdel-Rahman was issued a tourist visa to the US despite his name being listed on a U.S. State Department terrorist watch list. Rahman entered the United States in July 1990, via Saudi Arabia, Peshawar, and Sudan.

After the first World Trading Center bombing in 1993, the FBI with the assistance of an Egyptian informant wearing a listening device, managed to record Rahman issuing a fatwa encouraging acts of violence against U.S. civilian targets in the New York and New Jersey metropolitan area. The informant, a former Egyptian officer, received a one million dollar reward and was placed on the witness protection program.

The most startling plan, the government charged, was to set off five bombs in 10 minutes, blowing up the United Nations, the Lincoln and Holland tunnels, the George Washington Bridge and a federal building housing the FBI. Rahman was arrested in 1993 along with nine of his followers. In October 1995, he was convicted of seditious conspiracy and was sentenced to life in prison. (15)

In 1998, al-Zawahiri is believed to have formally merged Egyptian Islamic Jihad into al-Qaeda. He has worked in the al-Qaeda organization since its inception and was a senior member of the group's Shura [consultative] council. He is often described as a *lieutenant* to the head of Osama bin-Laden. By fourteen, al-Zawahiri had joined the Muslim Brotherhood.

Al-Zawahiri studied for his medical degree at Cairo University. By 1979, he had moved on to the much more radical Islamic Jihad, where he eventually became one of its leading organizers and recruiters. He was one of the hundreds arrested following the assassination of Sadat, according to al-Zawahiri's lawyer Muntasir al-Zayyat.

However, the Egyptian government was unable to prove any connection between al-Zawahiri and the assassination and he was released after serving jail time for illegal arms possession. On February 23, 1998, he issued a joint fatwa with Osama bin-Laden under the title of *World Islamic Front against Jews and Crusaders*. On October 10, 2001, al-Zawahiri appeared on the list of the *FBI's Top 22 Most Wanted Terrorists*.

Extremist Islamic militants get their intolerant self-righteous ideology from Wahhabism and Sayyid Qutb. According to Qutb,

"There are two parties in all the world: the *Party of Allah* and the *Party of Satan.* The Party of Allah which stands under the banner of Allah and bears his insignia, and the Party of Satan, which includes every community, group, race, and individual that does not stand under the banner of Allah."

According to the Islamists, the U.S. and its allies declared war on Islam, which makes Jihad against them a personal duty for every Muslim. In one of their communiqués, Islamists claimed there is even threat to Islam from the Muslims themselves! According to Islamists, *the believers*, (i.e. Sunni Islamists) face popular as well as institutionalized hatred, and "this hatred is no less [intense] than the hatred from Jews and Christians. Sometimes it is a hundred times worse than the hatred of the enemies of the nation, the Jews and the Christians."

Islamists consider democracy as a threat, an invention of the West and warn against "the Secular Threat: There is no doubt that one of the greatest threats to the hegemony of Islam and the dominance of Shari'a [Islamic law] is the American secularism that will be imposed forcefully on the region... The Islamic world will change from dictatorship to democracy, which means subhuman degradation in all walks of life."

Islamists also reject Sufism and warn against it. Sufis, according to Wahhabis, *are mostly infidels* and believe in monism, pantheism, re-incarnation, and observe laws that "appeared in night-dreams, wishful thinking, conscience, inspiration, and other endless falsehoods. Islamists also claim that Sufis oppose Jihad and do not oppose the infidels. (16)

The list of enemies of Wahhabis, or Islamists, continues to

grow including most Muslims, Sunnis and Shiites alike, which include what they call the *Threat of the Rational School.*

Islamists asserted that British imperialism planted this "deadly seedling that maintains that Islam is not opposed to atheism, and that Islam must get close to the infidel and coexist with him."

Islamists consider the Shi'a as enemies, as well: "The danger of the Shi'a to the region is no less than that posed by the Jews and the Christians. Throughout Islamic history, the Shi'a helped the Christians and the polytheists in their battles against Muslim countries. " (17)

Re-echoing Qutb's words, in Saudi Arabia, Wahhabi preacher at the Kaaba Mosque, Sheikh Abd al-Aziz Qari, delivered a sermon saying: "Two groups - the Jews and the Christians – are the main elements constituting the Camp of Kufr [unbelief] and will continue to be its two foundations until Allah allows their downfall and annihilation at the end of days." (18)

In a sermon at a Mecca mosque, preacher Sheikh Adnan Ahmad Siyami told worshippers, "[Islam] believes that there is no way to reach Paradise and be delivered from Hell except by walking in the path of our Prophet Muhammad and joining Islam. Any other way leads to Hell. " (19)

Some Islamist writings portray democracy to the gullible masses as a religion - one that contradicts and competes with true faith - and thus refer to all those who believe in democracy as infidels. The book *Democracy Is a Religion* was written by Abu-Muhammad al-Maqdisi, a pseudonym for Asem al-Burqawi. Al-Burqawi, Palestinian in origin, belongs to the Salafi movement. He lived in Kuwait but was expelled to Jordan after the first Gulf War, and in

November 2001 was arrested by the Jordanian authorities. (20)

Even the Sheikh of al-Azhar, Muhammad Sayyid Tantawi, during a speech at a 1999 conference at the Asyut University, was re-echoing a similar note. While stating that the Arabs should have nuclear energy but should use it only for peaceful purposes, he also quoted from the will of Caliph Abu Bakr. Sheikh Tantawi said that the Caliph had instructed the Muslim commander Khaled ibn al-Walid to fight the enemy with the sword if the enemy fought him with the sword, and to use the spear if the enemy fought him with the spear; thus justifying the obtaining and use of nuclear weapons against the assumed enemies. (21)

Sheikh Safar al-Hawali, a leader in conservative Saudi religious circles, told *al-Jazeera* on July 10, 2002: "Relations between America and us differ from the relations between us and all the other peoples or nations. These are relations between two very different nations: One is a nation that was chosen by Allah, and the other [America after 911] was tested and purified with disasters so that it will atone for its sins. "(22)

A WAHHABI WORLD VIEW

Following the bombings in Riyadh on May 12, 2003, the deputy editor of the independent Egyptian weekly *Roz al-Yousef,* Wael al-Abrashi, who is also an expert on Sunni terrorist movements, wrote several articles on Saudi Wahhabism and the development of Islamist terror.

In an article published on May 31, 2003, in *Roz al-Yousef,* al-Abrashi wrote: "A Wahhabi Saudi sheikh warned young people not to speak English and not to try to study it. He swallowed his saliva, wet his lips, and screamed: 'This is the language of the infidels, to the point where it has the word *blease* [please], which is derived from iblis [Satan]. This is the language of the devil.'"

Al-Abrashi also wrote: "I can state with certainly that after a very careful reading of all the documents and texts of the official investigations linked to all acts of terror that have taken place in Egypt, from the assassination of the late president Sadat in October 1981, up to the Luxor massacre in 1997, Saudi Arabia was the main station through which most of the Egyptian extremists passed and from Saudi Arabia terrorists emerged bearing with them Takfir [claiming someone infidel. They also bore with them funds they received from the Saudi charities. Based on the documents and the investigations in all cases of terror that harmed Egypt [in the 1980s and 1990s], I determined that there was not a single case in which Saudi Arabia was not the main station for the extremists." (23)

Al-Abrashi also said that "the Wahhabi sheikhs used the *fatwas* of Ibn Taymiyyah dealing with the Mongols and the conquerors for disseminating the ideology of Takfir and Jihad against the ruler. What is strange is that while the Wahhabis accused the rulers of heresy and called to fight Jihad against them in countries such as Egypt, Algeria, Tunisia, Morocco, and Jordan, they ruled that cooperating with the government in Saudi Arabia was a binding religious commandment and that the ruler is the [only] one authorized to declare Jihad, implement punishments, collect alms, and [enforce] the imperative of promoting virtue and preventing vice, and that it was an obligation to cooperate with it and obey it as long as it applied Islamic law."

"Wahhabism needs now an attack of another kind ...this time an ideological, cultural, religious, and political attack that will be led by the Saudi authorities themselves, and will not be forced from without. The attack must be Saudi, and not American. It must be more ideological and political than based on security. The attack on Wahhabism is an attack on terror, backwardness, and fanaticism. Wahhabism has moved from Takfir to destruction. We do not want it ultimately destroying Saudi Arabia which has supported the closed Wahhabi religious and ideological extremism and created the al-Qaeda organization. It persecuted the Shi'ite minority", Al-Abrashi added.

In another article, al-Abrashi wrote: "Although Saudi Arabia has adopted a strategy of exporting Wahhabism to the rest of the world, it has continued in recent years to claim that the ideology of the extremist Takfir was imported from abroad and was brought into Saudi Arabia, primarily from Egypt, and that it has no roots of any kind in Saudi culture. (24) Saudi Arabia created the monster, exported it abroad, and then lost control of it. Then, the monster turned on it...Saudi Arabia is in danger. It can neither relinquish Wahhabism nor leave it as it is; it can neither keep the American presence nor get rid of it", Al-Abrashi explains. (25)

Saudi Prince Khaled al-Faisal, governor of the Asir province, is one of the most prominent opponents of the Islamist worldview. He is the owner of the Saudi newspaper *al-Watan*, which is considered relatively open to all political views. Al-Faisal is also the head of the Arab Thought Foundation, which he founded in 2001 with the goals of raising Arab funds to support Arab culture and of providing a link between intellectuals and decision-makers.

In a number of recent interviews al-Faisal called upon the Saudi public and rulers "to fight against all the hidden deviant ideas that have infiltrated schools, [university] faculties, homes, and society in general, and to fight against extremism and excess of all forms." (26)

In July 2004, Saudi TV moderator Turki al-Dakhil hosted Khaled al-Faisal on his weekly program Idhaat (clarifications) on the Saudi *al-Arabiya TV*, which dealt that week with the spread of extremist ideologies in Saudi Arabia. According to Khaled al-Faisal, "this deviant ideology has begun to spread in the kingdom, in the schools, in the mosques, and everywhere. We now have TV channels which advocate an extremist ideology accusing [other Muslims] of heresy ... in our schools and mosques there are young men, 15-20 years of age, who deliver sermons as though they are senior clerics. At times these young men ...who call themselves missionaries for Islam, even offend the kingdom's senior clerics and attack them." (27)

Contrary to the Wahhabi self-serving, self-righteous interpretation of Islam, Mohammed Abed al-Jabri, a contemporary Moroccan critic and professor of philosophy and Islamic thought in Mohammed V University in Rabat, presents a different, moderate and a tolerant interpretation of Islam.

Al-Jabri's approach consists of the exploration of the conflict between modernity and tradition in the Muslim and Arab world. In his writings, al-Jabri focuses on the rationalism of the medieval Muslim philosophers such as Avicenna (980-1037), Averroes (1126-1198) and Ibn Khaldoun (1332-1406). He rejects what he calls *the current polarization of Arab thought between an imported modernism that disregards Arab tradition and a fundamentalism that reconstructs the present in the image of an idealized past.* According to al-Jabri, the Maghreb (the western Arab world) has a rationalist intellectual tradition based on the Greek philosophy. An example was the case of Averroes in the Zaherite school of thought. Al-Jabri calls for an empowerment of its reason to survive in the contemporary world, affirming that the modern Arab world needs a "new Averroism". (28)

Al-Jabri considered Averroism to be the way for the survival of the Arabo-Islamic tradition. Averroism had broken with the thoughts of Avicenna's Eastern Arab philosophy. Averroes separated religion from science and philosophy, and considered that the understanding of philosophy must have exclusively the same principles of philosophy as bases, and it should not be based on others fields like religion. Al-Jabri provided a controversial and unorthodox interpretation of Ibn Sina as not being the best representative of Islamic rationalism in the East, but as being a thinker who consecrated irrationalism not only in his texts on Eastern philosophy, but also in his philosophical legacy.

Al-Jabri contended that Arab political thought has not changed nor evolved since *Jahilia* (pre-Islamic times) where tribalism was the basis of governance. (29) The Arab and Muslim Worlds are caught in a state of sectarian wars fuelled by warlords, religious zealots, and nationalistic demagogues, with the masses paying the price; reminiscent of Europe's *Dark Ages*, the *Crusades* and the *Inquisition*. (30)

In an interview aired on *al-Jazeera* TV on February 21, 2006,

Arab-American psychiatrist Wafa Sultan summed up the conflict in the Middle East so eloquently by saying: "The clash we are witnessing around the world is not a clash of religions, or a clash of civilizations. It is a clash between two opposites, between two eras. It is a clash between a mentality that belongs to the *Middle Ages* and another mentality that belongs to the 21st century. It is a clash between civilization and backwardness, between the civilized and the primitive, between barbarity and rationality. It is a clash between freedom and oppression, between democracy and dictatorship. It is a clash between human rights, on the one hand, and the violation of these rights, on other hand. It is a clash between those who treat women like beasts, and those who treat them like human beings. What we see today is not a clash of civilizations. Civilizations do not clash, but compete."

"From Nasser to Mubarak, the use of legal-constitutional framework to curtail the influence and powers of institutions, groupings, and individuals, the distributions of state patronage to create a independent client list network, the presence of electoral malpractice, the use of state coercion to control the perceived challengers all point to this trend; the position of the president as the ultimate source of power and authority remains intact [the Pharaoh status]. On this basis it can be concluded that personal authoritarian rule in contemporary Egypt has become institutionalized".

- Maye Kasem,
Political Science Professor at the American University, Cairo.

6. THE OLD GUARD, CULTISTS AND THE UNDERGROUND: THE OPPOSITION

Egypt gained formal indepen dence from Great Britain in 1922. The 1952 military coup led Nasser overthrew the monarchy and established a military dictatorship until his death in 1970 marked by hostility toward the West, and two wars with Israel, in 1956 and 1967. Nasser and his successor Sadat established a strong presidential political system that was largely dependent on a pervasive security apparatus that maintained a firm grip on all aspects of civil society.(1)

Following the assassination of Sadat in 1981, Mubarak, who was then Vice President, became president and declared a state of emergency- which he has since renewed every three years. In the early 1990s, Islamic militant groups - in an effort to overthrow Mubarak - conducted a wave of terrorist attacks against the police, top government officials, the Christian Copts, and foreign tourists. The bitter fight against these groups lasted for several years; by 1998 the government had succeeded in destroying the militants' infrastructure in Egypt.

In the process, the government jailed thousands of suspected Islamists, and cracked down on political dissent. Although the armed sector of the militant Islamists was effectively destroyed by 1998, the Mubarak government continued to severely restrict civil and political liberties, while seeking to enhance its legitimacy by burnishing its Islamic credentials. (2)

THE EXECUTIVE, POLITICAL PARTIES AND ELECTIONS

Mubarak dominates the entire political arena. He is not chosen directly by the people in a competitive election, but is nominated by the People's Assembly and is confirmed in a national referendum. The last such referendum was in 1999 when Mubarak won his fourth 6-year term by 93.8% of the national vote. The President appoints the Prime Minister, the cabinet and the Governors of Egypt's 26 provinces. There are 17 legally recognized political parties.

Political parties based on religion are prohibited. The Muslim Brotherhood (MB) as an organization is banned. Hence its candidates run in the elections as independents, but their true affiliation is well known. Mubarak's ruling National Democratic Party (NDP) dominates the Parliament. All other parties are considered extremely weak, with many being parties in name only. It is attested to by the fact that in the national elections held in 2000 the opposition won only seven seats in the 454 seat parliament, the independents 13 seats, and the Muslim Brothers 17 seats; the remaining 417 seats (including the 10 appointed by the President) are taken by NDP members.

The assembly has limited effective power, restricted to introducing minor modifications to the bills which are invariably initiated by the executive. Many policies and initiatives, however, are simply carried out by administrative decree, by-passing the legislature altogether. With such extensive executive power and its dominance over the legislature, the constitutional right of citizens to change their government remains a purely theoretical one. Political parties cannot be established unless licensed by the NDP-dominated Political Parties Committee (PPC) which so far it has never done. Besides the Parliament, a 264-seat Consultative Council (*Maglis al-Shura*) of which two thirds are elected and one third appointed by the President- acts in an advisory capacity, and reports to the President on the proposed legislations. The main opposition parties in Egypt are the Wafd, the Socialist Labor Party, the Nationalist Unionist Progressive Party (Tagamu), and the Liberal Party.

National elections have been traditionally seriously flawed by extensive vote rigging and intimidation of opposition candidates and their supporters, especially those suspected of Islamist leanings. The elections of 2000 were offset by the arrest of hundreds of Muslim Brotherhood supporters prior to the elections, and the use of security forces to obstruct voters in pro-Islamist districts. These strong-arm tactics by the police led to clashes that left 10 dead and many more injured. As a result, in April 2002, the NDP won 97% of the seats in municipal elections. The suffocating grip of the regime over all political life has driven political parties, even those that stand at opposite ends of the ideological spectrum, to seek the formation of a common front.

The Judiciary, Trials, and Detention

Political and security cases are tried in either military or State Security Courts, which come under the strong influence of the executive, and in which many constitutional rights are denied. Under pressure from many Egyptian intellectuals, human rights organizations, and the criticism of Egypt's Western allies, Mubarak declared in 2003 that the government will submit a bill to the Parliament for the elimination of the State Security Courts, leaving in place the emergency military courts to try only cases of terrorism, and conspiracies designed to destabilize the regime.

The Emergency Law by which Egypt is ruled since 1981 restricts many basic rights. Its provisions allow for arrests without warrant and prolonged detention without charge. Mistreatment by the police is commonplace. In November 2003, Amnesty International stated that "everyone taken into detention in Egypt is at risk of torture." The authorities seldom investigated the complaints of abuse and torture— sometimes to death—many of which were recorded by the Egyptian Organization for Human Rights' 2003 report. On November 4, 2002, a report by Human Rights Watch estimated that since March of that year, no less than 13 died as a result of torture. But during 2004, the government convicted 14 police officers for abuse and torture of political prisoners. (3)

Civil Society and the Freedom of Association

Freedom of association and assembly is heavily restricted. NGOs cannot attain legal status unless licensed by and registered with the Ministry of Social Affairs (MOSA). Law 84 of

2002 also allows MOSA to interfere in the activities of NGOs and to revoke the license of any NGO by administrative decree, a power previously reserved to the courts. The law restricts the formation and activities of labor unions. There are 23 trade unions, all required to belong to the Egyptian Trade Union Federation which is the sole legally recognized labor federation. The International Labor Organization (ILO) has criticized single federations as an infringement on the freedom of association.

Civil society is ideally defined as a "mélange of associations, guilds, syndicates, parties and groups that can come together to represent the various and competing interests between the state and citizens". (4) Civil society also represents the competing ideologies and quest for power of political parties and the idealist concerns of society at large through human rights advocacy groups. The underlying core of civil society is the "peaceful management of differences among the individuals' collectivities sharing the same public space- i.e., the polity". (5) Under Mubarak and his predecessors, the state consolidated all the power in the hands of a central government represented in the president.

"The weakness of the civil society in the Arab world in general, and in Egypt in particular, is intrinsically linked to the authoritarian nature of the political systems that exist", says Maye Kasem. (6) "Egyptian civil society in its most basic form can be described as having been incorporated and almost distinguished under the populist policies of Nasser", adds Kasem.

Before Nasser's coup, there was a conglomerate of 500 trade

unions, with at least 15,000 members. Less than a month in after the coup, in August 1952, some members of the *Free Officers* visited a union meeting with workers in Kafr el-Dawar, a textile center near Alexandria. One of the disgruntled union members fired a shot at one of the officers. The reaction was swift and ruthless and determined the relation between the military institution and trade unions for the next fifty years. Two activist workers Mostafa Khamis and Mohamed el-Baqri were arrested and tried by a military court and executed on September 7, 1952.

The strong message sent shock waves throughout Egypt. It was a new age of total political intolerance, different from what existed during the Monarchy and even under the British mandate. (7) A similar incident happened the following year. About 2000 Textile workers in the Imbaba area of Cairo demonstrated asking for pay raise and improvement of conditions. Soon the strikers were confronted by full military force and tanks, and the arrest of 300 workers.

Nasser managed to contain and control the trade unions under a tamed entity loyal to his regime that he established called the General Federation of the Egyptian Trade Unions, GFETU, in 1957. Nasser provided the names of those to preside over the unions; a practice that was followed by his successors, Sadat and Mubarak. Nasser issued socialist decrees in July and October of 1961, which he boasted as a triumph of the Egyptian proletariat and described as *necessary to curtail the exploitative private sector bent on milking the public sector.* Yet Political scientist John Waterbury considers it a Machiavellian and demagogical attempt to consolidate Nasser's power and the military rule over Egypt. "Dismantling the upper reaches of the private sector therefore contributed to the regime's strength by placing the levers of economic control in its hands", Waterbury wrote. (8)

Nasser further managed to contain members of the Lawyers, the Artists, the Engineering, the Doctors and Journalists Syndicates who were required to join the ranks of Nasser's only political party; the *National Union* -renamed later as the *Arab Socialist Union*. Nasser issued a presidential decree in March 1958 stipulating that all syndicate members wishing to enter syndicate council elections must first be members of the National Union.

The strategies of containing and controlling that were implemented during Nasser were continued during the regimes of Sadat and Mubarak. "Under Mubarak, it's difficult to distinguish between the trade unions and the state. The co-optation of trade unions structure over the last two decades of Mubarak has resulted in a pattern whereby workers have little choice but to resort to wildcat strikes and spontaneous demonstrations in efforts to communicate their grievances to the government", says Kasem. The worst of these protests was a three-day strike-turned-riot in Kafr el-Dawar where the Central Security Forces were sent to disperse the rioters. Armed in heavy combat gear, using tear gas grenades and beating the rioters, three demonstrators were killed, hundreds injured and about five hundred arrested.

A similar scenario took place in 1986 when 17,000 workers at the Esco textile plant in Shobra el-Khima initiated a sit-in asking for a one day per week holiday. The Mubarak government responded with the same heavy handed technique.

Few months later a more violent uprising took place. This time it came from members of the Central Security Forces, CSF, which the government has used to quell any sign of disobedience. Thousands of the CSF recruits left their barracks in the desert and took to the streets looting and burning tourist businesses in the area of Giza near the Pyramids where many hotels and night clubs existed. The CSF soldiers, who are recruited for three years, mistreated and given meager rations and $5 a month salaries, vented their anger against their humiliating living conditions. Mubarak declared martial law and called in the military along with tanks to restore order.

Another apt example of workers opposition during the Mubarak's regime was the riots of the *Helwan Iron and Steel* factory in the summer of 1989. The workers demanded incentives to which they felt they were entitled. They staged a sit-in for a few days. The management at the state-owned factory refused their demands and fired the representatives of the workers. Then the workers occupied the plant and raised their demands again. The government-appointed board members fled the factory. At dawn the steel plant was stormed by the CSF in an extremely harsh manner. Mubarak's Minister of the Interior Zaki Badr said that if one per cent of the workers died during the storming of the factory he would have considered the operation successful. (9)

Mubarak continued using the strategy of weakening unions in order to contain them by co-opting union leaders into the political system. Many of the appointed union leaders come from Mubarak's NDP, like Sayyid Rashid, president of the GFETU. Twenty-one of the twenty-three heads of federations in Egypt are NDP members, and at least ten GFETU leaders entered the legislature as NDP deputies in 2000. Some of them are: Fathi Nemattalah, Fathi Abdelatif, Abdelaziz Mostafa, Mohamed Salama, Adly el-Meshnib, and Sayyed Rostum. Their primary role is to be the eye of the regime on unions, federations and syndicates. The incentives are high; the official record of a monthly salary for an appointed union leader is L.E. 30,000. It also entitles them to have a free hand in running the union and the state-owned establishment; which means an unlimited potential for corruption and cronyism, with hardly any accountability or oversight. (10)

While the Mubarak regime has managed to contain all signs of dissent and protest, it has also managed to mobilize and marshal masses of Egyptians on demand for a show of public support especially in major public events, celebrations, or the visits of foreign dignitaries, as a show of the assumed public support for his regime. School children, armed forces soldiers, union members and factory workers, are always given marching orders by their superiors, packed in buses and sent to chant for the president in football games, and especially during the mass orchestrated public celebrations of the president's birthday. Preparations for such events take months of elaborate preparations and cost the Egyptian treasury millions of pounds.

In this context, "the intertwined and conventional client list relationship between government and trade union leadership is increasingly maintained and reinforced in the post-populist era. The degree to which this strategy has preserved government domination is reflected in the unions' overtly passive attitude toward economic re-structioning since 1995", says Kasem. The controversial policy of the Egyptian government to *wholesale* its companies and factories to whoever has the cash has resulted into the layoff of at least 250,000 workers and the selling of at least 114 companies. The media reported the selling of many of these companies below market prices and the multi-million dollar commissions gained by many government officials. Yet, the Egyptian government internal debt crisis remains at approximately $30 billion, while external debts have reached $ 27 billion. About 150 strikes and work stoppages took place in 2001.

Freedom of Speech and the Media

Though the Penal Code and the Press Law contain vaguely worded statutes that would severely restrict freedom of speech, direct attack on the President is avoided since the law prohibits anything that may be construed as *undermining the dignity of the Head of State.* The Ibn Khaldun Center for Development Studies which dared to cross the final red line was shut down and its founder and chairman Egyptian-American Saad Eddin Ibrahim and 27 of the Center's staff were arrested and brought to trial in a State Security Court on charges that included *defaming Egypt abroad,* and receiving foreign funds without authorization ($250,000 from the EU).

On May 25, 2001, the *Cairo Times* magazine described the farce surrounding that trial, in an article titled *the Pharaoh's Prisoners* as "brazen in its disregard of legal norms, brazen in its disdain for international opinion, and brazen in its contempt for human rights". After three years and two heavily flawed trials that sentenced Ibrahim to 7 years imprisonment, Egypt's Court of Cassation finally, in a landmark ruling in March 2003, exonerated him and his colleagues of all charges.

Saad Elddin Ibrahim's plight seemed to have started after he wrote an article on June 10, 2000, titled *The Arab World's Contribution to Political Science.* In that article he sarcastically discussed the emerging trend within the Arab world of inherited presidency, which he dubbed *Gomolokia*, republican monarchy. In his article he discussed the practice of having Syrian President Bashaar Assad inheriting the presidency from his father Hafez Assad after the latter's passing away, and hinted at the possibility of Gamal Mubarak inheriting his father, as well.

The Penal Code and libel laws also prohibit criticism of the military or foreign leaders. Open public discussion of sectarian tensions between Muslims and the Christian Copts is discouraged as *a topic that fosters the divisiveness within the Egyptian society.* Under continuous pressure from the Journalists Syndicate, Mubarak, agreed to eliminate imprisonment for journalists as a penalty for defamation, but the bill was defeated when presented to parliament, indicating clearly that strong forces of the old guard within the ruling party felt threatened by increasing the margin of press freedom.

Egyptians are not unfamiliar with democratic practices, which prevailed during the first half of the Twentieth Century. At present, the entire political discourse, among both the public and within the government, is saturated with the call for reform, but little reform seems to be taking place. The odd phenomenon is that the opposition is totally ineffective in terms of causing any change. No doubt, partly, due to the severe constraints placed on their public demonstrations and contact with the masses. The malaise seems to reside in the great weakness of political parties. It is only when parties succeed in taking root among the general population and are able to aggregate and articulate the various interests in society that the hopes for a transition to a genuine democracy will be close to fulfillment.

So far the Mubarak regime keeps promising political reform but has exhibited a marked reluctance to take serious steps in that direction. But a ground swell is already underway driven by more vehement demands by opposition parties and numerous human rights organizations. It remains, however, that the most single element pushing the regime to democratize is the persistent pressure coming from the West, particularly the United States.

A Turning Point?

On September 7, 2005, Mubarak won a fifth 6-year term, with 88 percent of the vote, in the country's first multi-candidate presidential election marred by low voter turnout and charges of fraud. The November and December parliamentary elections witnessed significant opposition gains but were marred by violence, low turnout, fraud, and vote rigging. The civilian authorities generally maintained effective control of the security forces, which committed numerous, serious human rights abuses. (11)

An amendment to the constitution provided for the country's first multi-party presidential election in September 2005. The government did not permit international observers to monitor the election. Violence against peaceful opposition demonstrators by government supporters and/or security forces increased. They took place on May 25 and July 30 in Cairo, during the parliamentary elections, and on December 30 against Sudanese protesters in Cairo.

The National Council for Human Rights (NCHR) issued its first annual report in 2005, describing government abuses. The government responded in September by saying that it was fully co-operating and would investigate all complaints submitted by the NCHR, though by year's end the government did not appear to take any concrete action in response to the report's recommendations.

Mubarak's security forces killed a number of opposition voters and protesters during the parliamentary elections. The death toll was at least 11. The majority of the killings in the parliamentary elections resulted from the security forces' use of rubber bullets and live ammunition, as decried by human rights groups.

To obtain a warrant from a judge or prosecutor prior to 1981, the constitution provided that police had to show that an individual had *probably* committed a specific crime. The 1981 declaration of a state of emergency, and the imposition of the Emergency Law, nullified this requirement and provided that in order to obtain a warrant, police must show only that an individual *poses a danger* to security and public order. The Emergency Law allows detention of an individual without charge for up to 30 days, only after which a detainee may demand a court hearing to challenge the legality of the detention order, and may resubmit a motion for a hearing at one-month intervals thereafter. There is no limit to the detention period if a judge continues to uphold the detention order or if the detainee fails to exercise his right to a hearing. Incommunicado detention is authorized for prolonged periods by internal prison regulations.

In cases tried under the Emergency Law, access to counsel is often restricted or denied. Many detainees under the Emergency Law remained incommunicado in State Security detention facilities without access to lawyers. After these cases are transferred to trial, the court appoints a lawyer.

The Penal Code also gives the government broad detention powers. Prosecutors must bring charges within 48 hours following detention, or release the suspect. However, they may hold a suspect for a maximum of 6 months while they investigate.

Arrests under the Penal Code occurred openly and with warrants issued by a district prosecutor or judge. The Penal Code contains several provisions to combat extremist violence, which broadly defines terrorism to include the acts of *spreading panic* and *obstructing the work of authorities.*

In one notable case, Ayman Nour, Member of Parliament and leader of the licensed opposition al-Ghad Party, was arrested January 29, 2006, outside parliament on charges that he forged proxy signatures on his party's registration papers, which had been approved by the Shura Council's in October 2004. A request to strip Nour of his parliamentary immunity was endorsed the same day, apparently violating several significant procedural requirements in the process. Just before the arrest, State Prosecution already had teams initiating exhaustive searches of Nour's offices and residence.

Nour was initially held on a 4-day detention order, which was extended 48 hours later during his initial arraignment to the maximum of 45 days, after the court denied bail. Shortly after Nour's detention, EOHR issued a press release, alleging that Nour "was roughed up at the time of his arrest, thrown to the ground, hit and punched repeatedly in the face and back." At the police station, the statement mentioned that Nour was "shackled to a door frame and forced to bend for an extended period."

On March 12, the public prosecutor ordered Nour released on $1740 bail, 43 days after his January 29 arrest. On March 22, the government formally charged Nour and six codefendants with forgery and knowingly using forged documents. The case was referred to a criminal court for trial by a state security prosecutor beginning on June 28. The trial lasted for nearly six months, with a number of lengthy delays which permitted Nour to run, unsuccessfully, for president and for parliament. Nour was convicted on December 24 and sentenced to five years' imprisonment.

During the year of 2005, the government arrested and detained hundreds of persons associated with the Muslim Brotherhood, which has been an illegal organization since 1954. From February through June, during dozens of demonstrations across the country in which MB members demanded political reform, security forces arrested and detained hundreds of members of the organization, often holding them for at least 15 days, *pending fur-*

ther investigation.

In May, EOHR reported that it had documented the names of at least 498 Muslim Brotherhood members arrested during the course of peaceful demonstrations. Charges leveled against members during the year included membership in and revival of a banned organization; obstructing the laws and constitution of the country; inciting the masses against the government; organizing demonstrations critical of the government's policies; and possessing communiqués, booklets and tapes that propagate MB ideology.

In November and December the government detained hundreds more MB activists to limit MB success in the parliamentary elections.

Information about the number of detainees at any given time was often in dispute. For example, in June, the government announced that it had released approximately 300 MB members and supporters who had been detained after May demonstrations, and that 349 MB detainees remained in custody. The MB acknowledged the releases, but asserted that 2400 persons had been arrested and that 590 remained in detention. At year's end there were conflicting accounts of remaining Muslim Brotherhood detainees, ranging from several dozen to several hundred.

The government also arrested or detained several leaders of the organization, including Abdel-Moneim Aboul-Fotouh, on March 27, Essam el-Erian, senior leader and spokesman, on May 6; and Mahmoud Ezzat, Secretary-General and chief of the group's Cairo operations. (12)

Meanwhile, outside the legal opposition, the Muslim Brotherhood was reported by *Nahdet Masr* newspaper to have sunk a proposal for an alliance with the leftist Tagammu Party.

Abdelhalim Qandeel, editor of *al-Arabi* newspaper, told the Crisis Group that a social explosion could not be ruled out, and in this event an army intervention would be a strong possibility. He argued, however, that the army would not be able, or seek, to rule, as in Nasser's day, but would clean house and establish a new political framework, inclusive of all major forces, including the Muslim Brothers.

POLITICAL PRISONERS

Journalist Muhammad al-Sharqawi protested in front of the Press Syndicate in Cairo, May 25, 2006, about an hour before his arrest. His sign read *I want my rights.* He also called for the release of political detainees. Agents of the State Security Investigations (SSI) bureau arrested al-Sharqawi and Karim al-Shair as they were leaving a peaceful demonstration in downtown Cairo.

Severe beatings by security agents of political activists al-Shair and al-Sharqawi were reported by Human Rights Watch. Police also sexually assaulted al-Sharqawi, according to a written statement he smuggled out of prison. "The Egyptian government must investigate these attacks and punish the perpetrators. President Mubarak should put a stop to repeated outrages by agents of the state", said Joe Stork.

In his statement, al-Sharqawi wrote that at the Qasr el-Nil police station he was beaten for hours and then raped with a cardboard tube. Then he was sent to the State Security prosecutor's office in Heliopolis. His lawyer told Human Rights Watch that he saw al-Sharqawi at the prosecutor's office around midnight that night. "There wasn't a single part of his body not covered in bruises and gashes," the lawyer said.

Al-Sharqawi wrote in his statement that around 20 State Security officers surrounded him and began beating him furiously: "Their punches and kicks came one after the other... There were moments of so much pain, so many insults, so many blows... targeting all my body." Al-Sharqawi wrote that he was stuffed into a police van, after which "they ordered me to put my head between my knees. As soon as I did, they started hitting me on my back with all their strength."

Al-Sharqawi, wrote, "The beatings targeted particular places." One of the officers ordered al-Sharqawi's pants to be removed and began squeezing his left testicle, causing excruciating pain. "The pain was terrible. He kept doing it for three minutes, during which I was screaming and asking him to stop so I could catch my breath. He pulled my underwear down, tore it to pieces, and kept hitting me on different parts of my body. They ordered me to bend over. I refused, but they forced me." Al-Sharqawi said the officers then sodomized him with a roll of cardboard.

Eyewitnesses told Human Rights Watch that security agents beat al-Shair in the street. According to his lawyer, al-Shair said that the beatings continued once he was in police custody. The State Security prosecutor ordered both men to be held for 15 days pending investigations. The authorities released al-Sharqawi and al-Shair from Tora prison on May 2006.

Gamal Eid, a lawyer for al-Sharqawi and al-Shair, told Human

Rights Watch that when he saw al-Sharqawi that night. His lips were swollen and bloody, his eyes were nearly swollen shut, and you could see the imprints of shoes on his skin. He told me the beatings had continued for nearly three hours and that he had been unable to reply to police questioning because his mouth was full of blood and his lips were too swollen. It was pure sadism. Eid said he hadn't seen anyone that badly tortured in 12 years.

Eid said that he asked the prosecutor Muhammad Faisal to allow a doctor he had brought with him to examine and treat al-Sharqawi, but that the prosecutor refused. The authorities only allowed al-Sharqawi access to medical treatment four days later, on May 29.

Al-Shair was leaving the protest by car at around 4:45 p.m. in the company of three journalists and another activist. Dina Samak, a *BBC* journalist, was driving. "As we were leaving the Journalists Syndicate, Jihan Shaban, a journalist for *Sawt al-Umma Wal-Karama* newspaper asked if we could drop her and Karim [al-Shair] off downtown," she told Human Rights Watch. As we left the garage of the syndicate, a State Security officer pointed at our car and a taxi started chasing us. About 20 meters later, the taxi pulled in front of us, blocking the street so we couldn't continue. We were afraid. Everyone in the car locked their doors and closed their windows. Around 20 men in civilian clothes surrounded the car and started shouting "*stop the car, you bit..*" and all kinds of horrible insults. They threw Karim on the ground and started beating him violently.

Dina Gamil, another *BBC* journalist, was also in the car. "Around 20 men surrounded the car and smashed the windows with rocks and bottles," she told Human Rights Watch. They unlocked the doors through the smashed window and opened them. They pulled Jihan halfway out of the car so her head was on the ground. They tried to pull me out, too, but I had my seatbelt on.... They got Karim out of the car and threw him on the ground. When a crowd formed and judges started coming out of the Judges' Club to see what was happening, the security agents threw Karim in a car".

On May 27, 2006, a group of prisoners detained over the past month for participating in peaceful demonstrations in solidarity with reformist judges announced they were beginning a hunger strike to protest the treatment of al-Sharqawi and al-Shair, and to demand the release of all those held for participating in the recent demonstrations.

On May 30, visitors to the prison reported that 13 hunger strikers had been transferred to solitary confinement. Political prisoners included as many as 26 members of the illegal Islamic Liberation Party (Hizb al-Tahrir al-Islami), including three Britons. The members had been convicted in March 2004 by the Supreme State Security Emergency Court after being arrested in 2002. Sentences for most members ranged from 1 to 3 years' imprisonment. The three British prisoners received 5-year sentences. Several of the defendants, including the three Britons, alleged they had been tortured to compel them to sign confessions.

A New Enemy: Homosexuals!

In spite of the fact that the Mubarak regime has been cracking on Islamic fundamentalists, Mubarak has been trying to portray his rule as Islamic. A clear example of that double standard and schizophrenic behavior is evident in one of the most controversial and politicized cases in the last few years that generated a frenzy of coverage in the Egyptian and the international media, and caused an outcry of human rights organizations all over the world and pleas from forty U.S. senators.

On 10 May 2001, State Security Forces, with full combat gear, stormed a tourist night club vessel on the Nile called the *Queen Boat* and arrested fifty two young men. The young men were brought before the Emergency State Security Court and charged with *habitual practice of debauchery* - an archaic legal charge brought in prostitution cases.

The young men were accused of practicing acts of homosexuality - a big taboo in Egypt - with serious doubts about if even any homosexual acts were practiced in such a public place, to begin with.

Homosexuality has existed in Egypt, naturally like any other society, for as long as Egyptians can remember. But homosexuals in Egypt have to lead a much closeted double-life for fear of reprisal by the government or even family and society at large. The Egyptian government's exploitation of this case by bringing it to the public amidst pumped up accusation and harsh sentences, has increased Egyptians sense of conservatism and homophobia in their society.

On November, the court had swiftly handed down prison sentences up to five years to 23 of the defendants. Commenting on this mad situation, Ahmad Saif, director of Hisham Mubarak (with no connection to President Mubarak) legal aid center in Cairo which supported the defendants, said: "my personal speculation is that the government is trying to portray itself as a guardian of moral values. All this is hailed in official newspapers as upholding Islamic virtues. They say, *look we try to serve God, too*. In May 2002, the Military Governor (a title Mubarak claims) agreed to a retrial in a civil court for all but two of the fifty two defendants. (13)

Freedom of Speech and the Press

The Mubarak government continues to try and convict journalists and authors for libel, as well as for expressing their views on political and religious issues. According to human rights organizations, approximately 15,000 persons were detained without charge on suspicion of illegal terrorist or political activity. In addition, several thousand others were serving sentences after being convicted on similar charges. The government did not permit international humanitarian organizations access to political prisoners.

The long-forgotten Egyptian constitution provides for freedom of speech and of the press; however, Mubarak's government restricted these rights in practice. The government used the Emergency Law to infringe on citizens' civil liberties. Journalists and writers continued to practice some degree of self-censorship. The constitution restricts ownership of newspapers to public or private legal entities, corporate bodies and political parties.

The Mubarak government owns stock in the three largest daily newspapers, and the president appoints their top editors. These papers generally follow the government line. The government also controls the printing and distribution of newspapers, including those of the opposition parties. The Penal Code, Press Law, and Publications Law govern press issues.

The Penal Code stipulates fines or imprisonment for criticism of the president, members of the government, and foreign heads of state. The government continued to charge journalists with libel. An editor-in-chief found to be negligent could be considered criminally responsible for libel contained in any portion of the newspaper.

On April 13, 2004, Cairo Criminal Court sentenced in absentia three journalists from *el-Masry el-Youm* newspaper to one year imprisonment and a $1750 fine in damages for libeling Mohamed Ibrahim Soliman, minister of housing, utilities, and urban communities. Reporters Abdel Nasser el-Aoumi and Alaa el-Ghatrify were convicted for reporting in August 2004 that police had searched the offices of Housing Minister Soliman and denied him access.

During that year, the courts tried several prominent cases of libel. On April 7, a Cairo court acquitted Magdi Ahmad Hussayn, editor-in-chief of the suspended *al-Shaab* newspaper, of charges that he had *defamed* former agriculture minister Yusuf Wali. Hussayn previously published a story charging that Wali had conspired with Yusuf abdel-Rahman, a former under-secretary in the Ministry of Agriculture, to import carcinogenic pesticides into the country. On May 13, security forces arrested nine members of *al-Jazeera* news crew. They were detained in the Lazoughly state security office for seven hours after the journalists attempted to cover a general meeting of the Cairo Judges' Club.

On November 9, *al-Jazeera* journalist Ahmed Mansour was assaulted and beaten by two unidentified men as he prepared to interview an opposition politician. The Mansour case recalled a November 2004 incident, when unknown assailants abducted and beat Abdul-Halim Qandeel, editor of the Nasserist opposition party newspaper *al-Araby*, and left him stranded naked on a desert highway. Qandeel and many others in the media attributed the attack to elements of the State Security apparatus for Qandeel's editorial calls for public opposition to the government.

The Ministry of Information is empowered to ban ***particular issues or editions in the interest of public order.*** Under the law, the public prosecutor may issue a temporary ban on the publication of news related to ***national security.*** In August, 2004, the government imposed a local news ban on reporting on security operations in the Sinai against suspects allegedly involved in the July terror bombings in Sharm el-Sheikh.

Curbing Public Demonstrations

The Kifaya movement organized numerous demonstrations where 400 demonstrators gathered in front of the Press Syndicate building in Cairo demanding a repeal of the emergency law and holding banners rejecting another term for Mubarak. In late April, 2004, Kifaya held demonstrations simultaneously in 13 cities under the banner "no constitution without freedom." Hundreds of riot police and security forces surrounded demonstrators, arresting 50 in Cairo and over 1000 in other governorates. Security forces used batons and clubs to beat demonstrators.

On February 24, ten unidentified thugs in tracksuits disrupted a meeting, organized by the World Center for Human Rights, at Cairo's Pyramisa Hotel. The thugs threatened participants, overturned tables, and took cell phones and petty cash belonging to some of the participants. The meeting, which was attended by members of the al-Ghad Party, focused on the prospects for constitutional reform to permit the direct election of the president. Although the identities of the thugs were never determined, eyewitnesses said that their appearances and speech suggested that they were members of the security forces.

On April 19, dozens of university *professors for change* conducted public demonstrations on their campuses to protest the presence security police in campus life. On May 10, Cairo University professors staged a symbolical sit-in strike to protest the detention of two fellow professors.

On May 31, the public prosecutor vowed to investigate allegations of beatings and sexual assaults of demonstrators and journalists, including women, during the May 25 constitutional referendum. Twenty-two leading human rights NGOs with the Journalists' Syndicate, called for a full investigation into the attacks and the removal of the minister of interior.

ON TOP OF EGYPT!

The establishment and survival of personal authoritarian rule is inherently dependent upon the absence of autonomous political institutions and groupings that can challenge a ruler's personal monopoly on power. The institutionalization of Mubarak's personal authoritarian rule occurred when the powers of office established by the Sadat and Nasser regimes survived them. Mubarak found it advantageous to keep it intact.

To preserve his grasp over power, Mubarak maintained a weak political system that was never fully institutionalized in comparison to his own position. This formula had enabled him to rise above all other political institutions and to direct the policies of the state so that he is unhindered by formal constraints. (14)

Mubarak has an extreme and absolute power to hire and fire his cabinet which turned them into mere loyal bureaucrats subservient to their boss's will, whims and demands. In addition, Mubarak's domination over the legislature has rendered it little more than *a rubber stamp* to formalize the policies of the president.

The Judiciary does not seem to be more fortunate. The so-called 1969 *massacre of judges* illustrated presidential power in post-1952 Egypt taken to an extreme. Nasser dismissed hundreds of judges who refused to abide by his decree to join his sole political party by then, the Arab Socialist Party- which metamorphosed into the NDP in time of Sadat and Mubarak. Still, the Mubarak's regime has created exceptional powers to itself to literally ignore and circumvent court rulings and has established military tribunals, answerable only to the president, with un-appealable verdicts that in many cases handed down the harshest sentences including the death penalty.

Mubarak has used the military and the security apparatus as the backbone of his regime. The president who appoints the heads of these services remains the ultimate patron. This complexed relation is designed to make it difficult for another coup attempt; the "Byzantine complexity ...would have made a well-timed, carefully coordinated strike difficult and security leaks inevitable". (15)

The combination of repression and co-optation has weakened political parties, including Mubarak's party, the NDP. Consequently, electoral participation remains oriented toward parochial, individualistic, and patronage-based methods of cultivating voter support. Such a weak multiparty arena to ensure that the president's position and authority as the ultimate source of power will not be challenged, gives an edge to the illegalized Muslim Brothers to sweep through the elections.

The weakening of political parties during the Mubarak era contributed to the rise of the fundamentalist Islamic tide in Egypt and the rest of the Arab and Muslim worlds. Nasser's abolishing of all political parties that existed before him, and especially the MB, forced them to go underground and reemerge when the stage was set. The political void that was created after 1952, and the failure of many state policies, lack of a real political dialogue, disastrous wars that devastated the Egyptian economy, all led to the disgruntlement of Egyptians towards their government. Egyptians and Arabs in general, do not have much choice. To choose between a corrupt repressive regime and its only party or the fundamentalists - who claim a mandate from heaven- voters usually choose the latter, as a lesser evil.

The pattern has spread throughout the Middle East, with Hamas in Gaza, Hezbollah in Southern Lebanon, the Ayatollahs in Iran, Sudan and Algeria, and the Muslim Brothers in Egypt, as one analyst points out: “As the regimes of the Middle East grew more distant, oppressive and hollow in the decades following Nasser, fundamentalism’s appeals grew. The Muslim brotherhood and organizations like it tried to give people a sense of meaning and purpose in a changing world, something no leader in the Middle East tried to do. On the score, Islam had little competition. The Arab world is a political desert with no real political parties, no free press, few pathways for dissent... from Muslim Brotherhood to Hamas and Hezbollah; they actively provide social services, medical assistance, counseling and temporary housing. For those who treasure civil society, it is disturbing to see that those illiberal groups are civil society”. (16)

"The policies of scapegoating and finding excuses for not addressing domestic issues have been evident in the daily rhetoric of the state-owned media in Egypt. In a defensive reaction to President Bush's speech on the *New Middle East*, Egypt Government daily newspapers came out with similar headlines; *Saddam's Dictatorship is Preferable to Bush's Democracy*"

- Columnist Bassyouni Al-Hilwani
in the Egyptian government weekly *Aqidati.*

PART TWO:

DEMAGOGUES, ZEALOTS AND ANTI-SEMITES

7. Blame it on the Jews and the Imperialist Americans

On April 8, 2004, on the eve of Mubarak's scheduled meeting with George W. Bush in Crawford, Texas, the Anti-Defamation League (ADL) issued a report exposing the use of anti-Semitic caricatures, stereotypes and images in Egypt's media and wider society. "Anti-Semitism remains deeply ingrained in Egyptian society and continues to be a destabilizing force in the Middle East," said Abraham Foxman, ADL National Director. In Egypt, anti-Semitism remains virtually unchallenged by government leaders while mainstream publications give voice to the most vicious anti-Semitic caricatures and canards imaginable.(1)

The ADL shared its report with key members of the Bush Administration and members of Congress who serve in leadership roles dealing with foreign affairs and Middle East policy. According to the report, *Anti-Semitism in Egypt: Media and Society*, articles and caricatures in the Egyptian media routinely feature anti-Semitic depictions of Jews as stooped, hook-nosed, money-hungry and conspiratorial. Israeli leaders are depicted as Nazis. Articles deny or diminish the Holocaust. Anti-Israel and anti-Jewish conspiracy theories frequently surface, with references to the infamous anti-Semitic forgery *The Protocols of the Elders of Zion* and modern incarnations of the medieval blood-libel charge.

The ADL met with Mubarak on several occasions to urge him to speak out against anti-Semitism in media and society. "President Mubarak has shown a disturbing unwillingness to even acknowledge the extent of problem," said Foxman.

The ADL's report documented selected examples of anti-Semitic articles and caricatures that appeared in Egyptian newspapers from July 2003 through February 2004. Several common anti-Semitic themes were apparent, including conspiracy theories of Jews wanting to control the world, Western governments and controlling the world media; comparisons of Jews and Israelis to Nazis and comparing Zionism to Nazism; illustrations of stereotypical Jews along with Jewish religious symbols, such as the Star of David.

Since the international outcry over the airing on Egyptian television of an anti-Jewish drama based on the *Protocols of the Elders of Zion* in December 2002, important public discussions on anti-Semitism have taken place, leading to calls to condemn anti-Semitism and for Egyptians to avoid such manifestations. Nonetheless, vicious and hateful anti-Semitic articles and caricatures have continued to appear in the opposition and government press. (2)

The tragic phenomenon of anti-Semitic and anti-American propaganda in Egyptian and Arab media has been puzzling and disturbing to many in the West. It is a trend that mainly spread throughout the Arab world by the influence of the Egyptian media during Nasser's era and has continued through the Sadat and the Mubarak years.

Unfortunately, it became more ferocious during the last two decades of the Mubarak regime more than ever before. The practice of inflaming the Arab public's feelings against the Jews, the state of Israel and the United States, has been a steady feature within the Egyptian media.

For instance, on February 19, 2004, Fathi el-Baradi wrote in *al-Ahram;* "All of the Zionist economic and media forces that control the world were subjugated to stand behind this purpose, so that it would succeed in spreading this terroristic manner of speaking to the Western decision-makers, in addition to Christian churches, writers, thinkers and politicians..." (3)

President Bush's November 6, 2003 address, in which he called for democratization of the Arab world, elicited a negative response in the Arab press. In Egypt, which along with Iran and Syria was mentioned specifically by Bush, the speech enraged both the government and the opposition press. While excerpts from the address appeared in various Egyptian papers, the *al-*

Qahira weekly, published by the Ministry of Culture, printed the speech in its entirety. (4)

After the tragic events of September 11, 2001, policymakers in the United States and several Western capitals started to re-evaluate their relations with Arab regimes that were long thought to be allies. Among those regimes were Saudi Arabia and Egypt in particular. The Mubarak regime went in denial about its role of creating religious extremism in the region. It also felt targeted and threatened by the calls for democratization in Arab world. Instead of addressing the real issues behind extremism such as poverty, political oppression and violence - by both government and extremist groups- introducing economic and democratic reforms, it came up with the easy formula of conspiracy theory that blamed everything wrong on the Jews and the Imperialist West.

The policies of scapegoating and finding excuses for not addressing domestic issues have been evident in the daily rhetoric of the state-owned media in Egypt. In a defensive reaction to Bush's speech on the *New Middle East*, Egypt Government daily newspapers came out with similar headlines; *Saddam's Dictatorship is Preferable to Bush's Democracy*, wrote columnist Bassyouni al-Hilwani in *Aqidati*. Al-Hilwani further wrote: "It appears that the American president, *Little Bush*, relies on a group of hashish-smoking advisors. Not a week passes without him addressing the world with naïve proposals, false and random accusations, and idiotic demands, as if he were living on a desert island with his spoiled dogs. "

Al-Hilwani continued his inflammatory rancoring saying, "Bush has forgotten that the Arab and Islamic peoples prefer to be ruled by a dictator such as Saddam Hussein than by a democratic president of the likes of Bush, who lies to the world every day, deceives his people, sows hatred towards it in the souls of all the peoples of the world, and annihilates the lives of his people in battles that do not concern them at all. Oh Mr. Bush, if you were a democratic president as you claim to be, you would abandon your post immediately and disperse all your Zionist aides and advisors, since your lies, your fraud, and the fact that you do not respect Iraqi and Afghan human rights have been exposed to the eyes of the entire world – particularly since your forces, your planes, and your missiles have executed more than 50,000 Iraqis and Afghans who sinned not at all towards you and your people." (5)

Egyptian Foreign Minister Ahmad Maher commented on Bush's address in an editorial in the *al-Ahram* government daily in which he said: "The simplest rule of democracy is that it cannot be imposed from outside. Democracy means that the people rule itself by itself and for itself. Thus, it is inconceivable that anyone external [powers], whatever their intentions, can come to teach the peoples how to rule themselves!"

Maher further added: "Recently, voices have arisen in the American government demanding direct intervention in order to impose democracy on the peoples and on the governments, as if the peoples were minors or mentally retarded and needed their hands held! These demands... are in themselves a violation of the rules of democracy. This intervention is reminiscent of the abhorrent idea of previous centuries regarding the *White Man's* responsibility for the other peoples, for liberating them from ignorance and backwardness. The result was that this *White Man* maintained colonialism of these peoples for centuries, and this caused the backwardness from which the Americans want to rescue us today! Our people, whose civilization is 7,000 years old, does not expect others to give it lessons in democracy. Therefore, attempts to impose democracy from outside will fail." (6)

Continuing in the same vein in the government daily *Al-Gumhouriyya*, Maher suggested *exporting the Egyptian democratic model to other countries in the region*: "There is no doubt that in the next phase, Egypt will be witness to more than the democracy it is experiencing under Mubarak's rule, and this will come about of its own free will as opposed to imposition from outside. This democracy can be a model for implementation for other countries interested in democracy, as a way of development and welfare", Maher added. (7)

The opposition press in Egypt also took a harsh stance on Bush's words, but it also gloated over what it perceived as Bush's insult to Arab regimes that they have always accused of being pro-American. Ahmad Alwan, member of the supreme council of Al-Wafd, Egypt's biggest opposition party, wrote in the party daily *Al-Wafd*: "We will never accept a message from a tyrant who understands only force and whose use of weapons is the only way of spreading Bush's message. In contrast, we live on the land of the Arabs who understand the truth regarding Bush's greedy aspirations in our region… It is not our rulers' oppression of us that planted our hatred for the U.S., but American support for the Zionist state and, in particular, the current Bushist-Sharonist era, may Allah remove them from our path." (8)

In spite of their opposition to the Egyptian government, opposition journalists were found re-echoing the same tone of denial and defensiveness. The Nasserite opposition weekly *al-Arabi* featured an article by Egyptian Journalists Association member Gamal Fahmi saying: "Last Thursday, *Brother Bush* proved that although he is idiotic, stupid, fascist, and criminal; he is also base. He surprised the puppets of America's creation who play in our lands, the role of tyrannical leaders in his [i.e. Bush's] public statement... *Brother Bush* did not make do with this, but also swore to create democratic change in these regimes! It was said that the moment Their Highnesses, our malignant rulers, heard these words they were saddened and worried, and their bowels turned to water out of fear ..."

In the same article, Fahmi penned an imaginary dialogue between Bush and an emissary of the pro-U.S. Arab leaders, in which the emissary tries to ask the American president about democracy. "Don't you understand English?!" Bush says to the emissary, who responds, "We don't understand democracy and democracy does not understand us." Bush insists that the Arab rulers do something, and the emissary says that the U.S. was occupying Iraq, destroying it, and killing its people for the sake of democracy and that therefore "we ask your permission to do the same... Give us the order, and we will kill half of our peoples." Bush asks, "What about the other half?" "We will arrest them and put them in jail," the emissary promises, "and then we will declare democracy and release all the prisoners." (9)

For a Western reader, it is hard to comprehend the logic behind the attacks on Bush's call for democratization in the Arab World!

Isn't that what the Arabs want? Democracy and liberation from dictators like Saddam Hussein and his alikes? Why then the attitude of demonizing American policy and suspicions about it? The answer lies in the complex relation between the Arab governments and their media.

Arab state media will definitely repeat whatever the official line of their governments. State media journalists are hired by the government and cannot afford to lose their position, status, or the generous privileges that come with the job. On the other hand, the so-called Egyptian opposition press in spite of the fact that they hate the oppressive nature of the Mubarak regime, nevertheless they have drawn their own red lines that they cannot cross. They are longing for democracy, but they are limited by the official line of their party. They cannot also be seen taking side with the call for democracy that is coming from Washington, especially after Bush's call for a crusade.

There are so many other considerations that would explain the behavior of Egypt's opposition media and its hostile stand against American policies. For example, the Marxist Tagamu Party, has made it clear in its manifesto and literature, that nothing on earth would make them agree on a U.S. policy even if came with democracy.

The Muslim Brothers would never agree on an American-style democracy. Policymakers in Washington expected the Egyptian opposition to embrace Bush's call for democratization and run with it. But blaming everything on the Jews and the *Imperialist Americans* has been the easiest response for these struggling parties who would lie to appear more patriotic and nationalistic than the others. Hackneyed clichés would be very convenient; recycling old rhetoric that has perpetuated for at least half a century.

The reaction to President Bush's speech created similar waves in most Arab and Muslim capitals. Corrupt dictatorial regimes enjoying the aid and political protection of the U.S. gave instructions to their own media to pour its rage on the proposed American policy. Even the Palestinian Authority, that owes its very existence in the Palestinian Territories to the tireless American peace initiatives and aid, felt threatened by the call for democracy.

In an article published by the Palestinian Authority's *al-Ayyam*, a Palestinian journalist wrote: "Bush and his speechwriters are motivated by a *Yankee* and missionary zeal that propagates the values of democracy in the way of colonialism. This mentality blinds them to the facts of reality and history, because there is no one model for democracy. Democracy is the result of the economic, political, and social development of cultures, and it is not forced upon peoples by means of cruise missiles, tanks, and planes…" (10)

The reaction to Bush's speech in Syria was less surprising. The Assad's Baathist regime has been on U.S. State Department watch list for a long time as one of the states sponsoring terrorism. Syria has been aiding Hezbollah and sabotaging several peace initiatives attempts in the region. In the Syrian government daily *Teshreen*, Nasser Shamali wrote: "Bush's speechwriters are members of the Zionist gang that wrote the speeches of the war on Iraq and on the Arabs and Muslims. This is the same gang of usurers and bloodsuckers whose discourse on U.S.-style democracy refers to expanding its dictatorship all over the world, killing anyone it wants to, and robbing anyone it wants to." (11)

Syrian Minister for Immigrant Affairs, Buthaina Shaaban, published an open letter to President Bush in *Teshreen*, in which she wrote: "...The first thing that worried me in your speech was the statement that your adherence to democracy will be tested in the Middle East. Whether this hinted at Iraq or at the Arab-Israeli conflict, I say that what you are doing in both cases has created a real schism between the U.S. and millions of Arabs and Muslims. The second thing that worried me, Your Excellency the President, is your statement that the advance of freedom leads to peace. How can people taste the taste of freedom when they are occupied? There is no doubt that freedom and security are the natural fruits of peace, but the child cannot be born before his mother...The last and most important point, is your statement that democracy is the path to honor. The subject of honor is the most important factor in the misunderstanding between the U.S. and the Arab and Islamic world. If honor is the essence of democracy, why does the democracy of the U.S. not take into account the honor of the Arabs?" (12)

The position of the Egyptian media has been intriguing to many Western diplomats in Cairo and the Middle East. One of those who have been appalled by the contradictoins of the Egyptian media is the former American Ambassador to Egypt, David Welch, who had criticized the Egyptian media several times during his tenure in Egypt. (13)

On the first anniversary of the September 11 attacks, he published an op-ed in the Egyptian daily *al-Ahram* in which he criticized conspiracy theories in the Egyptian press. (14) Ambassador Welch met with *al-Akhbar* editor Jalal Daweidar and complained about the paper's extreme positions (such as the article accusing American forces in Iraq of cannibalism). (15)

On October 20, 2003 (16) Ambassador Welch delivered a speech at the American University in Cairo in which he addressed the conduct of the Egyptian press that celebrates martyrdom attacks and blamed the U.S. for the Najaf bombing in Iraq. (17)

In response to Ambassador Welch's article in *al-Ahram*, *al-Gumhuriya* columnist Gamal Badawi wrote: "Egypt is not one of the American states which are ruled by the Pentagon, and it is not subject to the influence of the Zionist gang that dominates the White House. Instead of frequenting coffee-houses and clubs, the American Ambassador should have analyzed the content of the Egyptian papers, because they accurately reflect the rage and fury that are simmering in the popular cauldron against America's policies. He should have related the missive to his country... Maybe he thought that he could perform in Egypt the same role that Bremer is performing in Iraq, or that he could act like Cromer the British Governor who used in the early 20th century to manage Egypt's affairs as if it were a British ranch..." (18)

Another harsh response came from Columnist Jamal Fahmi who wrote an article in the pro-Nasserist opposition weekly *al-Arabi* titled *the Ambassador from Hell in Cairo*. He wrote: "The American Ambassador in Cairo, David Welch deserves to be punished for being the representative of the gang that escaped from the *Trash Museum of the Old Colonialism* and entrenched itself in the White House. *Brother* Welch has the arrogance that befits an ambassador representing that imbecile in Washington, George W. Bush. The latest deplorable act of the honorable ambassador was his abhorred attack against the Egyptian press, especially *al-Gumhuriya*, because that paper described the recent *martyrdom* operation in Haifa as a *fedayeen* [suicidal] operation and not a terrorist one, which is what the ignorant President would have liked, based on the instruction of the blood-spilling Nazi, Sharon."

The ambassador intent of starting a dialogue with the Egyptian media backfired and caused a frenzy of more angry responses from several Egyptian journalists; another journalist in *al-Ahram* wrote: "Even though the audacious Ambassador, contrary to his President, does not lack the necessary intelligence to understand the difference between the behavior and statements of a respected ambassador and those of a jailer in Guantanamo, and even though – undoubtedly – he knows that his audacious act against the Egyptian press will not be helpful and will not make it [i.e. the press] take a stand contrary to the feelings of the Egyptian people and describe the heroic acts of the Palestinian people as terror. Despite all this, Mr. Ambassador does not want to abandon his terrorism and his disgrace, hoping to fulfill the desires of the murderer Sharon and hoping to be promoted from the ambassadorship to the position of a Zionist caretaker in charge of shackling and silencing us, so that we do not curse the neo-Nazis in Washington and Tel-Aviv…" (19)

Under the headline *Two Israeli Ambassadors in Cairo*, Even the Coptic journalist Adli Barssoum jumped into the bandwagon of bashers of Welsh and American foreign policies; he wrote in *Al-Gumhuriya*: "Sometimes, Ambassadors go to the government of the country in which they work and declare war with a smile on their faces... Mr. Welch thinks that part of his responsibility is to smack the hands of Egyptian journalists to teach them a lesson in discipline. Mr. American Ambassador knows very well, just like us, that the American press... is a press carefully orchestrated from above. In contrast, the Egyptian press is guided only by the national conscience, and when it determines that martyrdom operations [i.e. the suicide bombings] for the sake of liberating Palestinian territories are acts of courage – it is an historical testimonial... *Al-Gumhuriya* does not pretend to be the only paper describing the heroism of the Palestinian martyrs; this is the position of all the Egyptian papers because it accurately reflects the feeling of the Egyptian people..." (20)

In *Aqidati*, the government religious weekly magazine, columnist Bassyouni Hilwani wrote: "... It is surprising that the U.S., *the sponsor of democracy in the world*, wants the world, and especially our Arab world, to praise its crimes in Iraq... and wants the media to describe these honorable Fedayeen [suicide bombings] operations against the criminal occupiers in Iraq as terrorist acts that should be condemned... This is the lie that the U.S. is demanding from the Arab media. But it will not get it here in Egypt... where the blood is boiling in its son's veins, who witness every day the aggressions in Iraq and Palestine and the crimes committed by American weapons in the hands of the savage warriors on Iraqi land, and by the Zionist pigs on Palestinian land." (21)

Al-Gumhuriya columnist Lutfi Nassif added: "The Ambassador's Criticism is a Badge of Honor. What David Welch did is in harmony with the new American media policy following September 11, 2001. Since then, the American media took a new direction that has nothing to do with objectivity and impartiality. It persists in supporting the American strategy to dominate and impose it hegemony on the world, so it distorts the image of the rest of the nations… The ambassador's statements concerning the editor of *Al-Gumhuriya* are a badge of honor to Editor Samir Ragab". (22)

...If we really want to fight such incidents and to prevent

“them from occurring in the future, we must admit that we all – as the state, as intellectuals, and as a people – have failed to fulfill our duty... controlling the political orientation of certain publications helped to spread hatred of anything American and to disseminate the conspiratorial theory that Israel is behind every violent incident that occurs in Egypt. Thus, the state has failed to transmit its message regarding its strategic alliance with the U.S., as if it were afraid to confront the citizens with this truth.”

- Ahmad Nagi Qamha, researcher at the *al-Ahram* Center for Political and Strategic Studies, analyzing the causes for the April 7, 2005 terrorist attack at Khan al-Khalili, Cairo

8 THE AMERICANS: CO-CONSPIRATORS AND ACCOMPLICES?

In several writings that frequently appear in the Egyptian and Arab media, Americans are portrayed as *co-conspirators and accomplices with the Zionists* in a farfetched conspiracy theory beyond imagination.

Following the terrorist bombings in Sinai, there have been many reports in the Arab media involving conspiracy theories. This included former Palestinian President Arafat's national security advisor Jibril Rajoub, who pointed a finger at the U.S. and Israel, claiming that they stood to gain the most from the attacks. (1)

In a response to a journalist's question during his recent visit to Italy, Mubarak rejected the accusations against Israel and the U.S. Nevertheless, Egyptian Government paper *Al-Gumhuriya* came out with this headline: *The U.S. is the Main Culprit in All the Acts of Violence*. Coptic Columnist Adli Barsum wrote in *al-Gumhuriya*: "Who planned the bombings in Taba and who carried them out? Is it the al-Qaeda organization, which Israel hastened to hold responsible, even before the smoke of the fires had dissipated? Is it the Mossad? There are those in Tel Aviv who are not happy about Egypt's efforts to resolve the disputes between the various Palestinian factions, and there are those who are working to spread civil war between the Palestinians and Egypt. Is it the CIA? It may perhaps be interested in preoccupying the Arabs with the events in Taba instead of dealing with the recent scandalous U.S. veto".

The article continued its accusations to the U.S. by saying: "The answer to this remains in the hands of the investigative authorities ... Whether these authorities find the perpetrator swiftly, the political mind already knows what happened in Taba. The U.S. is the main culprit in all the acts of violence. It takes advantage of the call to fight terrorism in order to conceal what it is doing – the terrorism of a powerful country carried out by means of invasion, economy and brainwashing. Whether the U.S. is the main perpetrator, whether it is only the inciter, the planner, or the one providing behind-the-scenes encouragement, it strives to safeguard its interests and to stabilize its footing in the entire world by means of violence and counter-violence. This is in order for the conflicts to continue, for the fire to remain ablaze, and for the hatred to continue to rage. Thus the U.S. will feel itself to be the supreme power and will pull most or all of the strings and will set the world in motion as it wishes, in order to rake in riches upon riches, slaves upon slaves, and to attain more servants among the world's rulers who vie between themselves for its friendship and its appeasement... In truth, we are not interested in the matter of the Israelis who died in the explosions at Taba, and the U.S. does not have the courage to call upon us to say we are sorry for these

Israelis, because our Arab eyes will never be cheap, and they [will cry] only for the brave martyrs among us. In our eyes, Arab blood is a thousand times more precious than Israeli blood. If the U.S. does not want to see a thing except for Israeli blood, which is her business." (2)

The London Arabic-language daily *al-Quds al-Arabi* reported that a headline in the weekly *al-Mustaqbal al-Jadid*, the official organ of the NDP's Policies Committee under Gamal Mubarak, that read, *Proof of Mossad Involvement in the Explosions in Taba. Al-Quds al-Arabi* cited *al-Mustaqbal al-Jadid* as saying: "*Al-Mustaqbal al-Jadid* has obtained a number of proofs or first-hand evidence that proves Israeli involvement in the explosions in Taba and in Nueiba. Foremost among them was the extraordinary rapidity with which the ambulances were prepared to arrive at the site of the bombings, in addition to the story of Amira Shemi, who called immediately after the incident from the Taba Hilton to the Israeli Emergency Medical Service, so that they would transfer her to [their] hotline to speak with Israeli representatives. This in addition to other clear-cut proofs that the Mossad was involved in these explosions, of which the principle ones are the sidetracking of the investigation in a false direction and the dissemination of contradictory communiqués [in the name of groups claiming responsibility]…" (3)

Repeating the same conspiracy theories, Columnist Magdi Salem wrote in an article in the official religious weekly *Aqidati*: "For many years Israelis have been coming into Sinai, and especially to Taba, and nothing has occurred like what happened last week, not even during the high point of terrorist activity directed against

Egypt. All of this time, never once did the Israeli authorities warn the Israelis not to come to Sinai… does this not lead us to raise questions regarding Israel's stance concerning this action, as it seems that Israel knew about it? Did Israel inform the Egyptian authorities of the information in its possession or not? And from where did it acquire this information? I hope that we shall not overlook the extremist Israeli groups who have long experience in terrorism not only against Arabs and Muslims but also against Jews … especially if they are not religious." (4)

Dr. Abdallah Al-Ashal, former assistant to the Egyptian foreign minister and lecturer on international law at Cairo University, was quoted on the internet site Islamonline: "All of the signs indicate that Israeli hands were behind the attacks. The area is close to Israel, and Israel was the first to warn its citizens not to go to Sinai…" (5)

In the Egyptian weekly *Nahdat Misr*, al-Ashal said that Israel "is interested in embarrassing Egypt and in hurting Egyptian tourism, just as the Palestinian Intifada hurt Israeli tourism… It is in Israel's interest that there be [sic] an Egyptian response to what happened, since it wants Egypt to join the American campaign against terrorism… It is likely that Israel recruited some people in coordination with terrorist groups in order to hurt Egypt… Israel's goal in this operation was to bring terrorism back to Egypt…" (6)

General Fuad Allam, former deputy head of the Egyptian State Security Service, said to *Nahdat Misr*: "None of the suspects in these bombings – whether Egypt, Palestine, or al-Qaeda – have anything to gain from carrying out the bombings, except for

Israel. All of the evidence points to the conclusion that the Israeli Mossad is the first and last to gain from this operation… As for the Palestinian factions, no one suspects that they were involved in this incident – except for Israel, which accuses them – unless the Mossad got one of these factions involved in carrying out the attacks." (7)

Muhammad Abdel-Fattah Omar, former assistant to the Egyptian interior minister, said to www.islamonline.net: "For every action we need to search first for who stands to gain from it… Israel is the only one who benefits from these explosions. This is due to the fact that the only two elements that can enter the area with ease are the Israelis and their agents… The Israeli right was going through a crisis as a result of the American pressure on Sharon, after the veto that America cast at the U.N. to save Israel from the proposal to condemn it for the massacres it is conducting against the Palestinians in Gaza. Israel had no choice but to undertake an action that would ease the American pressure on the area and would put the ball in the Americans' court, at least until the elections…" (8)

Dhiaa Rashwan, from the Egyptian *al-Ahram* newspaper's Center for Diplomatic and Strategic Studies, said: "The events in Sinai were not planned by Islamists, neither Egyptian nor al-Qaida… The one who gained the most from this operation was Israel, and the one who was hurt most was Egypt. In addition, the intensive security presence prevents the importing of such huge quantities of explosives…This operation is the work of a security apparatus, or else was carried out in cooperation with a major security apparatus, and the one who gained the most was Israel, and thus one should attribute [the operation] to Israel." (9)

Chief Editor of the Egyptian opposition weekly *al-Osbu*, Mustafa Bakri, wrote: "There is a deliberate attempt to blame Egypt for what happened, through the statement that the car bombs arrived from Sinai. Allah be praised, this is Israeli information, and we understand that Israel wants to clear itself of blame. However, all the signs point to Israel being behind the event, even if the perpetrators say they belong to al-Qaida..." (10)

A communiqué from the Muslim Brotherhood said: "The main profiteers from these events and from similar events are the war criminal Sharon and his gang and his supporters in the U.S. administration who are interested in diverting attention away from the atrocious massacre being carried out by the Israeli forces for ten days... To link the legitimate resistance in Palestine with the monster of terrorism that is spreading worldwide through the U.S. administration's aggressive policy and to propagate anarchy throughout the world... Directing accusations here and there without evidence or proof does not clear the Zionist and world intelligence mechanisms from suspicion that they were involved in the operation], since they have tremendous capabilities in the planning of such abominable actions, the aims of which is to achieve the goals of their governments..." (11)

What causes this disease?

During his recent visit to Italy, President Mubarak said in response to a journalist's question about the conspiracy theories in the Egyptian papers concerning Israel's complicity in the Taba attacks: "What has been said regarding Sinai is groundless... I don't know what happened. First we need to investigate in depth... I cannot accuse anyone, Israel or others, until the investigations lead to results." (12)

Egyptian columnist Mamoun Fendy published an article in the Arabic-language London daily *al-Sharq al-Awsat*, in which he rejected the allegation that Israel was involved in the terrorist attack in Taba: "It would be logical to assume that it was the Israelis themselves who blew up the hotel in Taba – these are the words of a commentator on the *al-Arabiya* TV channel... He was speaking from Cairo... Instead of asking the seasoned commentator to give an explanation for this interesting revelation, the program's hostess allowed him to go off on a preposterous historical survey about the way in which Israel kills its civilians in order to achieve political gain. While this was going on, the hostess nodded her head as though agreeing to everything, " Fendy said.

Al-Arabiya was not the only channel to adopt this conspiratorial interpretation. *Al-Jazeera* repeated the same thing and its commentators, especially those located in Cairo, explained how Israel carries out conspiracies like these on a daily basis. How do these people want the world to believe them when they attempt to defend the Arab truth by concocting lies and absurdities? *Why do we forsake the facts and turn to lies instead?! What causes this disease?* Fendy exclaimed.

"Terrorism is terrorism and the killing of peaceful vacationers is terrorism; of this there can be no doubt. Is it the Israelis who blow up their own citizens for political purposes?! And was it the Americans or the Serbs who attacked the Twin Towers – or in the words of our journalists, the outstanding journalists of the Arab world, perhaps it was the Mossad who did it?! Some of us call these people *'onspiracy theorists* ... but the undisputed truth is that this is a group of people who are either paranoid or insane," Fendy explained (13)

Since September 11, 2001, conspiracy theories regarding the attacks have abounded in the Arab press, and especially the Egyptian press. The theories assert that the attacks were carried out by the CIA, the FBI, Jews, the Mossad, etc. (14) These theories again emerged in the Egyptian press on the first anniversary of the attacks.

Former American Ambassador to Cairo David Welch published an article in Arabic (15) in the leading Egyptian government daily, *al-Ahram*, decrying the dissemination of these theories. (16)

In that article Welsh wrote: "The commemoration of the one-year anniversary of the September 11 terrorist attacks has elicited a host of remembrance, commentary and analysis in the Egyptian media on the significance of the events and how America and the world have changed since that fateful day. Some writers offered Americans renewed condolences, for which we are grateful, as we are for the help Egypt has extended so far in bringing to justice those responsible for these crimes. Egyptians know first-hand the horrors terrorist groups can inflict. Egyptians also understand the need to pursue such terrorists before they can commit further atrocities. Unfortunately, the anniversary has also brought forth yet more voices in the media questioning who planned and committed the attacks, and positing incredible conspiracy theories without the slightest bit of evidence to back them up. Leading Egyptian newspapers and magazines in the past two weeks alone have published columns that suggested governments or groups other than al-Qaeda were responsible. A leading Egyptian professor of sociology, in a public lecture on September 11, spent nearly half an hour trying to cast doubt on al-Qaeda's culpability and even went so far as to implicate the American government by asserting that America had benefited from the attacks....", Welsh added.

"It is a fact that most of the world accepts the voluminous evidence of al-Qaeda's responsibility. No serious debate still exists about this. This evidence has been detailed in thousands of articles in independent media in many different countries, articles available to anyone with access to the Internet. Moreover, al-Qaeda itself fully admitted its culpability. It is difficult to fathom how commentators can simply disregard these confessions, coming on top of all the other publicly available evidence.", Welsh exclaimed.

"Sadly, such disregard for the facts in such a serious matter can tarnish the reputation of the Egyptian media in the eyes of the world. I hope editors will keep this in mind and exercise their editorial judgment when reviewing articles or columns to print in their publications. If nothing else, responsible media should be dedicated to telling the truth, not spreading falsehood, and knowing the difference between the two." Welsh concluded.

Following the publication of Welch's article, Egyptian intellectuals, authors, and journalists published a communiqué demanding that the U.S. government consider its ambassador to Cairo *persona non grata*. The communiqué was issued with the signatures of dozens of journalists, professors, and politicians. The signatories on the communiqué said: "…The ambassador spoke as if he were addressing slaves or the citizens of some banana republic, not those representing the voice and conscience of the Arab nation whose roots lie deep in history and whose culture is, as Western and American writers have acknowledged the cradle of the conscience of the entire world. It is odd that the ambassador of any foreign country, whether it is America or Micronesia, should dictate to free Egyptian intellectuals and journalists how to think and write, and tell them that they must believe everything America and its media think, even if it is lies…"

"A representative of the most powerful democracy in the world has gotten himself into trouble by destroying the fundamental principles underpinning the constitution of his country and the conventions of human rights - among them the right to freedom of speech… The Egyptian intellectuals are opposed to this disgraceful behavior on the part of the U.S. ambassador, and to his shameless interference in the affairs of the Egyptian press. They demand of him to give his advice to the press and government of his country, which see the truth only with one biased eye," they added.

"We hope that the American ambassador will ensure that he does not cross the lines drawn for him by international diplomacy, and will not try to stick his nose into the matters of the Egyptian press, because Egypt is an independent country, not a banana republic, and because the Egyptian journalists know their profession and need lessons from no one. Even if America thinks that it has conquered the globe, it will not succeed in conquering and subduing the free wielders of the pen. We demand that the U.S. government consider its representative in Cairo persona non grata, and recall him because he has harmed democracy and stabbed a dagger into the heart of his country's constitution. We advise the U.S. ambassador to try to salvage his country's reputation, shamed by its silence on Israel's crimes, which are in no way less than Hitler's crimes. If he has time to advise and interfere in Egypt's domestic matters, we say to him... that it would be better for him to return to his country", the communiqué said (17)

Dr. Muhammad al-Shadhli, a lecturer at the faculty of languages at Ein Shams University, Cairo, wrote in response to Welsh's article in the government daily *al-Gumhuriya*: "I am not justifying a mistaken reaction. A mistake is a mistake anywhere, at any time. But I hope that Mr. Welch will advise the editors of the American newspapers and the television stations to preserve the American media's reputation among the Islamic and Arabic peoples and the Egyptian people, primarily in light of the fact that the Arab and Islamic peoples pay for the American media's contempt for the facts in the spilled blood of thousands of their sons, in the degradation of their peoples, and in the usurpation of their legitimate rights. The American ambassador's interest in preferring truth over falsehood and in the reputation of the Egyptian media must be met with gratitude on the part of the Egyptians." (18)

In an article titled *The American High Commissioner*, Mostafa Bakri, editor of the opposition weekly *al-Osbu*, wrote: "The

American ambassador to Egypt has deviated from all diplomatic norms, beginning to talk to us about our newspapers as if he were a new high commissioner who issues orders that must be obeyed, delivering instructions that we must carry out.... My suggestion to the American ambassador in Egypt is that he read history well and understands that every time he deviates from his diplomatic tasks he will encounter rejection and struggle from all Egyptian circles. It is not the first time, nor will it be the last time, that this ambassador and his government have blatantly interfered in Egyptian affairs. " (19)

In a conversation with Egypt's Foreign Minister Ahmad Maher several days later, as reported by the government daily *al-Gumhuriya*, Ambassador Welch explained that he had not attacked the Egyptian press, which he respected and esteemed. He said, "What is important is to examine the facts and study them in an abstract and objective fashion, and to consolidate views based on these facts." (20)

Nevertheless, the bureau of the Council of the Egyptian Journalists' Union issued a statement saying that "The bureau wants to clarify to the Ambassador that his attempt to intervene in the Egyptian papers' publication policy is unacceptable and harms independence of the press..." (21)

Siding with the American ambassador was Egyptian journalist Nabil Sharaf al-Din, who responded to the Egyptian Journalists' Union statement in the London daily *al-Quds al-Arabi*: "Among the Egyptian journalists are many, who maintain that not everything that the American ambassador said was null and void, despite my objection to his call to review articles prior to their publication.

His words on the spread of the spirit of conspiracy are absolutely correct. It is not logical for us to continue to tell fairy tales with regard to the responsibility of organizations from here and there for the September 11 attacks while bin-Laden acknowledged responsibility. "

"The American ambassador acted like the ambassador of a country defending the interests of his country and his people should act. He did not wait for instructions and guidelines from above, as our diplomats do. After all, Welch only defended what he saw as the truth, and it would be well if our diplomats would act to correct the West's perspective regarding our nation and our culture the way the American ambassador did for his… If the honorable colleagues [i.e. members of the Egyptian Journalists' Union] think that the ambassador of America's importance is acting like our diplomats do, being self-absorbed while sinking into a life of luxury at the taxpayers' expense's… then they are deluding themselves" , Sharaf al-Din added. (22)

Exposing the lies and incitement against Israel, the U.S., and the West in Egyptian media, in an article titled *The Khan Al-Khalili Incident: Causes and Consequences*, published in *al-Ahram*, Ahmad Nagi Qamha, a researcher at the *Al-Ahram Center for Political and Strategic Studies*, analyzed the causes for the April 7, 2005 terrorist attack at Khan al-Khalili and proposed how to deal with such phenomena.

The writer emphasized that the fact that the terrorist attack was carried out by a single Egyptian citizen and that this is what highlights the serious nature of the problem, Qamha explaind that "the security apparatus does not have enough people to follow every citizen... It was surprised to find that the perpetrators of the attack at Taba were ordinary Egyptian citizens not affiliated with al-Qaida, with the Egyptian al-Jamaa al-Islamiya, or with the Jihad organization."

Qamha criticized the authorities for not letting the liberal Egyptian organizations to convey a message of openness to the Egyptian people, and for having allowed various factions *who live in the mentality of the past* to spread anti-Western incitement and to call for Jihad against anything American.

Qamha called upon the authorities to permit the activity of liberal organizations because this, in his view, would be the most effective response to religious and nationalist incitement. (23) "If we really want to fight such incidents and to prevent them from occurring in the future, we must admit that we all – as the state, as intellectuals, and as a people – have failed to fulfill our duty... Let me start with the state. For close to thirty years, Egypt has decided to play an active and primary role in establishing peace in the Middle East as a strategic option and for the benefit of all its citizens, including the Arab region and the three states in strategic proximity. In addition, Egypt has opted for special, distinctive relations with the U.S., taking precedence over the other countries... Since then we see that it has not been able to move society forward, except recently, and to be more precise, since 2002", Qamha explained.

Qamha further added that: "We see that Egypt has also failed to bring the substantial change to the awareness of the ordinary citizen. In this, the state has its justifications. Whenever things calmed down and moved toward real reforms, the state was taken by surprise by political acts of violence, beginning with the assassination of the late President Sadat, which pushed the state into the whirlpool of acts of terrorism, which continued until 1997. Consequently, the state took the step of imposing emergency laws and other laws restricting civil liberties... However, the state did not realize that by doing so it was preventing society's non-governmental liberal organizations from performing their duties and from transmitting a new message of openness to the citizens... These organizations could have helped to generate a dynamic of interaction between the citizen and the state, through which a liberal state can confront the political violence of Islamic groups without resorting to emergency laws. This liberal trend was the mainstay of the changes that have taken place from 2002 until now. The State behaves as if it is scared to tell its citizens about its decision to have a strategic alliance with the U.S. Restricting the activities of liberal organizations is not the state's only mistake. Its greatest mistake lies in the discrepancy between the state's policy and decisions on the one hand and what reaches the citizen's awareness on the other. "

"The consequence of this discrepancy is manifest in the way the state dealt with peace in the Middle East and with our relations with the U.S. Despite the strategic choices regarding these two issues that the country has openly adopted for the past thirty years, there is still a trend in the country that adheres to views of the past. This trend controls the political orientation of certain publications. It has helped to spread hatred of anything American and to disseminate the conspiratorial theory that Israel is behind every [violent] incident that occurs in Egypt. Thus, the state has failed to transmit its message regarding its strategic alliance with the U.S., as if it were afraid to confront the citizens with this truth. Yes, we are the U.S.'s allies, and this does not constitute a betrayal of any principle. This is an alliance aimed at reshaping the entire region on the basis of freedom and equality, and in order to change and awaken societies that deserve a better life. What is wrong with presenting this message loud and clear? Yes, we are the U.S.'s allies, and this alliance grows with every crisis in the region. This alliance is based on principles which permit no-one to interfere with our affairs. It is our policy and our reform alone that leads us to join the policy lines of our strongest ally – politically, economically, and socially – for the sake of a society that is free in every sense of the word", Qamha added.

" The state has made a mistake by letting its voice be weaker than the publications inciting jihad against anything American or Western., on the basis of attitudes shaped in a past era, which the authors of these publications refuse to believe has gone, never to return. It is therefore now the duty of the liberal forces to enter the ideological fray against the authors of these publications, in order to clarify the past, present, and future changes in the state, and to explain that the inciting, inflammatory and violent language is the language of one who is unable to develop and to maintain a dialogue with intellectuals world-wide. One must expose the lie behind the inciting claims that the U.S. is the *Great Satan* with eyes for Israeli interests alone, that the changes and reforms currently taking place are merely the result of external pressures, and that the U.S. is only looking for some opening that would enable it to exert additional pressures on the Egyptian state and to intervene in its political decisions. Exposing all these lies is the opening shot for the phase of an ideological breakthrough that would enable the Egyptian mind to examine everything rationally and to reach rational conclusions instead of being pushed toward a policy of suicide, sacrificing society and its citizens, like at the Khan Al-Khalili market," Qamha further explained.

As for the role of the Egyptian people, Qamha believes that: "the citizens were collectively swept away because the inciting writings and agitation rely upon the religious and pan-Arab nationalist dimensions. That is why the time has come for each and every one of us to relinquish collective thinking and to search, with his individual mind, what will lead to the realization of the interests of the Egyptian state, as well as his own interests... We are required today to think rationally and to imagine where such inciting publications might lead us, and to ask ourselves whether we are ready to accept that each of us harbors within himself a latent terrorist who would destroy the state's and the citizens' property. Or else it is incumbent upon each of us to harbor within himself a modern enlightened citizen, who behaves with openness toward others, who is interested in acquiring an education and in modernization, and who is not afraid of the West, but who influences and is influenced by it. "

"All society's political organizations must be allowed to express themselves. This way the state would respond most forcefully to the inciters and would protect the minds of others from falling into the clutches of this kind of destructive thinking. Thus, the state would begin to confront the most serious obstacles preventing communication between it and its citizens, who all oppose criminal actions like these", Qamha concluded

"Despite the information accumulated about the identities of the perpetrators of the September 11 terrorist attacks – officials, journalists, and religious leaders throughout the Arab and Muslim world have continued to claim that the perpetrators of the attacks were not Arabs or Muslims. The claim that American and or Jewish/Israeli elements carried out the attacks has become an accepted, common myth in the Arab world. According to some versions of this grotesque fantasy, it is President Bush and Secretary of State Colin Powell are the ones who masterminded the attacks."

- Menahem Milson,
Professor of Arabic Literature at the
Hebrew University of Jerusalem

9. A Knight without a Horse: Propagandists and Spin Doctors in al-Jazeera Age

The rise of anti-Semiticism in Egypt and the region

The rise of anti-Semitism in the Mubarak era has been alarming. Mubarak has clashed several times with former Israeli prime ministers in recent years and called his ambassador from Tel Aviv back to Cairo. In several interviews, he emphasized that "cold peace will remain colder for a long time to come". It has been accompanied with the Egyptian media beating the drums of possible war with Israel and launching ferocious campaigns of anti-Semiticism only comparable to the Nasser's era!

What went wrong?

To media analysts and observers in the West, it has been appalling to hear talking about possible war with Israel in the Egyptian media. Even young school children and fresh college graduates parrot the same rehtoric. The *broken record* that has been heard over and over through the Egyptian media for the last fifty years, and especially during the Mubarak era, is the obsession with a conspiracy theory that *Jews and their puppets, the Americans*, are behind everything that has been going wrong. When some Egyptian school girls in Egypt felt some strange symptoms after chewing gum, the response came fast and as usual. Egyptian media pointed the fingers at the Israeli MOSSAD (Intelligence Service). In other cases, Egyptian media would give much credit to the CIA for any conspiracy, as believed by the Egyptian media pundits.

In reality, the Egyptian media has done the Israel's MOSSAD a great service; free publicity within the Arab World. Many Arabs believe that the MOSSAD and the CIA are running the whole world with a keen eye on the Arabs especially. Conspiracy theories are rampant among Arabs. Arabs do even suspect their own rulers to be moles of the CIA or in other cases to the former USSR during its super power status.

Conspiracy theories in the Arab World have a tendency to shift and evolve to a higher conspiratorial level. This makes it difficult for the average Arab to trust their own government and even to determine their own political orientation. Many Arab leaders have shown a tendency to switch roles and change alliances and loyalties in a heartbeat. Nasser tried to win American support in the early years of his presidency. Actually, American diplomatic pressures drove the British, the French and the Israelis from Sinai and the Suez Canal area in 1956 after the Suez Campaign. When Nasser did not receive the additional support he hoped for from the U.S. —weapons and finance for his pet project the Aswan High Dam—he switched his allegiance to the USSR during the height of the Cold War. Nasser embraced the comrades in Moscow, Havana, Belgrade, and became redder than the Reds themselves.

Nasser, who once pledged allegiance to Hassan al-Bana; former leader of the Muslim Brothers, rounded up tens of thousands of them and hanged their leaders. Communists did not receive a happier fate than their fellow faithful compatriots. Political parties that thrived before 1952 disbanded and illegalized. Newspapers nationalized. Military censors had their offices in every newspaper monitoring every word published.

Then, Nasser discovered a new medium that launched him into stardom as the new leader of pan-Arabism. Egypt's TV and Radio service beamed songs praising Nasser's every decision as an embodiment of wisdom. Famous popular Egyptian singers, like Um-Kulthum, Abdel-Wahab, and Abdel-Halim Hafez, were competing to idolize Nasser. Nasser's military machine intervened to support coups in several Arab countries; in Yemen, Algeria, allegedly to *liberate the freedom loving people of the yoke of imperialism and reactionary regime,* as his media claimed.

Nasserism was in full gear. Nasser championed his favorite cause; the Palestinian issue, that he added to his roles. Efforts to elevate Nasser to the stature of a superhero were well-planned, calculated and carefully orchestrated. Nasser spared no effort to import former Nazi experts of propaganda who fled Germany after the fall of the Third Reich. Many of them settled in Cairo and Damascus. Nasser even hired some of them as military experts to make him the super missiles that he hoped to use to solve the *Jewish Problem* in Palestine. Years later, Saddam Hussein had attempted to build his *Super Gun* and nuclear missiles, Nasser's way.

The Nazi propaganda experts, along with their Russian counterparts sent by Moscow during Nasser's Socialist years, cooked up a new image for the leader of the Arab world. They recycled crude anti-Semitic propaganda and rebottled it for the consumption of the Arab masses. After all, the new Arab leader and hero needed an enemy and the new old enemy was the Jews.

The Nasser years witnessed the rise in Nasserism in Egypt and throughout the Arab region. Copycats of Nasser, and Nasser-wanabes would stage a coup in an Arab country and then broadcast their allegiance to him over the radio. Several *Free Officers* movements started all over the Arab world in the fifties and sixties; in Yemen, Libya, Syria, Iraq, and Sudan. The Arab world became infatuated with Nasser. He managed to silence any kind of opposition in Egypt, threaten fellow Arab rulers, badmouth *Western imperialists*, and promised to *throw the Jews in the Mediterranean*. Arabs had not witnessed anything like that in their near past.

It was the time that most Arab countries came out of European colonization and before that they were under the Ottoman Turks for hundreds of years. Democracy was considered a Western invention that was not tested even in a single Arab country. The Arabs, although were eager to have their own self rule, were doubtful about democracy. Promoters of democracy would be looked down upon as mouthpieces and moles of the West.

To the present day, the Arabs only have experienced the rule of either a military dictator or an absolute monarchy. Arab masses rejected socialism because they were told that it was an invention of *Satan and the Godless communists.*

Before the oil boom of the seventies, most Arab governments had limited financial means. Nasser's propaganda machine was far-reaching. The Cairo radio station *Sawt al-Arab* (the *Voice of the Arabs*) reached every household in Arab countries, even to Bedouins in tents. Nasser threatened any Arab leader who did not get in line and adhere to Nasser's policies and whims. Egypt had its influence as the cultural capital of the Arab world with huge government subsidies printing books, producing *revolutionary* songs, movies and theatrical shows. Nasser exported hundreds of thousands of teachers, media and political consultants to Arab countries who transported his version of pan-Arabism.

But Nasser's humiliating defeat in 1967 by Israel, after he had promised to *throw the Israelis in the sea*, brought his regime to an abrupt end. The armies of Egypt, Syria, and Jordan were crushed. The Arabs felt betrayed by their hero and pharaoh. It was a big blow to the Arabs' sense of pride and dignity that they value above all things; even life itself.

The psychological scar seemed never to heal. Later, Sadat would shock the Arab psyche again when he landed in Ben Gurion airport in Tel Aviv asking for peace. He seemed to have broken a taboo and breached the three famous *No's* of the Arabs. Arab leaders long since Nasser had vowed to *no peace with Israel*, *no recognition of the state of Israel*, and *no concessions about*

Palestinian land.

Sadat had broken the sacred vow and shattered the Arabs sense of tribalism that found its manifestation in Nasser's pan-Arabism. They called Sadat a traitor.

Ironically, years later, other Arab leaders followed suit with Sadat after long years of renouncing him. The late King Hussein of Jordan and *PLO* leader Yasser Arafat were eager to reach peace with Israel. Many other Arab leaders announced their peace initiatives hoping to make history in their own.

With the resurgence of anti-Semiticism in Egypt, and the Arab and Muslim worlds at large, it seems that Nasserism has been reborn in the Arab media, simultaneously led by the Egyptian media. The rebirth of Nasserism came due to many factors; in part by the Arabs' disillusionment in their rulers, the perception of being invaded by a foreign superpower like the United States in various episodes of the Gulf War in Iraq, and the persistence of the Palestinian problem.

In a global village where the internet and satellite dishes are in every street in the Arab lands, the younger generation that count to almost sixty percent of the population have never seen Nasser, but they heard about him from their parents and teachers. Many of the young generation are educated, jobless, unmarried, sexually repressed, and see no end to the status quo; where dictatorship, corruption and cronyism are the daily norm.

They are confused. They do not know in what to believe. Should they believe in what fundamentalist preachers tell them day and night while they are listening to their state media blaming the Jews and the Imperialist Americans? Is democracy good for them?

Nasserites played an important role founding media outlets in most Arab countries. Even a satellite network like *al-Jazeera* funded by the Qatari government is no exception to that. In fact, the editorial staff of *al-Jazeera* has been taken over by Nasserite Palestinians so much so that most of *al-Jazeera* coverage revolves around what's happening in the West Bank and Gaza. *Al-Jazeera* has been broadcasting on a daily basis, a stream of graphic images of Israeli soldiers and tanks against young Palestinian children. Adding to the fury of the Arab masses, with the Iraqi war, *al-Jazeera* added to its favorite topics daily graphic images of American soldiers chasing, bombing and torturing Iraqis. To the ordinary Arab viewer, these images and inflammatory commentary give a sense of being targeted and invaded once more by the *Franks*; reminiscent of the crusaders in the Middle Ages.

Taking the sudden popularity of *al-Jazeera* into account, other state TV channels mushroomed throughout the Arab world; *al-Arabia* in Saudi Arabia, *Nile Sat* in Egypt, and the Lebanese *LBC*. Even Hezbollah has its *al-Manar TV,* competing with the successful formula proved by *al-Jazeera* to incite the Arab street.

Arab state media had to compete as well. Most of the contemporary journalists and senior editors in the Arab state media are a product of Nasserism. They grew up as Nasser's youth and were members in his Arab Socialist Union in Egypt and Syria, and in similar official state parties like the Baath in both Iraq and Syria - an offshoot of pan-Arabism.

Many Arab governments found the *al-Jazeera* phenomenon to serve their purposes; in part it does deflect the public's attention from nagging domestic issues like failing economies, inflation, unemployment, corruption, etc. In another way, it does vent the anger of the Arab masses (or the *Arab Street*) towards the two favorite old targets, the Jews and the imperialist Americans that Arab media describe as *have invaded and defiled Arab sacred land.*

The formula proved to work like magic. Since Nasser till Mubarak, little effort was needed; only the recycling of crude anti-Semitic conspiracy theories to fit the new angry audience. The old Arab sense of tribalism has been revived and the Jinni has come out of the bottle angry and looking for enemies.

Arab autocratic régimes have managed to tame, neutralize and contain their intellectuals, members of academia and artists, alike. Those who dared to sing outside of the choir, other than the official tune, were ostracized, deemed traitors to their country, and even imprisoned. Some were sent to lunatic asylums, like the late Egyptian poet Naguib Soror.

Those who complied and played by the rules of the game have been generously compensated and gained wealth and fame that they do not venture to lose, and do have a personal interest in keeping the oppressive sponsoring regime; regardless of what they may believe.

The result has been the creation of masters of double talk, who would say something, believe in something, and do something else; creating a climate of fear, paranoia, and a schizophrenic behavior.

Therefore, anti-Semiticism seems to be a convenient tool for the Mubarak regime and other regimes in the region. On November

6, 2002, on the first night of Ramadan, several Arab television channels aired the first segment of a 41-part serial called *A Knight without a Horse*. It was based on the infamous forgery of *The Protocols of the Elders of Zion*.

The U.S. State Department called on the Egyptian government to prevent the broadcast – a demand that was rejected out of hand by Egyptian Information Minister Safwat el-Sharif. The series was viewed and approved for broadcast by a committee appointed by the *Egyptian Censor*. A committee from the Egyptian Radio and Television Association declared the series *a landmark in the history of Arab drama*. The Egyptian Information Minister stated that "the dramatic views expressed by the series contain nothing that can be considered anti-Semitic." (1)

In Ramadan 2003, also for prime-time screening, there was a series devoted to smearing the Jews and allegedly *exposing their evil machinations*. The Syrian-produced series, *Al-Shatat* (*The Diaspora*), purported to show Jewish life in the Diaspora and the emergence of Zionism, and was broadcast by Hezbollah's *al-Manar TV*. It included gruesome scenes such as the ritual murder of a Christian boy and the ritual murder of a Jew who married a Gentile.

The series also shows how Amschel Rothschild, the founder of the purported secret world Jewish government, allegedly instructed his sons from his deathbed to start wars and corrupt society all over the world to serve the financial interests and the political goals of the Jews. (2)

Blood libel accusations in the Arab media, which claim that on the Jewish holiday of Purim Jews use human blood for their traditional pastries, are most commonly encountered in the context of criticism of Israel's actions against the Palestinians. One instance of this caused the Paris Supreme Court, in August 2002, to subpoena Ibrahim Nafea, former editor of the Egyptian daily *al-Ahram*. Nafiea was charged with incitement to anti-Semitism and racist violence for having permitted the publication of an article entitled *Jewish Matza is Made from Arab Blood* in the October 28, 2000.

The article connected the 1840 Damascus blood libel with Israel's activity in the occupied territories. (3) The charges against Nafea aroused a storm of protest and outrage throughout the Arab world. They were described in the Arab media as *intellectual terrorism, a blow to freedom of expression, a Zionist attack on the Egyptian press, extortion by the Zionist lobby in France*, and even as *an insult to the entire Arab press.*

Despite the information accumulated about the identities of the perpetrators of the September 11 terrorist attacks – officials, journalists, and religious leaders throughout the Arab and Muslim world have continued to claim that the perpetrators of the attacks were not Arabs or Muslims, says Menahem Milson, professor of Arabic Literature at the Hebrew University of Jerusalem.

"The claim that American and or Jewish/Israeli elements carried out the attacks has become an accepted, common myth in the Arab world. According to some versions of this grotesque fantasy, it is U.S. President George W. Bush and Secretary of State Colin Powell who masterminded the attacks", Milson explains. (4)

Arab governments and intellectuals responded to protests and outside pressures. Usama el-Baz wrote articles in December

2005, in which he denounced anti-Semitism. Equally significant is the news published in the Saudi daily *al-Watan* on March 14, 2003 that the Institute of Islamic Studies at Cairo's religious Al-Azhar University recommended that Muslim preachers refrain from comparing Jews to pigs and apes. It is doubtful that either of these steps would have been taken were it not for the recent protests and criticism in the U.S. Congress and media, explains Milson. (5)

A common insult directed at Jews, not only in Friday sermons, is that they are, or are descended from, apes and pigs. This abusive reference claim that a Quranic verse which states that some Jews were turned into apes and pigs by God, as a punishment for violating the Sabbath. (6)

In one of his sermons, Saudi Sheikh abd al-Rahman al-Sudayyis, imam and preacher at the Kaaba mosque in Mecca, the most important shrine in the Muslim world, said: "Read history and you will understand that the Jews of yesterday are the evil fathers of the Jews of today, who are evil offspring, infidels, distorters of [God's] words, calf-worshippers, prophet-murderers, prophecy-deniers... the scum of the human race whom Allah cursed and turned into apes and pigs… These are the Jews, an ongoing continuum of deceit, obstinacy, licentiousness, evil, and corruption..." (7)

Salim Azzouz, columnist for the Egyptian opposition daily *al-Ahrar*, which is affiliated with the religious Liberal Party, described Israel's withdrawal from Lebanon in May 2000 as follows: "They fled with only the skin on their bodies, like pigs flee. And why say *like*, when they actually are pigs and apes?"

The image has pervaded the public consciousness, even that

of children. In May 2002, *Iqraa*, the Saudi television station interviewed a three-and-a-half-year-old *real Muslim girl* about Jews, on *The Muslim Women's Magazine* program. The little girl was asked whether she liked Jews; she answered, *no*. When asked why not, she said that Jews were *apes and pigs*. Who said this? The moderator asked. The girl answered, *Our God.*" "Where did He say this? *In the Quran*. At the end of the interview, the moderator said with satisfaction: *No [parents] could wish for Allah to give them a more believing girl than she... May Allah bless her and both her father and mother.* Nevertheless the station claims to *highlight aspects of Arab Islamic cultures that inspire admiration ... to highlight the true, tolerant image of Islam and refute the accusations directed against it.* (8)

Another very popular anti-Jewish traditional motif is the *Promise of the Stone and the Tree*. A widely quoted prophetic tradition (hadith) affirms that before the Day of Judgment, the Muslims will fight the Jews and kill them. Seeking refuge, the Jews will hide behind stones and trees, and the stones and trees will call out, "*Oh Muslim, oh Servant of Allah, a Jew is hiding behind me. Come and kill him.*" Shortly before the war in Iraq, a preacher in Baghdad's largest mosque quoted this hadith on television, as he brandished a long sword; his cry, *We shall cut off their heads* swept his audience of thousands into ecstasy.

The most common trend today in Arab anti-Zionist writing is equating Zionism with Nazism. Articles and public discussions in the Arab world point out an ostensible similarity between the two ideologies, particularly with regard to racism. They claim that just as the Nazis believed in the superiority of the Aryan race, the

Zionists believe in a *Chosen People* – i.e. the Jews.

An additional outrageous claim is that the Zionists collaborated with the Nazis to annihilate the Jewish people; since the Zionists considered Palestine the only appropriate destination for Jewish emigration, they refrained from engaging in strictly humanitarian efforts to rescue Jews.

Astonishingly, such claims were the focus of a 1982 doctoral dissertation by Palestinian Authority President Mahmoud Abbas, at Moscow's Institute of Oriental Studies. (9)

"The so-called *Golden Age of Egyptian Cinema* is a testimony of that long bygone area bemoaned as *la belle epoch.* The names of the star-studded big budget silver screen musicals of the day remain a testimonial to that cosmopolitanism: Farid al-Atrash, famous singer/actor/producer and his sister, singer/actress Asmahan became the darlings of Egyptian cinema. Actresses Nagma Ibrahim and Raqia Ibrahim; actress/singer Layla Murad Nagma Ibrahim, and the early director Togo Mizrahi, all of whom were Egyptian Jews who played immortal and unforgettable roles on the screen.

- Joel Gordon
In *Revolutionary Melodrama;*
Popular Film and Civic Identity in Nasser's Egypt

10. THE JEWS OF EGYPT: ROUNDING UP THE USUAL SUSPECTS

Egyptian Jews are the oldest Jewish community in the world. The Jewish population of Egypt has been reduced to 100 people, down from between 75,000 and more than 100,000 in 1948. The ancient Hebrew name of Egypt is *Mitzrayim, Mazor, or Misri.*

The Bible calls Egypt also land of Ham in Genesis. (1) *Misr*, the Arabic and official name for modern Egypt, is of Semitic origin directly cognate with the Hebrew *Mitzráyim*, meaning the two straits, and means a country or a state in Arabic.

The ancient name for the country, Kemet, or *black land*, is derived from the fertile black soils deposited by the Nile. This name became *Keme* in a later stage of Coptic and appeared in early Greek as *Chymeía*. The English name Egypt came via the Latin word Aegyptus. It was formed by the combination of the two words meaning home of the *Soul of* god *Ptah of Memphis.*

The Jewish connection to Egypt is ancient. The Biblical stories of Abraham, Joseph, and the Exodus incorporate Egypt into the sacred geography of the Jewish tradition. The history of the

Jewish people has been linked, since the remotest times, to that of Egypt.

Already in the time of the pharaohs of the first dynasties, Joseph sold by his brothers becoming, because of his great wisdom and profound judgment, a powerful minister in the valley of the Nile. The children of Israel went to Goshen of Egypt at the call of Joseph.

Moses emerged from the womb of Egypt (2) The Jewish people have taken root in Egypt and many Jewish figures resided came seeking refuge: Joseph, the first minister of supply in history, Moses, Philo of Alexandria, Maimonides, and many others. The Torah was given on Mount Sinai in Egypt. (3)

Egypt became home to large numbers of fugitive Semites who settled in the land. According to biblical accounts, after 1700 B.C. Egypt had constantly a large Semitic element of population, especially along the eastern frontier of the Delta.

Jews immigrated to Egypt in the Ptolemaic era, settling especially around Alexandria. The Jews in Alexandria enjoyed a greater degree of political independence there than elsewhere.

In 629 AD, the emperor Heraclius had driven the Jews from Jerusalem which was followed by a massacre of Jews throughout the empire. The Treaty of Alexandria in 641 sealed the Arab conquest of Egypt. It stipulated that the Jews were to be allowed to remain in that city; and at the time of the capture of that city. In his letter to Caliph Omar, Amr ibn al-Aas, relates that he found there 40,000 Jews.

The Fatimite rule was in general a favorable one for the Jews, except the latter portion of al-Hakim's reign. The mad caliph al-Hakim (996-1020) vigorously applied the Pact of Omar, and compelled the Jews to wear bells and to carry in public the wooden image of a calf.

By the beginning of the twelfth century a Jew, Abu al-Munajja ibn Shayah was at the head of the Ministry of Agriculture. He is especially known as the constructor of a Nile sluice (1112), which was called after him *Bahr Abi al-Munajja.*

The rigid orthodoxy of Saladin (1169-93) did not seem to have affected the Jews in his kingdom. A Karaite doctor, Abu al-Bayyan al-Mudawwar (d. 1184), who had been physician to the last Fatimite, treated Saladin also; while Abu al-Ma'ali, brother-in-law of Maimonides, was likewise in his service.

In 1166 Maimonides went to Egypt and settled in Fostat, where he gained much renown as a physician, practicing in the family of Saladin and in that of his vizier Qadi al-Fadhil al-Baisami. The title *Ra'is al-Umma or al-Millah* (*Head of the Nation, or of the Faith*), was bestowed upon him. In Fostat, he wrote his *Mishneh Torah* (1180) and the *Moreh Nebukim.*

Historian al-Maqrizi relates that the first Mameluke, Sultan Baibars (1260-77), doubled the tribute paid by the *ahl al-dhimmah* [literally, *People of the Book*, non-Muslims]. At one time he had resolved to burn all the Jews, a ditch having been dug for that purpose; but at the last moment he repented, and instead exacted a heavy tribute, during the collection of which many perished, says Professor Joel Benin.

On Jan. 22, 1517, the Turkish sultan, Selim I, defeated Tuman Bey, the last of the Mamelukes. Selim made radical changes in the affairs of the Jews, making each community independent, and placing David ibn abi-Zimra at the head of Tewish community of Cairo. He also appointed Abraham de Castro to be master of the mint.

According to Manasseh ben Israel (1656), "The viceroy of Egypt has always at his side a Jew with the title *zaraf bashi*, or treasurer, who gathers the taxes of the land.

According to the official census in 1898, there were in Egypt 25,200 Jews in a total population of 9,734,405. During British rule, and under King Fuad, Egypt was friendly towards its Jewish population. Jews played important roles in the economy, and the Jewish population climbed to nearly 100,000 as Jews settled in Egypt while fleeing increasing persecution in Eastern Europe.

One of the most famous Jews of this period was Yaqub Sanu who advocated the removal of the British, and he edited the nationalist publication *Abu Nazara* even after his exile. "This was one of the first magazines written in Egyptian Arabic, and it consisted of mostly satire, poking fun at the British as well as the Monarchy as a puppet of the British", Benin said.

The story of Yusuf Aslan Qattawi Pasha (1861-1942), is shows the atmosphere of tolerance that pervade in Egypt before 1952. Qattawi was the president of the Sephardic Jewish community council of Cairo, was the most visible Egyptian Jew of the interwar era, because of his leadership of the community, and his extensive business and political activity. He studied engineering in France, returning to Egypt to work for a time in the Ministry of Public Works, and then left to study the sugar refining industry in Moravia.

Returning to Egypt, Yusuf Qattawi became a director of the Kom

Ombo Sugar Company which developed and cultivated sugar on 70,000 acres in Aswan Province. Building from this base in the sugar industry, the Qattawis established several industrial, financial, and real estate enterprises in collaboration with the Suarèses and other Jewish families, amassing considerable economic and political power. (4)

Talaat Harb, the founder of Bank Misr and father of Egyptian economic nationalism, began his career in the employ of the Suarès and Qattawi families. Harb first worked at the Dairah Saniyeh Company, and then as a managing director of the Kom Ombo Company. (5) He acknowledged his debt to the Suarèses and Qattawis and maintained close relations with the Cairo Jewish business elite.

When Harb established Bank Misr in 1920, he invited two prominent Jews with whom he had collaborated on the Executive Committee of the Egyptian Chamber of Commerce and the Commission on Commerce and Industry, Yusuf Qattawi and Yusuf Cicurel, to join him as founding directors, and Qattawi became Vice-President of the board.

The Qattawi family claimed residence in Egypt since the eighth century. (6) Though Yusuf Aslan's grandfather acquired Austrian citizenship, Yusuf was an Egyptian citizen. His French education was a symbol of modernity and progress common to the sons of the elite, the business community, and many leading intellectuals of the early twentieth century.

The Qattawi family's Egyptian identity was reinforced by its ties to the royal family and political activism. Yusuf Aslan received the title of Pasha in 1912. He was elected to the committee to draft the

1923 Constitution. He served as a minister in two pro-monarchist governments in 1924-25, though he was forced to resign because he maintained personal relations with Egyptian nationalist Saad Zaghlul. King Fu'ad appointed him to the Senate in 1927. His wife, Alice was first lady of honor to queens Farida and Nazli, narrates Professor Benin.

His sons, Aslan Bey (1890-1956) and René Bey (1896-?) succeeded him in both the political and business arenas. Both were educated in Switzerland, but like their father they insistently asserted their Egyptian identity and cultivated the family's relationship with the royal family. When Yusuf Aslan Pasha retired from the Senate in 1938, King Faruq appointed younger Aslan to take his father's place. The same year René was elected deputy for the Kom Ombo Sugar Co. Both retained their positions until 1953, when the parliament was dissolved by the regime of the Free Officers, as told by Benin.

René Qattawi inherited his father's leadership of the Cairo Sephardic Jewish community. He urged Jews to see themselves as an integral part of the Egyptian nation and in 1935 encouraged the formation of the Association of Egyptian Jewish Youth whose manifesto proclaiming *Egypt is our homeland, Arabic is our language* called on Jews to take part in the Egyptian national renaissance. (7)

The Association of Egyptian Jewish Youth and its newspaper, *al-Shams*, supported René Qattawi for the presidency of the Cairo Sephardic Jewish community council as the candidate best able to promote the *Arabization* and *Egyptianization* of the community. (8) He was elected and served from 1943 to 1946.

René Qattawi aggressively opposed Zionism, which gained significant support for the first time during World War II. In November 1944 he and Edwin Goar, vice-president of the Alexandria Jewish community, sent a *Note on the Jewish Question* to a meeting of the World Jewish Congress in Atlantic City, arguing that Palestine could not absorb all the European Jewish refugees and noting Egypt's *exemplary treatment of its Jews.* (9)

In late 1944 and early 1945, Qattawi carried on a sharp correspondence with Léon Castro demanding that Castro close the camps operated by the Zionist youth movements. Qattawi was unable to impose his will on the Zionist elements of the community council, and this was apparently the cause of his resignation in August 1946. (10)

The Qattawi family maintained extensive business relationships with all the leading Muslim families in the emerging Egyptian bourgeoisie of the inter-war period. Such inter-communal business alliances were common among other wealthy and powerful bourgeois Jewish families: Adès, Aghion, Goar, Mosseri, Nahman, Pinto, Rolos, and Tilche. (11)

In 1909 Moreno Cicurel, an immigrant from Izmir opened a large department store in the heart of the European section of Cairo. (12) Moreno's three sons were born in Cairo, and the family had become Egyptian citizens by 1920, when his second son, Yusuf Cicurel, became a director of Bank Misr. Although Yusuf Cicurel participated in several of Bank Misr's ventures in the 1920s, his younger brother Salvator devoted most of his attention to the family business.

The Cicurel store became the central concern of the family

after the 1920s, when it developed into Egypt's largest and most fashionable department store chain: *Les Grand Magasins Cicurel et Oreco.* In addition to managing his family business, his active sports life, and his service to the Egyptian state on various economic commissions, Salvator was an active leader of the Jewish community. He served on Cairo's Sephardic Jewish community council and succeeded René Qattawi as president from 1946 to 1957.
(Source: Benin)

The Cicurel store had a foreign cultural character due to its exclusive and largely imported merchandise, and the use of French by employees and customers on the shop floor. Nonetheless, a memorandum submitted to the Ministry of Commerce described the firm as *one of the pillars of our economic independence.* (13).

At the outbreak of the Suez War in 1956 with Israel, the Cicurel firm was placed under sequestration. The store was quickly reopened, but the Cicurel family soon ceded its majority holding to a new group headed by Muslim Egyptians. In 1957, Salvator Cicurel left Egypt for France.

Jews in Egypt feared the intolerant positions of Young Egypt and the Muslim Brothers who were, by the late 1930s, antagonistic to the Jewish presence.

Between the two world wars, many Jews felt no contradiction between Zionist and Egyptian national commitments. In an open letter to Haim Nahum Effendi, the Chief Rabbi of Egypt, the editor of the Arabic/French pro-Zionist periodical *Israël*, Albert Mosseri, asked the rabbi to, "Please explain to our brothers that one can be an excellent patriot of the country of one's birth while being a perfect Jewish nationalist. One does not exclude the other." (14) Rabbi Nahum, a consistent anti-Zionist throughout his tenure in office (1924-60), did not accede to this request.

The secularist slogan of the 1919 nationalist uprising – *Religion is for God and the homeland is for all* invited Jews to claim their place as citizens of the Egyptian nation.

By the late 1930s, the limited character of the independence achieved in 1922 eroded liberal territorial conceptions of the nation. British collusion with the monarchy and the continuing military occupation, the privileged position of Europeans, the intensifying Arab-Zionist conflict in Palestine, and the rise of fascism and communism in Europe led many Egyptians to rearticulate their nationalism in either pan-Arab or Islamist terms. (15)

Such orientations excluded Jews from membership in the nation, either because they were not Muslims or because Jews were uncomfortable with militant pan-Arabist/anti-Zionist and the pro-German sentiments of some Arab nationalists.

Several Egyptian Jews did participate in both national movements. Léon Castro conducted propaganda for the Wafd Party in Europe after the 1919 nationalist uprising and founded and edited a pro-Wafd French language newspaper, La Liberté. He was simultaneously the head of the Zionist Organization of Cairo and the representative of the Jewish Agency for Palestine in Egypt.

Félix Benzakein was a member of the Wafd, a deputy in parliament, a member of the Alexandria rabbinical court, and president of the Zionist Organization of Alexandria. Despite his Zionist commitments, Benzakein remained in Egypt until 1960, when he immigrated to the United States. (16)

During the summer of 1948, the property of those suspected of Zionist activity was sequestered, pro-Zionist Jewish newspapers were closed, and Zionism was declared illegal. The government did little to protect Egyptian Jews and their property from bombings and other attacks generally attributed to the Muslim Brothers.

Between 1948 and 1950, 20,000 Jews left Egypt, of who 14,428 reached Israel. (17) By the turn of the twentieth century, Jews were entitled to Egyptian citizenship by the 1929 nationality law. (18) (19) Many of the poor, Arabic-speaking residents of the Jewish quarter [harat al-yahud] in the Gamaliyya district of Cairo or the residents of the port district [harat al-liman] of Alexandria were among the stateless Jews. (20)

The Karaite Jews (21) have lived in Egypt for over 1,000 years, mainly in Cairo's harat al-yahud. They were fully integrated into Cairo's ethnic division of labor and typically worked as goldsmiths and jewelers. Remnants of their historic role persist in the Karaite family names of firms in Cairo's gold market, like al-Sirgani, and few Egyptians are aware of the origin of these names.

In the twentieth century, wealthier Karaites began to move to Abbasiyya and Heliopolis and to adopt elements of bourgeois, francophone, cosmopolitan culture. But in all respects except religious practice, the daily life of the Karaites of harat al-yahud was indistinguishable from that of their Muslim neighbors. (Source: Benin)

By the 1940s, the situation worsened, as a number of pogroms were launched against the Jewish population, incited by Amin al-

Husayni, the Grand Mufti of Jerusalem, starting in 1942. Hostility for the Jews increased as the partition of Palestine and the founding of Israel drew closer. Rising nationalism led to attacks against all *foreigners*.

Most of the older Jewish bourgeoisie embraced loyalist, Egyptianist sentiments who enjoyed comfortable lives and prominence in Egypt. In 1943, when Jews constituted less than 0.5 percent of Egypt's population, they comprised over 15 percent of all directors of joint-stock companies. (22)

The Egyptian *Who's Who* list of the most prominent names in commerce, industry, law, and politics, identified fifty-two percent of those names as Jewish in the 1947. (23)

After the foundation of Israel in 1948, bombings of Jewish areas killed 70 Jews and wounded nearly 200, while riots claimed many more lives.

In July 1954, Israeli Military Intelligence ordered an espionage network of Egyptian Jews it had formed three years earlier to launch *Operation Susannah,* a campaign to fire bomb the main Alexandria post office, the Cairo train station, and several movie theaters. The ring members were quickly apprehended and brought to trial in December 1954.

The verdicts and sentences were delivered in January 1955. Sami (Shmu`el) Azar and Musa (Moshe) Marzuq were sentenced to death along with the Israeli handlers of the network – John Darling (Avraham Dar) and Paul Frank (Avraham Seidenwerg) – who tried in absentia. Me'ir Meyuhas and Me'ir Zaafran received seven years in prison.

Moshe Marzuq, who was executed for his role in *Operation*

Susannah, was a member of the underground self-defense Haganah organization. As a physician in Cairo's Rabbanite Jewish hospital, the son of a wealthy family, and a French citizen, his social and cultural milieu was not limited toghetto world. (Benin)

Victor Levy and Philip Natanson were sentenced to fifteen years in prison. Marcelle Ninio and Robert Dassa received a life sentence. Max Binnet, apprehended with the network, but not directly involved in its operations, committed suicide in jail after severe torture. (24)

Giving his version of the story to the Egyptian media, Egyptian Minister of Interior Zakariyya Muhyiel-Din claimed that "some Jews approached by Israeli agents had refused to act against their homeland". (25) He vowed that the government would deal harshly with the minority of Jews who committed espionage and sabotage on Israel's behalf.

The Lavon Affair named after Israeli Prime Minster; Pinhas Lavon led to his resignation. *Operation Susannah* was exploited by Nasser's media to exacerbate the Egyptian public's distrust of the indigenous Jewish communities.

In 1956 Nasser's government expelled almost 25,000 Jews and confiscated their property and 1,000 more Jews were imprisoned. On November 23, 1956, a proclamation was issued stating that "*all Jews are Zionists and enemies of the state*," and it promised that they would be soon expelled.

Thousands of Jews left, forced to sign declarations that they were doing so voluntarily, and allowing their property to be confiscated. After 1967, more confiscations took place.

After the 1956 Suez/Sinai War, the Jewish community in Egypt completely disappeared. Only a hundred or so remained. Most Egyptian Jews fled to Israel (35,000), Brazil (15,000), France (10,000), and the U.S. (9,000) or Argentina (9,000).

The once flourishing Egyptian Jewish community that represented *le crème de la crème* vanished. The cosmopolitan climate that existed in Egypt before the 1952 revolution ceased to exist. "Looking back now, many Egyptians bemoan the demise of that cosmopolitanism during the Nasser years when economic nationalization, pan- Arabism and the intensification of the Arab/ Israeli conflict led to the dispersal of minority population and a more narrow focus on what it meant to be Egyptian.

The so-called *Golden Age* of Egyptian cinema is a testimony of that long bygone area bemoaned as *la belle epoche*. The names of the star-studded big budget silver screen musicals of the day remain a testimonial to that cosmopolitanism.

Farid al-Atrash, famous singer/actor/producer and his sister singer/actress Asmahan (who fled Lebanon after the rebellion of their grandparent Sultan Pasha al-Atrash) became the darlings of Egyptian cinema. Actor Stefan Rosti, the son of a Viennese nobility; actress/producer Asya Dagher, Mary Queenie, and comedian Mary Munib; all Lebanese Christians who became stars of the Egyptian cinema and their roles are still being admired and memorized to the present day. Actresses Nagma Ibrahim and Raqia Ibrahim, actress/singer Layla Murad, and the early director Togo Mizrahi, all of whom were Egyptian Jews who played immortal and unforgettable roles on the screen. (26)

Layla Murad's stardom and popularity in Egypt was an example of the success of the Egyptian Jews. Murad starred in many immensely successful movies that attracted major names in acting and singing. Some of the best actors and singers even took supporting or a guest star role just to be in her movies. In 1946, Murad married Anwar Wagdi, the leading actor/producer of his era.

Murad disappeared *Greta Garbo-style* from the public eye after her last movie in 1955. Not even a single picture of her was published in Egyptian media after that date. Ironically, Murad later married a *Free Officer.*

The *Golden Age* of Egyptian cinema had ended. Movies that followed were just simply raw propaganda for the *Free Officers* that eerily resembled movies produced by communist parties in *Bolshevik* Russia and in China during Chairman Mao's *Cultural Revolution.*

The religious and political tolerance that existed was quickly replaced by a form of hyper-nationalism, ethno-centric pan-Arabism; that scared away the remnants of the communities that lived in Egypt for centuries; Armenians, Turks, Kurds, Italians, Greeks, French and many others. It started the brain drain phenomenon where the best talents left Egypt seeking refuge and more political and religious tolerance elsewhere in the West.

Today, the Egyptian Diaspora all over the world is almost five million people who left Egypt after 1952; not only Jews, but Christians and Muslims, as well. The Jewish population in Egypt is minimal – the last Jewish wedding that took place was in 1984.

"The value of freedom that has been stolen is that Man lives in two prisons, the prison of his own soul and the prison of his government, from cradle to grave. A man who stretches out his hands to ask for freedom is not begging; he is seeking a right that has been stolen from him by human greed. If he obtains it, it will not be as a favor from anyone, and he will not be beholden to anyone.'

- Egyptian writer, Mostafa Lotfi Al-Manfaluti

11. Gatekeepers and Infidels: The Religious Right versus the Intelligentsia

Why, do Arabs have so little freedom? What has led Arab democratic institutions to become stripped of their original purpose to uphold freedom? Some analysts seek answers in the fraught and ambiguous relationship between *East* and *West*, portrayed as a stark split. The first pole is usually associated with "despotism" as a supposedly inherent characteristic of "the East" and "Eastern" civilization, while the second is linked to freedom, purportedly a fundamental quality of "Western" civilization.

Some have claimed that Arabs and Muslims are not capable of being democrats, for the very reason of being Arab or Muslims. However, a recent research effort, the World Values Survey (WVS), has exposed the falseness of these claims by demonstrating that there is a rational and understandable thirst among Arabs to be rid of despots and to enjoy democratic governance. Among the nine regions surveyed by the WVS, which included the advanced Western countries, Arab countries topped the list of those agreeing that "democracy is better that any other form of governance" according to the UN's Arab Human Development

Report (AHDR) in 2003.

"Since when have you compelled people to enslavement, when their mothers birthed them free?" Caliph Omar bin al-Khattab said more than fourteen centuries ago.

But it seems that his saying has been long forgotten by both the oppressive regimes throughout the Arab and Muslim worlds, and notably in Egypt. Arab journalists affiliated with the state rigorously impose self-censorship in their writings and public speaking to conform to the official policies of their regimes and especially religious authorities setting the tone for the public's mood and emotions.

Political rights, of Arabs and Muslims, the realization of justice and equality, the assurance of public freedoms, the right of the nation to appoint and dismiss rulers, and guarantees of all public and private rights for Non-Muslims and Muslims alike do not exist in the Arab and Muslim worlds. Political forces, in power and in opposition, have selectively appropriated Islam to support and perpetuate their oppressive rule, the UN's Arab Human Development Report (AHDR) stated.

That statement would partially explain why Ali Salem, Egypt's most prominent playwright has been shunned and banished from his country's cultural circles by none but his own colleagues, artists and intellectuals. Ali Salem, who won the courage award in 2008, has been ostracized and banished from his country's cultural circles due to his views favoring normalization with Israel. (1)

Salem's views became widely known after he visited Israel in 1994, and published his favorable impressions of Israel in a book titled *A Drive to Israel*, that became a best seller in Egypt. Since then, he has visited Israel 15 times, and in 2005 he was awarded an honorary doctorate by Israel's Ben Gurion University.

Since his first trip to Israel, Salem has been unable to find producers for his work in Egypt, and none of his 25 plays have been performed there for many years. There has been a semi-official boycott of his works by the Egyptian TV that used to broadcast his very popular stage plays.

In a debate broadcast on *al-Jazeera,* Egyptian peace activist Said Jalal (member of the Egyptian society the *New Call*) faced international relations expert Dr. Rifat Mustafa, who is an opponent of normalization with Israel. (2)

Dr. Mustafa accused Israel of trying to destroy the Arabs along with the peace process. He repeated claims frequently heard in the Arab media that Israel is poisoning the drinking water in Palestine and Jordan, spreading disease-carrying germs, infecting children in Beirut with the HIV virus, spreading diseases in Egyptian agriculture, trying to take over Arab economy, etc.

Jalal replied that most of the accusations are baseless and hurt the Arab credibility. After the broadcast, Egypt's opposition press attacked Jalal charging him with treason and claiming he had requested political asylum in Israel.

The attacks expanded to Western oriented groups, institutes and intellectuals that arose in Egypt during the 1990's. These groups turned away from Arab world-oriented Nasserite ideology, endorsing the classical and modern values of the West: liberalism, separation of religious and political authority, democracy, human rights, free-market economy, and civil society.

While concern for Egypt's future is the motivating factor behind this movement, they also call for greater acceptance for peace and broader normalization with Israel. Most of these activists are from the mainstream of the Egyptian cultural elite.

The neo-Nasserite and radical Islamist opposition, however, view them as an enemy. The neo-Nasserite weekly *al-Usbu* led the attacks on Jalal. One *al-Usbu* columnist, Yasin Husam al-Din, dubbed Jalal as *Said Dayan* (referring to Israeli leader, Moshe Dayan). Another writer, Zuheir al-Arabi, compared Jalal to Zionist leader Ze'ev Jabotinsky. (3)

Al-Usbu editor, Mustafa Bakri, dedicated his weekly column to attacking not only Jalal, but to peace activists in Egypt as if they were foreign agents or saboteurs. Bakri said: "I don't know from what swamp Jalal came. His face is bleak and horrible; his tongue articulates lies and hatred for everything that is Egyptian or Arab. ...I saw him in front of me in *al-Jazeera*. He looked mad, moving sideways; I sensed that he was directing his black face towards the place he desires – Tel Aviv. (4)

Bakri continued his rants saying: "Many people asked me: what right has he to appear on the screen, betray his people and damage Egypt's reputation? But he is not the only one betraying Egypt and its people. The Arab satellite channels are filled with such characters. They compete to strip away the nation's clothing, distort its symbols and reputation, its history and struggle...Take, for example, this vagabond: dressed as a professor but stabbing the nation in the back every day. ... [Bakri refers to Saad Al-Din Ibrahim, the head of the Ibn Khaldoun Institute] (5). He is one Egypt's leading proponents of turning towards the West. What have you done against this suspicious man? Have you locked him up for the crimes he commits against the nation? How can you let this man stroll around the country claiming he runs a committee to monitor the elections... while he is trying to appropriate the hundreds of thousands of dollars flowing to his suspicious institute? (6) One of them even formally asked Israel for substantial financial support in order to publish a newspaper called Change, under the guise of advocating peace and normalization [Bakri referring to an initiative by the Egyptian intellectuals Wahid Ghazi and the late Sharif Kamel]". Bakri continued his inciteful rhetoric against peace activists.

"What have you done against the man who, together with the Israeli embassy, shamelessly established the Egyptian-Israeli Friendship Association [Bakri refers to Nabil Foda, founder of The Egyptian-Israeli Friendship Association]? Where is Egyptian national security? Who will guard the nation? ...They print books, papers and magazines and distort the national memory. They publish Zionist ideas ...and question our national convictions. I know that the USA, the West and the Zionists, who consider hurting these people to be an offense against their authority, protect them." Bakri called for retaliation against peace activists. (7)

Egypt's opposition press did not only attack Egyptian peace groups, but also attacked *al-Jazeera* for hosting the peace activists. The editor of the Islamist opposition weekly *al-Ghad al-Arabi* [*Arab Tomorrow*], Adel al-Jawjary, wrote: "What are the limits of Faysal al-Qasem (host of the show on which Jalal and others have appeared)? For some time he has presented creatures to us, and you never know where they came from. Are they from outer space or were they smuggled from the Qatari-Israeli border? There are no more then 20 such people who support normalization with the Israeli enemy... Al-Qasem has forced Western creatures on us, such as Said Jalal, who became a star on *al-Jazeera*".

Continuing on the same vein, al-Jawjary added: "the station hosted the Copenhagen supporters of normalization. (8) One can call them the Egyptian *Peace Now* movement. Al-Qasem is entitled to present them, because they grant his show a unique flavor that one does not find on other Arab stations. Al-Jazeera destroys the Egyptian people's struggle against normalization when it compares the Egyptian people's struggle to those trapped into normalization. I do not know why al-Qasem invites those people time and again. " (9)

THE SWORD OF THE RELIGIOUS RIGHT

Marking the 16th anniversary of the Fatwa calling for author Salman Rushdie's death issued by Ayatollah Khomeini, the Iranian Revolutionary Guards announced: "The day will finally come when the apostate Salman Rushdie will receive his due punishment for his disgraceful and slanderous move against the Quran and the Prophet." Iran's Leader Ali Khamenei stressed that the death sentence following the publication of Rushdie's *The Satanic Verses* is irrevocable. (10)

The accusation against Muslims intellectuals, artists, and writers of unbelief (an accusation known as *takfir*) recurs in the Muslim world. The traditional punishment for an apostate (*murtadd*) set in early Islam was capital punishment. This punishment was implemented on a large scale in the period following the death of the Prophet Muhammad, when Muhammad's successor Abu Bakr fought wars against the tribes that abandoned Islam.

In modern Muslim history too, there are several cases of charges of apostasy against intellectuals who allegedly *deviated from the dictates of Islamist circles*, says Aluma Dankowitz director of the Reform Project in Washington. (11)

Section 228 of Iran's Islamic Penal Code, states that "an apostate should be excuted if it is proven to the court that the blood of the victim was permitted." An example of the implementation of this law is the cash prize of over $2 million set for the murder of Salman Rushdie, who was accused of apostasy.

Other prominent examples include the 1985 execution of Sudanese Sufi philosopher Muhammad Mahmoud Taha on charges of *ridda*, and the 1992 assassination by Islamists, following similar accusations, of secular Egyptian intellectual Farag Foda. When Muslim Brotherhood leader Sheikh Muhammad al-Ghazali was asked for his view on this assassination, he simply said that "the sentence for ridda that the country's ruler refrained from carrying out has now been implemented." In 1994, Islamists made an attempt on the life of Egyptian Nobel Prize laureate Naguib Mahfouz. (12)

In other cases, conservative Muslim activists exploited the *Hisbah* law enabling anyone to file suit in a court of law against anyone else in the name of society. Thus, the charge of *ridda* was filed against several intellectuals. If found guilty; the court could force them to divorce their spouses, presuming that if one party to an Islamic marriage became an apostate, the marriage was nullified.

Thus, in 1995 an Egyptian court forced Dr. Nasser Hamed Abu-Zayd, who had published critical research on the Koran, to separate from his wife. In 2001, a similar suit was filed against feminist Egyptian author Nawal Al-Saadawi.

In an interview with the Egyptian weekly *al-Ahram al-Arabi*, Sheikh Yousef al-Qaradhawi, a spiritual leader for the Muslim Brotherhood, discussed the view of modern religious law on carrying out the punishment for *ridda*, and permitted the murder of Muslim intellectuals whose views differ from those of Islamist clerics.

Asked, "In Muslim society, has an individual the right to change his religion as he wishes?" Al-Qaradhawi drew a distinction between two types of *ridda*: "One of the freedoms that Islam does not accept is the freedom of *ridda*. Limited *ridda* is the apostacy of the individual who switches religion. According to Islam, the punishment for this individual is Hell. But the other ridda, is a ridda in which the individual who abandons Islam calls upon others to do likewise, thus creating a group whose allegiance is not to the Islamic nation", Qaradhawi added.

"Thus, the Muslim sages agreed that the punishment for the murtadd who commits ridda... is execution" Qaradhawi further added. (13)

In his book *Islam and Secularism*, al-Qaradhawi wrote: "The Muslim sages agreed unanimously that anyone who denies something that is known in the religion ... is an apostate who abandons his religion. The Imam must demand of him to repent, and recant his deviation from the righteous path, or the laws of apostacy will apply to him."

Egyptian intellectual Sayyed Al-Qimni cited the above quote in an article in the Egyptian weekly *Roz Al-Yousef*, explained what it meant: "According to al-Qaradhawi, [the ridda] punishment does not apply only to someone who decides freely to leave Islam for what satisfies his heart and his conscience, it applies in principle also to the Muslim who clings to the laws of his religion … but disagrees with those who have appointed themselves the priests of Islam and who call themselves religious sages … especially when the disputes concern the understanding of a particular matter in Islam. Because those priests have determined that their understanding of the Holy Scriptures is the only permitted understanding and the absolute truth, and anything else is absolute falsehood… Any attempt at new thinking in reading the scriptures is thrust away on the pretext of accusations of abandoning the religion … and the punishment for new thought or expressing a different opinion is death." (14)

The issues of *ridda*, *takfir*, and *tafriq* [forcing separation of spouses] are a constant concern in the Muslim world. The latest affair to take Egypt by storm concerns statements by Egyptian author and TV writer Usama Anwar Ukasha, who allegedly slandered one of the Prophet's Companions, Amr ibn Al-Aas, who commanded the forces that brought Islam to Egypt.

Ukasha called him *the most contemptible figure in Islam* for causing divisiveness and internal conflict in Islam. Attorney Nabih al-Wahsh, who in the past filed a suit against Egyptian author Nawal al-Saadawi, filed a similar suit to separate Ukasha from his wife, claiming that by attacking ibn Al-Aas, Ukasha had left the fold of Islam.

Egypt's shapers of public opinion are divided on the affair. For example, Dr. Abd al-Sabour Shahin, lecturer on Islamic law at the University of Cairo, stated that Amr ibn Al-Aas has an important place in Islam and therefore "we will not permit any secularist to deride him." He expressed support for legal measures against Ukasha in order to *put an end to the distortion of the image of Islam heroes.*

In contrast, Islamic intellectual Gamal al-Bana, the brother of the founder of the Muslim Brotherhood movement Hassan al-Bana, firmly rejected all demands to ostracize any individual or to make charges of apostasy, arguing that criticizing the Companions of the Prophet was legitimate. He said: "The lawsuits we are seeing today to ostracize and prevent different ideas recall previous eras. We must understand that Islam has given man freedom of thought. Islam's history proves that no one is immune to error. The Companions of the Prophet made errors, and therefore it is not right for them to be exempt from criticism. This does permit us to describe their deeds in political terms. It is known that Amr ibn Al-Aas had a controversial political history; therefore, there is nothing to prevent us from opposing him." (15)

Gamal al-Banna himself recently made headlines when the Islamic Research Institute of Al-Azhar University in Cairo banned his book, *The Responsibility for the Failure of the Islamic State.* (16) He authored a study about what he called *Sunna deniers* posted on www.mojahid.net.

Al-Banna' study reviewed the history of Sunna [sayings of the Prophet] denial that began in the second century of Islam (the eighth century), which sees the Quran as the only source of Islamic legislation and rejects the Sunna as an additional source for religious rulings. The study presented the various groups that rejected the Sunna, in part or in whole (17). It goes on to review the development of Sunna denial in different countries, and discusses the important centers of Sunna denial in India, Pakistan, Iran, Iraq, and Egypt. (18)

The study also focused on the main figures who advocated and still advocate this approach, including the prominent reformists of the late 19th and early 20th centuries: Egyptian scholar Muhammad Abdu (d. 1905) and his disciple, Syrian scholar Rashid Rida (d. 1935); Egyptian writers Taha Hussein (d. 1973), Ahmad Amin (d. 1954); Tawfiq Al-Hakim (d. 1987); former Al-Azhar University lecturer, fired for his anti-Sunna views, Ahmad Subhi Mansour; and liberal Syrian intellectual Muhammad Shahrou.

Following its review of Sunna denial, the study determined that the doubts raised by *opponents of Sunna*, past and present, should be studied and that it must be clarified that they are all disproved, and that their writings must all be subjected to a thorough examination. Further, al-Banna said that they must all be decreed apostates and Allah's laws must be applied. He also added that the punishment for *introducing forbidden innovations into Islam* must be applied to those who oppose the proper Islamic traditions, and they must atone or be condemned. (19)

A similar view was expressed by Al-Azhar University member Sheikh Mahmoud Ashour, who stated in an interview with the Egyptian paper *al-Masri al-Yawm*: "Anyone who calls to rely on the Quran alone and ignore the Sunna is an apostate. Anyone who says that the Sunna should be ignored is beyond doubt an apostate." (20)

The issue of rejection of the Sunna as a source of legislation was discussed in a workshop on *Islam and Reform*, held in Cairo on October 5-6, 2004. The workshop's stressed "the importance of implementing both religious and political reforms in order to achieve comprehensive reform." It called for "creating a new intellectual context for Islamic thought based on clear assumptions and unity that will take into account all the changes in Muslim society throughout the past 11 centuries."

To this end, the statement said, there must be "a profound reexamination of Islamic heritage, including all the Islamic sciences established during the past three centuries of Islam – Quran commentary, the Hadith the roots of the religion, and religious law," and "reliance on the Quranic texts as the only authentic source for the purpose of reexamining all of Islamic heritage."

The concluding statement further called for "confronting all the institutions that claim a monopoly on the religion and on the proper interpretation of the holy text. Instead, there is a need for a new trend that will establish everyone's right to implement *Ijtihad* [free thinking], under the banner of Islamic reform that is right for this century." (21)

The concluding statement was signed by leading progressives and reformists in the Arab and Islamic world: Saad al-Din Ibrahim; Gamal al-Banna; Sayyed al-Qimni; Muhammad Shahrour; Dr. Radhwan Masmoudi, executive director of the Center for the Study of Islam and Democracy in the U.S.; Dr. Najah Kadhim, director of the Islamic Forum for Islamic Dialogue in Britain; Sharifa Macarandas, president of the Mindanao Women's League, the Philippines; Tunisian intellectual Salah al-Din Al-Jurashi; Dr. Abd al-Hamid al-Ansari, former director of the Faculty of Shari'a Law, Qatar University; Dr. Fabyola Badawi, director of the European Arabian Union for Democracy and Dialogue in France; and Abdallah Ali Sabri, editor-in-chief of the Yemenite *Saut Al-Shura* daily.

The workshop and its recommendations enraged Egypt's religious establishment. In a statement to the Kuwaiti daily *al-Rai al-'Aam*, the Sheikh of Al-Azhar Muhammad Tantawi said that the workshop had sounded like "an explicit call to deny the Sunna of the Prophet, and the Al-Azhar establishment and Egyptian society rejects this."

Tantawi added, "These centers whose representatives participated in the workshop have a destructive influence on Egyptian society, and their activity must be stopped and their representatives must be brought to trial... This is an explicit call to abandon the main source from among the sources of religious law in Islam – the Sunna of the Prophet. This is a danger that some of our foreign enemies are interested in promoting." (22)

In response to Sheikh Tantawi's statements, the Ibn Khaldun Center issued a communiqué arguing that it was not seeking to abolish the Sunna of the Prophet, but calling to issue religious rulings based solely on the Quran when disputes arose. In answer to Tantawi's statement that the workshop participants were "a group of separatists, one of whom was in the past charged with treason," the communiqué explained that Tantawi was obviously referring to a case against Saad Al-Din Ibrahim and the Ibn Khaldun Center employees, and clarified that Ibrahim had not been charged with treason but with other false charges and the Egyptian Supreme Court had found him and the center's employees innocent.

The communiqué further exclaimed: "Is the Al-Azhar Sheikh entitled to accuse some of the Muslim intellectuals of separating from Islam? Doesn't that mean accusing us of apostasy and endangering our lives? Weren't similar charges responsible for the assassination of Farag Foda, and for the assassination attempt on the world-renowned author Naguib Mahfouz? We call on Al-Azhar not to descend to that path taken by the violent and extremist groups". (23)

About a month after the workshop, Al-Azhar Sheikh Tantawi again attacked the Sunna deniers who see the Quran as the sole source for religious rulings, calling them *ignoramuses, liars, and hypocrites* and warning the public not to listen to their views, which were aimed at fomenting confusion.

In statements delivered on November 5, 2004 at a conference organized by the Supreme Council for Islamic Affairs, Sheikh Tantawi also said, "The attack on the Sunna is a means employed by the enemies of Islam, because the Sunna is only a clarification of the laws appearing in the Quran... Thus, anyone who raises doubts about Sunna is hostile to Islam." (24)

Islamic circles refer to the critical or scientific approach to the Quran as apostasy as well. For example, a weekly talk show on *al-Jazeera* dealt with removing certain Quranic verses from the school curricula in Arab and Muslim countries. Al-Azhar University lecturer Ibrahim al-Chula accused a program guest, the progressive author and journalist Shaker al-Kabulis, of *denying Allah*, and said that he should be expelled from the fold of the Muslim community.

Speaking by phone from the U.S., Dr. Kabulis stated: "There should be a distinction between the Quranic chapters, most of which were revealed in Mecca during the first 10 years of the Prophet's activity, and the chapters dealing with legislation or the life of the Prophet and his relations with his wives and his Companions, and so on. That is, there are chapters that cut across history, and these are the verses revealed at Mecca … and there are circumstantial verses of legislation that were revealed at al-Medina as a result of events that took place 1,400 years ago and which are no longer in existence. Frankly, there are many verses that we call political and military verses, that is, *verses of the sword*, that are connected to circumstances that existed in the past but exist no longer. The verses revealed at Mecca, about the Jews, the Christians, and the People of the Book, for example … were usually verses of support for them, but the verses concerning the Jews and Christians at the stages of the revelation at Al-Medina were contrary to these verses. Why? Because the verses revealed at Al-Medina were the result of the changing political relations of the People of the Book and the Muslims"

Kabulis further said that: "Politics are fluid, not static; therefore, the laws built on a political foundation are also subject to movement, and are not static. On the contrary, most of the verses revealed at al-Medina regarding this matter the People of the Book contradict each other. What is happening now in the Arab world is not the removal of the permanent verses of belief that cross history, but an attempt not to emphasize or teach the circumstantial verses that incite to accusing the other of apostasy and to hatred of the other. Why was the Second Caliph Omar, 1,400 years ago, more courageous than us when he eliminated even the verses connected to the heart of the faith, not only circumstantial verses… Why was Omar capable of doing this 1,400 years ago, while today Ibrahim al-Chula calls anyone who eliminates any verse or chapter of the Koran an apostate?"

Ibrahim al-Chula rejected al-Kabuli's statements out of hand, saying "He doesn't understand Caliph Omar, and he *spoke nonsense that is unworthy of a response*. Neither Omar nor any of the *Sahaba* [disciples of the Prophet] ever dared to eliminate even a single letter of the Koran. What changed were the circumstances of the words of the Quran".

According to al-Chula, "al-Kabulis and Hamid Abu-Zayd and their gangs, speak of the historic aspect of Quranic scripture… Abu Zayd went so far as to say that the Quran is a human text that developed and crystallized, and is a cultural product. This is a lie, [and therefore] the Egyptian court's sentence regarding him was the sentence of apostacy– and had he not left Egypt he would have been executed… Al-Kabulis is not worth holding a discussion with, or of me mentioning him. He lied when he said that there are Quranic verses that contradict one another. When you say that in the Quran there are verses contradicting one another, you commit apostasy, and you leave the fold of the Muslim community through its widest gate. I take responsibility for these words." (25)

In the wake of the recent wave of terrorist bombings in Egypt, al-Qimni published an essay in the weekly *Roz al-Yourself* in which he argued that the responsibility for terrorism in Egypt lies not just with the terrorists themselves but also with those who create a cultural atmosphere conducive to terrorism.

Thus, in al-Qimni's opinion, the fight against terrorism requires combating extremist trends among Muslim clerics and in the Arab media. At the end of his essay, al-Qimni presents a famous episode in early Muslim history to support his argument. When Ali became caliph in 656, he was opposed by a number of the Prophet's closest companions, including Muhammad's wife Aisha. In the first intra-Muslim fighting in history, these opponents met Ali at what is known as the Battle of the Camel, in 656. Although killing animals in war is generally forbidden in Muslim law, and despite the aura of sanctity attached to Aisha, Muslim tradition relates that Ali ordered his followers to bring down the camel on which Aisha rode, as he considered this necessary in order to win the battle for the caliphate. Al-Qimni uses this episode to urge Egyptians to oppose those who threaten society, even if they speak in the name of religion. (26)

A Barrier Separates the Muslim's Mind from the Real World, Making Him Lose the Capacity to Distinguish Good from Evil...

In his article, al-Qimni tried to explain terrorism and the roots behind it: "This suicide bomber was not a lone drop-out from society. He was certainly part of a cell. Nonetheless, it is now possible that an isolated individual can carry out a bombing, as indeed occurred when an Egyptian citizen stabbed a tourist who was kissing his own wife, one week prior to the explosion. It is taught by the schools, on television, in the mosques, and within the family that this scene of a husband kissing his wife – which touches the hearts of people all over the world, and makes them overflow with feelings of humanity – is ugly, promiscuous, and immodest. Thus, the terrorist act of that citizen was merely a result of what we planted in him. He was unable to resist the generator of hate and repugnance within him, so he stabbed the couple with a switchblade. "

Al-Qimni further added that: "The generator of hatred, revulsion, and cruelty is like a generator of energy; it explodes if internal pressure rises. That is what happens to the poor Muslim when he is exposed to the enormous pressure of the religious people in our country, which is far greater than that to which people of other religions in the world are exposed. While for the Christian it is enough to make the sign of the cross, which only takes one second, the Muslim is required to be a mechanical instrument, performing the same action every day. He is required to go to the mosque five times a day, and is required to constantly read the Quran, and to force himself to weep if he cannot weep, and to spend an entire work day in the mosque. No one can make him work so long as he is reading the Quran and reciting endless supplications and devotions. Such recitations accompany his every motion and position, from the moment he gets up at dawn to the moment he retires to the conjugal bed... There is a barrier separating the Muslim's mind from the real world around him, so that he falls into a state of constant hallucination and, as a result, loses the capacity to distinguish between good and evil. He only recognizes the value of *halal* and *haram* [i.e., permissible vs. prohibited] ".

The Muslim Is Fenced-in to the Point Where His Mind Is Paralyzed

Al-Qimni contends that Muslims are burdened with many repressive restrictions. Freedom of thought and expression are fenced in by Islamic restrictions. There are stipulations and rules concerning clothing, such as the veil heap…

"Muslims are forbidden to participate in carnivals which bring together all fellow citizens to meet each other in the streets in an atmosphere of mutual love and love for the homeland… Muslims are forbidden to enjoy refined dance… forbidden to enjoy cinema, novels, theater, and music… The Muslim is fenced in to the point where his mind is paralyzed, and thus he surrenders his mind to the deputies of Islam upon Earth, because there is someone else to think for him… As for the Muslim woman, she is consigned to wretched slavery, she is like a prisoner in a man's possession", al-Qimni said. (27)

Commenting on the current status of Muslim women in today's society, al-Qaradhawi stated on *al-Jazeera*: 'The woman is subject to more restrictions than the man because the man is not a source of temptation as is the woman, who is required to cover her hair, bosom, and neck and to wear clothing that is neither transparent nor tight-fitting...'

"Muslim women have surrendered their minds and spirits and

believe that these are religious duties that are obligatory for them, to such an extent that women academics from al-Azhar University accused al-Qimni of apostasy when I spoke about the rights to which they are entitled by virtue of their being full-fledged citizens just like men", al-Qaradhawi added.

Responding to al-Qaradhawi, al-Qimni stated: "Through the media, education, mosques, and voluntary religious associations, they have been able to take control of peoples' minds, and thus direct them however they wished. We have become their instruments, which they use however they want. If they want, they make us fight for their glory, and if they want, they turn some of us into walking explosive devices. Among them there is a group engaged in *preaching and guidance*, and it is the most dangerous of all, because it prepares the intellectual ground for terrorism. Another group is responsible for justifying terrorist acts through the media. This group mouths condemnation of terrorist acts while finding the worst sort of excuses for them... but when they are hard-pressed, they claim that they [i.e. the terrorists] are a minority who have nothing to do with Muslims and that Islam is not to blame for them, and that they blow themselves up around us and amongst us... because they have been deprived of freedom."

"Now do you see the achievements of the *Blessed Islamic Awakening*? Do you see that we have now reached a record level of backwardness among the nations, and we have earned the height of the world's contempt? They have deluded our youth into believing that despotism is of recent advent, invented by the current Arab governments with the support of the infidel countries, headed by the American Satan. Qaradhawi and his followers have appointed themselves the *deputies of Allah.* When we ask ourselves: who is the real criminal murderer in the terrorist incidents, we are at a loss to answer. (28) Is it al-Qaradhawi, of Muslim Brotherhood and their brethren of various sorts?", al-Qimni exclaimed.

In response, Qaradhawi on *al-Jazeera,* said: 'They [the reformists] claim that it is in the people's interest to permit prostitution and to permit the selling of alcohol so as to encourage tourism. First of all, prostitution and alcohol is contrary to Islam. '

Al-Qaradhawi continued saying, "Mecca was also like this [i.e., with prostitution and alcohol], but the Prophet forbade this kind of income and replaced it with another kind of income – jihad for the sake of Allah, in order to gain an income which is greater and better, by conquering other countries. And Allah said: *If you fear poverty, then know that Allah will enrich you from his bounty* [Quran 9:28], meaning that if you are afraid of suffering dire financial straits, the *Lord will deliver you from these straits* – and in fact, Allah enriched them through conquest and spoils. "

Refuting Qaradhawi's claims, al-Qimni wrote: "Consider how Qaradhawi brazenly attempts to deceive the Muslims. The substitute for income from tourism according to Qaradhawi, then, is jihad in order to conquer the entire world, after tourism is banned from our country... Qaradhawi's position against Egypt is certainly not merely his own personal position... because he is part of a whole band, mostly in Egypt, that constantly repeats the same message. Qaradhawi opines: *'There are people who strive to break Islam into pieces.* Naturally, Qaradhawi does not tell us that there is no legal Islamic statement on political matters or on the nature of the regime… However, Qaradhawi and his followers say that political affairs should be under Allah's rule and not under human rule, and since Allah does not rule in person, they have appointed themselves to rule as His deputies! "

Al-Qimni also claims that: "Qaradhawi has misled our youth with this idea of Islam's *shumuliyya* [the notion that Islamic law covers every aspect of life] and that this is the essential principle of Islam, so that if you do not accept it, you commit outright apostasy. But then reformist thinkers forced him to admit that it had never been an essential principle of Islam… and that the idea of Islam's *shumuliyya* was in fact introduced in 1928 by Hasan al-Bana [the founder of the Muslim Brotherhood and that the concept of *hakimiyya* [i.e., the idea that Allah is the sole sovereign] appeared relatively late, in the writings of Sayyid Qutb [a Muslim Brotherhood leader executed by the Nasser regime in 1966]. These concepts of *shumuliyya* are nothing more than ideas and beliefs of an outlawed group that is soiled with blood." (29)

Al-Qimni further exposed the fallacies behind Qardawi's contensions: "According to these concepts we should refer to the seventh century in all our affairs. *Who is responsible for the terrorist acts? We let terrorism grow and flourish when we allowed Islamist thought to infiltrate our media and schools…* Terrorism grew when we allowed the Islamists to plant in the minds of Muslims the concept that citizenship and patriotism are reprehensible innovations, and this is because the Islamists do not recognize [individual] countries, for they are the Islamic nation of *la ilaha illa Allah* 'There is no God but Allah', wherever they may be. The issue of the ideology of hatred got out of hand when we allowed the Egyptian Fatwa Authority to decide in matters outside its jurisdiction ".

Al-Qimni also stated: "This cancer spread when we allowed them to steal the souls of our children… The virus thrived when we allowed the current of hatred to be directed against the very interests of the people, when we charged the souls with the current of hatred for the advanced Western countries– to the point where our peoples now hate everything associated with the West –instead of hating those Islamic sheikhs and armed militias who have dragged our honor in the mud for the whole world to see."

Has the Arab Media Given the Islamists Legitimacy to Kill Innocent People?

Commenting on the accomplicity of of the Arab media and their attitude of repeating the same rhetoric often used by Islamits, al-Qimni argued in his article that: "We have once again given the Islamists legitimacy to kill innocent people, because all the Arab media have been using the term *resistance* to refer to what the Arab infiltrators and the remnants of the bloody Baath in Iraq are doing against our own people. Thus the Islamists compare the *resistance* in Iraq with the French resistance against the Nazi occupation! The Arab media supported the Sunnis in Iraq when they refused to participate in the elections – even if some media outlets did not say so explicitly, but this was implied. "

"We know that the Sunnis do not want partners in ruling Iraq – not Kurds, nor Shi'ites, nor Christians, nor Assyrians, nor

Chaldeans, nor Mandeans... They are striking at the majority of the Iraqi people, who courageously went to the polls while saying to the Sunnis, *No! Your time and the time of your monopoly on rule is over.* However, the Sunnis aren't giving up, because they are convinced that rule over Iraq is theirs and theirs alone, "al-Qimni added.

Qaradhawi has been one of the theorists behind fundamental movements in the last decades. On one of his programs on *al-Jazeera*, Qaradhawi declared: 'One should sacrifice one's life and one's country for Islam, because Islam takes precedence over human life'... In one of his books, Qaradhawi states: 'Our goal is to establish a Muslim state that will be governed by Allah's Shari'a. The Islamist activists need to exert their best efforts to prepare public opinion to accept their ideas and to pave the way for their state.' In another book, he says: 'Fighting apostasy, heresy, secularism, and immorality, and fighting their foreign and domestic supporters, is the religious duty of these times and the order of the day.'

But outspoken and controvercial Islamic scholar al-Qimni has been ostracized for daring to speak out and expose what has been taken for granted by the clergy and the Islamists. Al-Qimni's courageous views stirred a lot of debate in Egypt and the Arab and Muslim worlds. He believes that: "Proper education and teaching create an individual who loves life – not one who hates life and thus destroys himself and others. However, our universities have turned into religious associations that discuss what is permissible and what is prohibited, and they research religious commentaries instead of researching the laws of physics and mathematics. Our universities now research the issue of the head covering, the veil, modesty, virtue, and the pillars of Islam... The universities have forgotten their role as the primary place for scientific research – that is, to examine the country's ills, whether in medicine or in culture, in order to fight against them... The universities have abandoned their field of expertise and have assumed the role of the mosque. "

"To be specific, when you visit the University of Zaqaziq - which is where the suicide bomber from the Al-Azhar incident studied– you will find slogans everywhere, none of which have anything to do with science. They are all about hatred, the veil, and jihad. We nurtured the seed of terrorism when we allowed our laws, our media, and our schools to divide our people into two camps, with the country belonging to only one of them. This one group is in possession of the absolute truth, and is obligated to correct the others, or, if it can't correct them, to destroy them. "(30)

Al-Qimni finally concludes that; "This is the same trial which Muslims faced at the beginning of their history, at the Battle of the Camel... *Aisha's* [widow of Prophet Muhammad] camel was the symbol of rebellion against the legitimacy. Therefore, Ali called out: *Bring down the camel! As long as the camel lives, people will die.* My dear countrymen*: bring down your camel! Bring down the camel, even if it be sacred, to keep Egyptians from dying.*"

“The basic issue is: Do the Copts in Egypt suffer from serious problems in their own country? The only possible answer is: Yes. Yes, Copts fear for themselves, their families, their property and their safety”

- Reformist Egyptian thinker and Muslim activist Tarek Heggy

12. THE COPTS: STRANGERS IN THEIR NATIVE LAND!

The issue of the Copts of Egypt has gained coverage by the international media in the last decades. Reports of persecution and discrimination against them in their native country of Egypt have made headlines around the world. Amidst that, the Mubarak government has maintained an official line of denial that the problem even exists! Anti- Coptic sentiments, similar to anti-Semitic sentiments, have been on the rise and often promoted by the Egyptian state media branding the Copts as *un-loyal* to their home country of Egypt. It promoted a public discourse about Muslim-Coptic relations in Egypt, their role in Egypt and the role of the Expatriate Copts in the West.

WHO ARE THE COPTS?

According to copts.org, a grassroots U.S.–based organization, the Copts, Egypt's indigenous, pre-Arab, pre-Islamic Christians, are a native ethno-religious group of Egypt. Egyptian Christians trace their ancestry to the indigenous Pharaonic-era population of Egypt, which was converted to Christianity by St. Mark, one of Christ's earliest disciples. In modern usage, the word Copt—originally meaning simply Egyptian denotes any indigenous Egyptian Christian, including traditional Coptic Orthodox, as well as members of the Coptic Protestant (Evangelical) and Catholic communities.

Today Copts of all denominations number approximately seven to twelve million people and constitute between 10% and 15% of the Egyptian population, making them the largest indigenous Christian community in both Africa and the Middle East.

As targets of both the Egyptian government and the increasing threat of Islamic extremists, Copts have long struggled for human and civil rights and religious freedom in their homeland. Despite the censure of the U.S. Department of State, the U.S. Commission on International Religious Freedom, and international human rights organizations, the Egyptian government continues to deny Copts basic rights such as judicial and police protection from persecution, freedom of religious expression and worship, and equal opportunity employment. (1)

In 641 A.D., Muslim Arabs conquered Egypt and began a centuries-long process of ethnic and cultural assimilation, converting, intermarrying with, and absorbing large segments of the Egyptian population into the Arab-Islamic culture. Successive Arab and Turkic (Ottoman) Islamic dynasties levied a punitive tax *jizia* against Egyptians wishing to maintain their Christian heritage. Several of these regimes instituted policies to eradicate the native Egyptian culture and language and initiated violence against the indigenous, non-Arabized population. (2)

In an article on the plight of Egypt's Coptic community, reformist and Muslim activist Tarek Heggy describes the discrimination against Copts. Heggy wrote an article that urged equal treatment of all Egyptians regardless of religion or gender. The article was written as a lead-up to Heggy's participation in a conference on the issue, which was held on November 16-19, 2005 in Washington, D.C.

Members of the Coptic community and other individuals convened in Washington, D.C. to discuss the problems facing Copts in Egypt. "This security-service mentality, which tends to abandon the heart of the matter and pursue marginal issues, suspicions and conspiratorial thinking, is one of the factors that contributed to the collapse of objectivity and rationality in our thinking. It also caused this kind of thinking; to be so far removed from objective and civilized modes of analysis which are one of the achievements of human civilization", says Heggy.

"The basic issue is: Do the Copts in Egypt suffer from serious problems in their own country? The only possible answer is: Yes. Yes, Copts fear for themselves, their families, their property and their safety much more than Muslims do, though the latter, too, are not completely safe. Yes, Copts suffer from a public atmosphere of fanaticism, which is not characterized by friendliness towards them. Yes, Copts encounter exceptional obstacles in various stages of their lives - in acquiring education, obtaining a job and getting promotions - merely because they are Copts", Heggy explains.

"Yes, Copts feel that, even though the qualifications of many of them may exceed the average level of the Muslims, they do not hold important public offices such as governor, mayor, university president, college dean, or even most of the secondary-level positions in the Foreign Ministry, Defense Ministry, Ministry of the Interior, etc. Copts feel that, as soon as a Copt utters his name, which reveals his Coptic identity, he often feels a sharp decline in the degree of friendliness shown towards him", adds Heggy.

"Yes, Copts feel that it makes no sense that, even though they constitute about one sixth (15%) of the population, Coptic MPs constitute less than one percent of the parliament. One does not need to be exceptionally bright in order to realize that this cannot be a mere coincidence, but can only be the result of motivations that are nefarious, irrational, unjust, inhuman and contrary to the basic concept of citizenship. Yes, Copts feel that it is an insult to the intelligence of all Copts and all Egyptians to claim that *everything is all right* now that Sheikh Al-Azhar has been seen embracing the Coptic Pope. Yes, Copts feel that it is strange that the taxes they pay are spent on building mosques and on the Al-Azhar Islamic University, while at the same time they must invest huge efforts to build churches at their own expense ", Heggy further explained.

"Yes, Copts, and especially those above the age of 60, feel that the attitude displayed today towards themselves, their wives, their daughters, and their sons is totally different from what they experienced over 40 years ago in the very same Egypt. These are the essential aspects of the subject. To accuse anyone who speaks of these matters of being an agent of parties hostile to Egypt, or of being involved in a plot against Egypt, is simply a joke, an insult to the truth and an affront to reason. As an Egyptian it is my obligation to do so - because Egypt today is ill. She will never get on the road to recovery so long as Copts and women do not take part in treating Egypt's problems from a position of full and unimpaired citizenship. A person who is oppressed and whose rights are denied cannot participate in pushing forward the broken-down wagon. I was sure that this visitor did not understand what I told him, because he was trained to treat the Copts as a threat to Egypt, despite the fact that they are the original Egypt." Heggy delivered his emothinal plea.

"To come back to the issue of the Copts in Egypt, I contend that the fact that most senior officials continue to ignore the Coptic issue will bring Egypt to crises which I can almost make out on the horizon. They are similar to the crises of others in the region - others who fell [sic] prey to the temptation to ignore some problems, and especially to ignore the realities of today's world, that is, the post-Cold War world. This is a world in which the idea of sovereignty in its old sense, which had been stable for the many decades preceding the fall of the Berlin Wall, is no longer of any use to anyone. There are those who understand this new world, and there are those who are unable to understand and take in all dimensions of this change", Heggy explained to the international media that covered the conference on religious minorities in Washington, D.C.

The sincere and emotional remarks of Heggy caused a storm back in his native country of Egypt. The Egyptian media in its frenzied coverage of the event called the conference and those participating in it conspirators and traitors. Egypt's media considered the event that aimed at starting a rational dialogue about the status of its Copts as a *conspiracy to pressure and defame Egypt*.

As usual, the Mubarak regime does not deal with incidents related to the Copts not as a phenomenon that needs serious deliberation and governmental measures to correct the wrongdoings inflicted on the Copts, but rather it downplays and sweeps it under the rug.

On February 10, 2002, the news agencies reported attacks on Copts in a village in the al-Minia district. Copts' homes, cars, and churches were burned, and 10 Copts were hurt. An Egyptian writer living in New York City wrote a critical account of the Egyptian government's treatment of its Christian Coptic minority, in the London daily *al-Quds al-Arabi*. "Lack of a clear penal policy: In self-respecting societies, there is no dialogue or compromise whatsoever with a criminal who commits an act punishable by law. Yet in Egypt… the real criminal ends up going free, and the ones brought to trial are youths against whom the judge has no evidence whatsoever… All this, when everyone knows who really committed the crimes – not one of whom, for some unknown reason, is brought to trial or punished", explained the writer. (3)

"Equal treatment for attacker and attacked: Since President Sadat's espousal of the accursed policy of equalizing the attacker with the attacked – which developed into claims about clashes between extremists from both sides, our lives became a nightmare. By what logic, law, or religion is the attacker compared to the attacked? After every brutal attack on the Copts come arrests of groups from both sides; this show ends in the victim relinquishing his rights… This means that the state is not neutral, and it encourages crime against the Copts", the writer added.

Did the Mubarak government attempt to protect the Copts? Asked the writer: "Rewarding the aggressor...: Every time, the state rewards the extremists for their crimes instead of punishing them. Thus, the extremists manage to impose their will. In the village of al-Timsahiya, in the Assyut district, when the Muslim mob went wild because of the height of a church, it was agreed to make the mosque's minaret higher so that it would be taller than the church. In exchange for rebuilding the church destroyed by a Muslim mob in the recent attack, the housing minister launched a fundraising campaign for the construction of a mosque. Why should they [the Muslim mob] refrain from running wild if it ends in the burning of Christian homes and churches, while at the same time they accomplish their goal building a mosque?" the writer exclaimed.

Exposing the oppressive nature of the Mubarak regime and its double standards in dealing with Copts, the writer added: "Oppressive, arbitrary laws: Clearly, the laws for establishing Christian houses of worship in Egypt are oppressive and unconstitutional. Because of this injustice, the Christians have paid dearly, in blood and property, for attempts to establish houses of worship. Government behavior that fosters extremism: When the government destroys a four-story church in Shubra al-Khayma, that same government destroys the walls and foundations of the al-Ubur Church; when the government prevents the Church of the Virgin in al-Zeytoun from being made higher on the pretext that it would interfere with air traffic – although the church is quite far from the airport!; when it builds a mosque in the middle of the road in al-Abbasiya so that it faces the cathedral; when the government thinks with this kind of mentality – what signals does it send to the Muslim mob?"

Is it enough to have the Sheikh of al-Azhar embracing the Coptic Pope in front of TV cameras as a *Sign of National Unity* as the Egyptian government claims? On that, the Egyptian writer from New York sarcastically calls it the *Embracing Show*. He adds that: "The Egyptian government maintains that the Copts should be satisfied and thank God for gestures that are a great honor for them. What is the matter with this Coptic greed?! Isn't it enough for them when the sheikhs embrace the priests in front of the television cameras? After all this, they whine about the burning of a few houses, the destruction of a church, and a few people wounded or murdered when a church is opened or rebuilt?! We, Muslim Egyptians have a philosophy according to which we burn the Copts' homes and churches and then apologize to their clerics. Be grateful to Allah that we do not annihilate you!"

The writer further added: "Interest in image, disregard of essence: All that interests the Egyptian regime is its image abroad; the facts on the ground are a secondary issue. To this end, the regime recruits businessmen to take out advertisements in leading American and European newspapers on various occasions, to say that all is well. It launches delegations at the expense of the Egyptian foreign ministry and with funds from the Coptic taxpayer to say that everything is just fine and we have come to establish a cultural dialogue!! They deny the known facts and disseminate words of deceit. Unfortunately for them, since September 11 these methods are of limited effect. The renovation and rebuilding tax: For every attempt to build or rebuild a church,

Copts must pay in lives and property, even though they have building permits. In July 2000, Coptic citizen Fakhri Ayad paid with his life for his attempt to build a church in the village of Sol in the Al-Fayyoum district. The same thing happened in August 2000, at the Qasr Rashwan Church in al-Fayyoum. The church was attacked, and then seven Coptic homes were attacked. Four people were wounded. Thus, while a church is being renovated, some Coptic homes are burned in exchange, or people pay with their lives."

Do attacks on Copts have a certain pattern? The writer further claims that: "Recurring rituals: Special rituals have begun to emerge in all attacks on Copts. One of these is incitement against the *infidel Copts* from the mosques' loudspeakers…Likewise, the security apparatuses are soft on the aggressors, and collaborate with them. Furthermore, telephone lines are cut so that no calls for help are possible. An additional ritual is blaming the Christians for provoking the Muslims – as if it were they who started the attacks. By God, how can a church bell calling people to prayer every week constitute provocation of Muslims? Is the mere existence of the Copt also a provocation? Saudi Arabia provided financial backing for religious radicalism in Egypt. Unfortunately, three decades later… Egypt has become the largest exporter of extremist sheikhs… The Saudi funds helped paint Egyptian life in the colors of religious extremism. In conclusion, I will say openly that the state is mistaken, and everyone in Egypt is mistaken, if they think that encouraging the majority to persecute the minority will lead to the submission of the Copts. This behavior will lead to collective suicide and the destruction of Egypt", the writer concluded.

Where does the hatred come from?

But were does all that hatred towards the Copts come from? What went wrong in Egypt, a country that prided itself on the assumption of peaceful co-existence between its co-religionists who fought together against foreign invaders and celebrated each other's holidays? Where the incitement of hatred does has come from in the last decades?

Many Egyptian intellectuals have pointed fingers towards fundamentalist preachers in the last three decades who have been branding Christians and Jews as *non-Believers*. The wide-brush branding has been allowed and even encouraged by successive regimes after 1952, starting with Nasser and ending with Mubarak. Adding to that, official alliances drawn between the Mubarak regime and Saudi Arabia, and accepting and allowing the propagation of the Saudi Wahabi doctrine, encouraged fundamentalist groups along with Egypt's al-Azhar mosque to OK the gospel of hatred. Generous endowments of money changed hands between the Saudi government, some of the al-Azhar Sheiks, and fundamentalists bent on demonizing Christians and Jews, and a whole market was established that many people were beneficiaries.

The Mubarak era witnessed the emergence of preachers given access on national TV, radio, and press, publicly denouncing Jews and Christians. The Mubarak regime helped create several mega star Sheiks from al-Azhar or academia, who competed for public recognition which meant a stardom status within the Arab and Muslim worlds. The stardom status meant official invitations by wealthy Arab Gulf countries, royalties from books, TV and radio shows, and syndicated newspaper columns. The whole phenomenon turned into an elaborate lucrative industry that turned religion into hatred for others.

The intolerant sermons recieved the blessings of many Arab regimes who found the intertwined nationalist and fundamentalist tides useful in venting the public's anger towards an outside enemy, rather than against their failing governments.

Explaining this phenomenon, in a July 9, 2006 article on elaph.com, Egyptian Coptic intellectual Magdi Khalil discussed the attitude of Dr. Muhammad Salim al-Awa, a prominent figure in political Islam in the Arab world, towards Egypt's Copts. In his article, Khalil refers to al-Awa's recent book, *Religion and Homeland - Chapters in Muslim Attitudes towards Non-Muslims*, that was published in March 2006. (4)

Dr. Muhammad Salim al-Awa is secretary-general of the International Association of Muslim Scholars, which is headed by the Islamist sheikh Dr. Yousef al-Qaradhawi. Al-Awa is a member of the *Arab Group for Muslim-Christian Dialogue* and belongs to many Islamic institutions, and is a founder of Egypt's Islamic *al-Wasat* party. Al-Awa frequently appears on Egyptian television and on *al-Jazeera*, and his articles are published by many Arab papers. He is also a regular columnist for the Egyptian opposition weekly *al-Usbu*.

In his article, Magdi Khalil attempted to expose the real views of al-Awa, who usually presents himself as a moderate Muslim, and to show that these views are essentially no different from extremist Islamist views. Under the title *The first thing that draws attention*, Khalil wrote, "is the title of al-Awa's book: *Chapters in Muslim Attitudes towards Non-Muslims* inflammatory? According to al-Awa, the status of the Copts is connected to Islam: They are non-Muslims. Throughout the book, al-Awa sets out the status of the Copts in all areas of life as if they are adjuncts to the Islamic system and religion - and that they must adapt to Islam's laws, customs, rules, and culture. Al-Awa devotes his book to *the unpretentious... who, when they hear the words of revelation of the Prophet Muhammad, their eyes fill with tears because of the truth that they know... and they say: Our Lord, we believe in Islam.* "

Khalil also stated that, "al-Awa aims his books at *Copts who believe in Islam* - knowing that no Christian in the world believes in the Prophet of Islam and his mission, just as no Muslim in the world believes in Jesus' divinity, crucifixion, and resurrection, and that He was sacrificed for the sake of all mankind. Every religion has its own beliefs, so there is no point in arguing about these beliefs or in pressuring one side to recognize the beliefs of the other..." Khalil explains.

Khalil's main argument in his article is that al-Awa views Copts as citizens "not in accordance with the rules of a modern state, but in accordance with the rules of citizenship that apply to non-Muslims in a Muslim state... and he declares this openly in the preface to his book: 'We defend the Copts out of our Islamic belief'... He does not recognize modern social concepts, and according to him, 'the treatment of people in the Islamic state is based on their faith - whether they are Muslims or non-Muslims'."

In his rebuttal of al-Awa, Khalil wrote: "although al-Awa stresses, at all his meetings and in all his writings, that the *ahl al-dhimma* [individuals with protected status] belong to a history that no longer exist, he preaches that there is now a new protection apparatus that eliminates citizenship. According to this apparatus, all rights and obligations stem not from citizenship, but from religion: 'Islam gives the Copts the protection of Allah, and does not set them under the protection of the government, the police, or the local authorities. Whoever attacks a Copt attacks the overall protection provided by Islam. Islam obliges the Muslims to protect the Copts in Egypt even before the law does. In the first chapter of his study, al-Awa explicitly states that the Koran is the fundamental and primary source for all Islamic laws, values, and virtues and that 'the Koran is what determines the nature of the relations between Muslims and non-Muslims of all other religions. Thus, in a society that is largely Muslim, Christian clerics are forbidden from discussing matters of religion, religious law, and Islamic sharia, and from accepting what they like and objecting to what does not suit their inclination".

Khalil further explains that: "al-Awa condemns Coptic Pope Shenouda's opposition to the imposition of sharia on the Copts, and the discussion of its details, saying: 'With regard to specific issues raised by Pope Shenouda regarding sharia and its implementation, his dealing with these issues means admitting that he is entitled to discuss the subject of the Islamic sharia and its laws. We do not agree that Pope Shenouda, or any other non-Muslim, may do this. According to Al-Awa, the Copts are infidels. In his book, al-Awa states that the Koran determines that those of *ahl al-kitab* are infidels."

However, Khalil sarcastically explained that, "although we are infidels, a Muslim man can marry a Christian woman whom he likes, because a Muslim man is entitled to marry a Christian or Jewish woman who believes in her religion without getting into the details of her faith. But a Muslim woman is absolutely prohibited from marrying a Christian or a Jewish man. First, this is because he rejects her religion, and second, because of the principle of guardianship. The Muslim man must be the guardian in the relationship, and because the man is the guardian of the woman, a non-Muslim man must not have guardianship over a Muslim woman. Similarly, the Muslim man must be uppermost in bed..."

In this context, Khalil added that, even regarding neighborly relations, al-Awa determines that "it is preferable to have a Muslim for a neighbor than a non-Muslim. Similarly, if one of a child's parents is a Muslim, the child is also considered Muslim, since a non-Muslim does not have legal authority over a Muslim. Al-Awa refuses to give the Copts a fair part in the media so that their partners in the homeland will recognize their religion. He sees this [i.e. Copts in the media] as missionary activity - which is prohibited in an Islamic country: 'The state must not give in to the demands that are sometimes heard to permit Christian religious preaching in the government media. This is because Egypt is a Muslim country according to its constitution, and the Islamic sharia is the primary source for legislation. The Copts are entitled to preach only in their churches, amongst their co-religionists, and in their own neighborhoods'."

Khalil says that, while al-Awa prtends to discuss the rules regulating relations between Muslims and others, his book is full of lies, invention, mistakes, and provocation of hatred." According to al-Awa, adds Khalil "the Copts control 60% of the Egyptian economy... This is not a problem if an individual has economic power as a result of his own efforts... but if this [superior] economic situation is the result of external help, is linked with external forces, or stems from help that is contingent upon conditions that must be met - herein lies danger."

In four places in his book, al-Awa reiterates that the Copts constitute only 6% of Egypt's population; this figure is in line with that given by all the Islamic streams. However, Egyptian government figures state that Copts constitute 10% of the population, while according to the Copts themselves; they are 15% or more.

According to al-Awa, the Copts have privileges that, by right, Muslims should enjoy: "If the state is fanatical, it is fanatical in the Copts' favor. There is no oversight of the churches, and the Egyptian security forces protect them - even though no one knows what is going on inside them. In contrast, the security forces come to every prayer service in the mosques to oversee what is going on - and this is in addition to the 10 conditions for the construction of mosques set by the Ministry of Religious Endowments."

In addition, al-Awa justifies the acts of the young and violent Muslims who damaged Coptic property during the incidents in Alexandria, and even called upon Muslims to visit them in prison: "The best sacrifice to Allah is to visit them in prison on holidays, and for everybody to ease their situation as best they can. Even if they committed an offense, it was done out of fanaticism for the religion, and in order to defend their religion," al-Awa said (5)

In concluding his article, Khalil completely rejects the *moderate Islam* presented by al-Awa: "We do not agree to rights originating in the religious texts. The only acceptable source of rights is citizenship as defined by modern international law, and rights as set out by the international treaties. A man receives his identity with his birth, and this identity gives him the right of citizenship. In contrast, religion is a personal matter, and a man can adopt it or change it as he wishes, at any time. He is not committed to a specific religion at birth, except in backwards countries..." Khalil concluded.

PART III:

THE BEGINNING OF THE END

13. THE MUBARAK DYNASTY: THE UNHOLY TRIO

President Mubarak is the 4th President of Egypt. He is in office since 14 October 1981. He is presiding over the most populous country in the Middle East and the second-most populous on the African continent, with nearly 79 million people. Born on May 4, 1928 at Kafr-el Meselha, al-Monufia province, Mubarak, was appointed Vice-President of Egypt after moving up the ranks of the Air Force. He automatically ascended to the Presidency, succeeding Sadat, following the latter's assassination.

Upon completion of high school, he joined the Egyptian Military Academy, where he received a Bachelor's Degree in Military

Sciences in 1949. In 1950, he joined the Air Force Academy and earned a Bachelor's Degree in Aviation Sciences. He received part of his pilot's training at the Soviet pilot training school in Frunze in Soviet Kyrgyzstan. He then moved up the chain of command, holding the positions of pilot, instructor, squadron leader, and base commander. In 1964, he was appointed head of the Egyptian Military Delegation to the USSR.

Between the years of 1967 to 1972, during the War of Attrition between Egypt and Israel, Mubarak was appointed Director of the Air Force Academy and Chief of Staff of the Egyptian Air Force. In 1972, he became Commander of the Air Force and Deputy Minister of War.

In October 1973, following the October War, also known as Yom Kippur War, Mubarak was promoted to the rank of Air Chief Marshal. In April 1975, he was appointed Vice-President of Egypt and, in 1978, he was selected as Vice-Chairman of the National Democratic Party (NDP).

Following the assassination of Sadat in 1981, Mubarak became president and Chairman of the NDP. Mubarak has escaped no fewer than six assassination attempts.

Under the 1971 Constitution of Egypt, Mubarak has exercised strong control over the country. He has been re-elected by a laughable 99.999 % majority votes in referenda for successive terms on four occasions: in 1987, 1993, 1999 and 2005. The results of the referenda are of questionable validity.

Due to increased domestic and international pressure for democratic reform in Egypt, on February 26, 2005 Mubarak asked the largely rubber stamp parliament to amend the constitution to allow multi-candidate presidential elections by September 2005.

Previously, Mubarak secured his position by having himself nominated by parliament, then confirmed without opposition in a referendum. The September 2005 ballot was therefore a multiple candidate election rather than a referendum, but the electoral institutions, and security apparatus remained under the control of the President. The official state media, including the three government newspapers and state television also express views identical to the official line taken by Mubarak.

Mubarak started to lose support in Egypt in the mid-1990s. According to the list of countries lagging in development, the Human Development Index, Egypt ranks 119 out of 177 countries and rates 0.659 on the index.

On July 28, Mubarak announced his candidacy, as he had been widely expected to do. According to civil organizations that observed the elections, the election involved mass rigging. Reports have shown that Mubarak's party used government vehicles to take public employees to vote for him. Votes were bought for Mubarak in poor suburbs and rural areas. It was also reported that thousands of illegal votes were allowed for Mubarak from citizens who were not registered to vote.

On September 8, Ayman Nour, a dissident and candidate for al-Ghad party, contested the election results and demanded a repeat of the election. On September 9, the Egyptian Electional Committee, consisting of several independent judges denied the demands of Nour. Nour was later given a five year jail sentence.

On the day of Nour's guilty verdict and sentencing, the White House Press Secretary released the following statement denouncing the government's action: "The United States is deeply troubled by the conviction today of Egyptian politician Ayman Nour by an Egyptian court. The conviction of Mr. Nour, the runner-up in Egypt's 2005 presidential elections, calls into question Egypt's commitment to democracy, freedom, and the rule of law. The United States calls upon the Egyptian government to act under the laws of Egypt in the spirit of its professed desire for increased political openness and dialogue within Egyptian society, and out of humanitarian concern, to release Nour from detention."

Mubarak and Corruption

A dramatic drop in support for Mubarak occurred with news that his son Alaa was favored in government tenders and privatization.

Fear of the Mubarak family dictatorship has increased among Egyptians. Around the year 2000, Mubarak's second son Gamal started rising in the National Democratic Party. Due to Gamal's increasing visibility and influence, rumors about his being groomed for the presidency became common. Many believe that his succession would mean a hereditary pseudo-monarchy.

In the 1991 Gulf War, Egypt was a member of the allied coalition and Egyptian foot soldiers were some of the first to land in Kuwait to evict Iraqi forces. Egypt, like many other countries was promised economic aid or debt forgiveness. Some reports alleged that sums as large as $500,000 per soldier were paid to the Mubarak regime by Gulf countries in order for Egyptian military to participate in that war effort.

About how the Mubarak regime benefited from the first Gulf War, the *Economist* cites: "The program worked like a charm: a textbook case, according to the IMF. In fact, luck was on Hosni Mubarak's side. When America was hunting for a military alliance to force Iraq out of Kuwait, Egypt's president joined without hesitation. His reward, after the 1991 Gulf War, was that America, the Gulf States and Europe forgave around $20 billion-worth of Egypt's foreign debt, and re-scheduled nearly as much that amount." (3)

Being that Egyptians were some of the first to land in Kuwait, Egyptian forces are believed to having suffered more casualties than reported. A blackout is usually forced on such news. According to Reporters without Borders; Egyptian media ranks 133 out of 168 in freedom of the press.

Mubarak and his dynasty have reaped so many titles only worthy of a Pharaoh. Mubarak claims these titles among others: Chairman of the G-15, Chairman of the Arab Summit, Chairman of the Organization of African Unity, President of the National Democratic Party, Commander-in-Chief of the Armed Forces and Military Ruler.

SUZANNE: LET'EM EAT BEANS!

Suzanne Mubarak, (birth name: Suzanne Saleh Thabet) born February 28, 1941, is married to Mubarak and holds the title of the first lady of Egypt. The daughter of an Egyptian doctor and a Welsh nurse, Suzanne was born in the al-Menya Governorate.

She studied at St. Claire School in Heliopolis during high school and moved on to study at the American University in Cairo. She received a Bachelor's degree in Political Science in 1977.

Suzanne Mubarak and Jihan Sadat (former first lady) have several similarities; both benefited from several years of priming as wife of incumbent Vice Presidents and both of them have British mothers. It is said that Jihan was the one who discovered Suzanne and her husband and introduced them to the late president Sadat from her close social circle. Suzanne had Jihan as an intimate mentor. Jihan Sadat was the first to invent the role of First Lady in Egypt. Before her, Nasser's wife, Tahiya kept a low profile and hardly appeared in public.

Both Jihan and Suzanne have claimed every title possible in social life and headed almost every social association, club, or a charity organization. Allegations of their corruption have been circulating for many years. No other Egyptian female public figure would dare to head a renowned social association or a charity without the personal permission or concession of the First Lady, Suzanne, and Jihan before her. The late well-known Egyptian singer, Um Kulthum, was said that she had to abandon her ownership of the charity organization, *al-Wafaa wal Amal* that she founded to Jihan Sadat.

According to the official public records, Mrs. Mubarak holds a long list of titles and sits on the boards of countless associations and organizations that make it impossible for her to find time for all of that! For example, she serves as a patron of the children's television series, *Alam Simsim,* Egypt's version of Sesame Street. Mrs. Mubarak is the honorary president of Rotary Clubs of Egypt, and her brother General Munir Thabet is the Rotary International district 2450 governor. Her son Gamal Mubarak is also an honorary member of Rotary Clubs and Founder and Chairperson of the Association for the Development Services in the Community of Heliopolis.

Mrs. Mubarakis Founder and Chairperson of the Egyptian Society For Childhood and Development, Initiator and Founder of Egyptian Children's Literature Centre for Documentation Research and Information, Founder of the National History Museum for Children, President of the Advisory Board to the National Council for Childhood and Motherhood, President of the Egyptian National Women Committee, President of the First and Second National Conference on Women, Initiator of the Unified Law on Children, President of the Egyptian Section of the International Board of Books for Young People, President of the Egyptian Red Crescent Society and the National Campaign for Safe Blood Transfusion, Vice President of COMEST, and President of the National Council for Women, to mention a few.

Suzanne Mubarak heads hundreds of charities. As the president's wife, Suzanne Mubarak receives countless donations that reach on average $5 billions a year. Allegations of funneling portions of these charity donations to personal bank accounts have been circulating.

The increasing role of Mrs. Mubarak, her over-exposure, and extravagant life style has made some Egyptians liken her to Queen Marie-Antoinette, wife of King Louis XVI and best remembered for her legendary excesses. Marie-Antoinette was executed by guillotine at the height of the French Revolution in 1793. She is famous for her saying: *Let'em eat cake* after being told that the French people could not find bread to eat. The Egyptian people do not have the luxury of having French pastries; in their case, it would be mere bread and beans.

Gamal: The Heir to the Throne of Egypt?

Gamal-Edinn Muhammad Hosni Mubarak, a.k.a. Gamal Mubarak, born 1963, is the younger of the two sons of President Mubarak. Gamal Mubarak graduated from the American University in Cairo with a Business Degree. He started working for *Bank of America* in Cairo and London becoming an investment executive.

Gamal Mubarak branched out with a few colleagues to set up *Medinvest Associates Ltd.*, which manages private equity funds, and provides corporate finance consultancy.

Gamal is on the board of almost every charity organization including his pet project *Future Generation*, an NGO that provides job training to young people. (1)

Gamal married Khadiga el-Gammal, daughter of Egyptian construction tycoon Mahmoud el-Gammal in May 2007. Gamal was nominated by his father in 2002 to become the General Secretary of the Policy Committee: the third most powerful position in the party and the kitchen for most of the government's actions. (2) After the July 2004 cabinet shuffle and the appointment of Ahmed Nazif as the new Prime Minister of Egypt, the cabinet was named *Gamal's cabinet*, as most of the new ministers were chosen from the policy committee of the NDP.

ALLEGED CORRUPTION OF THE PRESIDENT'S SONS

Alaa Mubarak, or Alaeldin Muhammad Hosni Mubarak, is one of two sons of Mubarak. He keeps a much lower profile than his younger brother Gamal, and is not involved in politics. A lot of claims relate Alaa to weapon trading, many corruptions and bribe scandals in Egypt, which led him out of public life and news.

THE BIG PEOPLE AND FAT CATS

According to Kefaya's published report on corruption in Egypt, both Alaa and Gamal Mubarak allegedly participate in *bullying* their way into major privately-owned companies with free shares that reach 50% of the capital. Gamal and Alaa are partners in the biggest trade and industrial companies in Egypt, practically paying nothing. They have to be paid their share that reaches 50% in case of loss-or- gain. Of the companies in which Gamal and Alaa have shares are: *Marlborough* and *Chilis* chain restaurants owned by Mansour family, *Hyndai* and *Scoda* auto dealerships with Shafeek Gaboor, *El-Ezz Steel Industries* with Ahmad Ezz, *Dream* with Ahmad Bahgat, *ART TV* with Saudi billionaire Saleh Kamel, *First Co.*, with Kamel and Kholi, *Movenpic* hotel chain with Hussein Salem, *El-Togari* with al-Malawani family, *Vodafone* with Nuseir, *Siramica* with Abul-Einien, *El-Nasagoon Oriental Waevers* with Ahmed Khamis, *Mobinil* with Sawerus, *Al-Ahram Beverages* with el-Zaiyat, *City Stars Hotels and Luxury Housing* with Saudi billionaires El-Sharbatly and Shokobkshi, *Americana* with al-

Kharafi and al-Alfi, *McDonalds* with the Mansour and Sawerus families, and others.

Kefaya alleges that Mubarak's sons opened the banks for their partners to obtain loans with no guarantees or a prosecution investigation like other debtors, though their due debts exceeded 50 billion pounds.

The two brothers own free shares in other business with the sons of Esmat Sadat (brother of former President Sadat). Rumors and allegations have been circulating for quite some time about shady dealings of the president' sons in monuments smuggling with Zahi Hawas (Director of Egypt's Archeological Authority), Farouk Hosni (Minister of Culture), Kamal el-Shazli (former Speaker of Egyptian Parliament), and arms dealing with Kholi, Salem and others, according to Kefaya.

Kefaya also alleges that Gamal Mubarak eyed major companies in Egypt and managed to obtain partnership in those companies, and started *harassing* other businessmen. Those who rejected having partnership with him were ultimately forced to oblige through fabricated charges, imprisoning them; like Hussam Abul-Fettouh, Magdy Yakoub, and others.

Kefaya further alleges that Gamal uses several intimidation techniques like fabricating charges of tax evasion against those who do not oblige to his wills. Kefaya also alleges that even murder attempts against those business owners who would not budge to coercion were orchestrated, like Mahmoud el-Sherbeni, the former owner of *El-Dekhila Iron and Steel Co*, who rejected to have a partnership with Gamal with a rate of 50%. It is alleged that el-Sherbeni was killed in a truck accident and the whole company was taken over for free and given to Ahmad Ezz, a Palestinian refugee to run it. A special nationality act was passed for Ezz - to grant him Egyptian citizenship, while tens of thousands of Palestinians born in Egypt to Egyptian mothers were denied Egyptian citizenship and treated like aliens in their country of birth for decades.

An example of influence peddling was provided in the recent issue of *Rose El-Youssef* involving the sale of B.M.W. franchise in Egypt. The owners, the Abul-Futuh family and their partners, were asking for about $40 million to sell their shares. The buyers offered much less. When the sellers refused to go below the offer, charges of tax evasion and owning pornographic material were brought against Abul-Futuh. Minister of Industry and Technology, Ali al-Saidi intervened and the sellers accepted the offer. The buyers of the company were Qatari individuals (with 80 percent interest), a German company (with 15 percent), and Gamal Mubarak (with the remaining 5 percent), who has also assumed the role of chief executive of the new company, renamed as *Bavaria Egypt.* (3)

Kefaya alleges that before deciding to suddenly reduce the value of the Egyptian pound at 53%, Gamal Mubarak had advised his partners to convert their liquid money to dollars. As a result, Gamal got a commission that reached half of the profits his partners gained. This greatly increased commodity prices consequently harming Egyptian economy and consumers.

The role of the Mubarak's family in business circles in Egypt draws similarities to the role previously played by the Suharto family in Indonesia. General Suharto, former Indonesian dictator, caused the political purges and deaths of millions of Indonesians. Suharto's almost unquestioned authority over Indonesian affairs slipped dramatically when the Asian financial crisis lowered Indonesians' standard of living and fractured his support among the nation's military, political and civil society institutions. After internal unrest and diplomatic isolation began to drain his support in the mid-to-late 1990s, Suharto was forced to resign from the presidency in May 1998 following mass demonstrations.

In May 1999, *Time Asia* estimated the Suharto's family fortune at $15 billion in cash, shares, corporate assets, real estate, jewelry and fine art. Of this, $9 billion is reported to have been deposited in an Austrian bank. The family is said to control about 36,000 square kilometers of real estate in Indonesia, including nearly 40 percent of the land in East Timor. Over $73 billion is said to have passed through the family's hands during Suharto's 32-year rule. According to Transparency International, Suharto embezzled more money than any other world leader in history.

Inheritance of Power

Huge billboards carrying pictures of the Egyptian president's son, Gamal Mubarak, have appeared in central Cairo in recent years. The billboards show the young Mubarak flanked by the country's Olympic champions, who were given a hero's welcome after returning from Athens with five medals. The billboards appear to be part of the strategy to promote Gamal Mubarak as a symbol of success and hope in a country struggling to cope with mounting economic and social problems. (4)

On February 26, 2005, Mubarak ordered the constitution changed to allow multi-candidate presidential elections before September 2005 by asking parliament to amend Article 76 of the Egyptian constitution. This change in the constitution is seen by some analysts as a ploy to seamlessly allow Gamal Mubarak to inherit the top position in Egypt.

The view is that Gamal Mubarak would be one of the candidates in coming presidential elections and would enjoy full backing from the ruling party and the government-controlled media. The other serious candidates would be disqualified by the NDP-controlled People's Assembly leaving the less popular candidates.

Ayman Nour Attacks Mubarak's Intention to Nominate His Son Gamal as Next President

In an article in May 2007 published on al-Ghad Party website, Ayman Nour criticized the steps taken by Gamal Mubarak, in the ruling NDP to ensure his succession to his father's rule. Following the article's publication, the Egyptian authorities prohibited Nour from writing and publishing. (5)

The Succession Scenario According to Nour

In September 2002, Gamal assumed the role of head of the Central Committee and head of the Higher Council for Political Affairs - whereas advancement in the party from rank and file to leadership normally takes several times longer than it took Gamal.

"Gamal brought his friends on board in the party and cabinet, using them, as a prelude to the beginning of the succession scenario... which began in April 2006. The scenario reveals that Gamal's succession plan begins with neutralizing the opposition", Nour said. (6)

Article 76 of the Egyptian constitution sets the condition that anyone who puts forward his candidacy for the presidency from any political party must have been a member of that party's Central Committee for at least one year. "This condition led Gamal Mubarak to expel from the party's Central Committee - in one fell swoop - eight people who do not belong to his group and whom he does not trust… and to replace them with a group of his own people." Nour explained.

"For instance, Kamal el-Shazili, former Parliamentary Affairs minister and assistant secretary-general was the first to be expelled from the party's Central Committee. The previous secretary-general, Yusuf Wali, was expelled from his post as secretary-general and expelled from membership in the Central Committee. The list of expellees features: former Culture and Education minister Hussein Kamel Bahaa al-Din, former Communication Minister Mamduh el-Beltagi. Only Secretary-General and Shura Council head Safwat el-Sharif remained. Why should we accept Gamal as president? Because he is the son of President Mubarak, who has ruled Egypt for a quarter of a century?! This is the first reason that will lead us to oppose Gamal! We have dozens of reasons to cry out against Mubarak's continuing in this path. However, even if there might be other reasons for electing Gamal they would be reasons like his age, his generation, and his education, which is of course different than his father's education. Yet Egypt has 80 million citizens, of whom over 40% are Gamal's age or younger, and thousands of talented and experienced people who did not just appear suddenly, and do not enjoy the protection of reputation, the authorities, and influential people."

In his article, Ayman Nour lists seven steps that he expects will be taken in the near future in order to ensure that the presidency is transferred to Gamal Mubarak:

"1. Throughout April, 2006, we witnessed the end of the last of the *Kamalists* in the NDP. The *Kamalists* are not just Kamal el-Shadhili's people, but rather everyone who is not defined as a *Gamalist*! The fact that el-Shadhili left his posts... and the party's Central Committee brings Gamal closer to achieving his goal, which requires the purging of those whom Gamal's people term the *lackeys of Kamal Al-Shadhili* - whereas their real goal is to establish a strong group in the various electoral districts that will take the lead in calling for the transfer of power to Gamal.

2. September 2006: the end of the era of Safwat el-Sharif. El-Sharif will not get out unscathed, as is the case with all those who get out of the hell of the ruling party… The attack on el-Sharif began as early as February 2006, when he came under a heavy attack led by the *Roz al-Yousef* newspaper, which is Gamal's mouthpiece. The newspaper declared war on el-Sharif… and made it clear that the media attack against him was preparation for his expected dismissal, so that Gamal Mubarak would inherit el-Sharif's position... This, in follow-up to el-Shadhili's dismissal, is meant to produce a one-man rule, and Gamal or one of his men

will be appointed to the party's Central Committee and the High Press Council.

3. Zakaria Azmi, MP and director of President Mubarak's office, will, replace current parliamentary head Ahmad Fathi Srur. Zakaria Azmi enjoyed great popularity because of his reputation in parliament as a dedicated fighter against corruption... This led Azmi to develop aspirations that might threaten Gamal. The threat can be defused only if Azmi is appointed parliamentary head. In this way, he will not be entitled to present his candidacy in the presidential elections... This will ensure that Gamal will be able to take advantage of Azmi's connections with the Republican Guard and with the presidency in order to strengthen the guarantees that Gamal will take power...

4. Referendum on the amendment to the constitution. Certain amendments will be introduced into the current constitution. The most important of them will be the repeal of the percentage, stipulated in Article 76, for a party to be able to participate in the presidential elections. According to the new amendment it will be enough for a party to have representation in the parliament, and that it has no internal struggles and differences of opinion. The first condition - that of representation in parliament - denies all parties; the right to have a candidate for the presidency, except for al-Wafd, al-Tagammu, and al-Ghad parties. The second condition denies al-Ghad and al-Wafd the right to have a candidate in the presidential elections. Thus, there will remain only one rival party allowed to participate in the presidential elections against the ruling party- that is, al-Tagammu which is weak...

5. An announcement by President Mubarak in that he will

step down from the presidency. This announcement will include an immediate choice of three MPs to be his partners in being in charge of affairs of state. The prevailing prediction is that the first of them will be Field Marshal Tantawi, and the other two will be chosen from three MPs, among whom are current Prime Minister Ahmed Nazif, the Copt Nadia Makram Ubayd, and Minister Umar Suleyman head of the Egyptian intelligence apparatus. This pronouncement is a preparation for the following stage in the process of the power transfer, which will come when the number of candidates for the presidency shrinks to include only members of the party's Central Committee. This will completely rule out the candidacies of Field Marshal Tantawi and Umar Suleyman, who are the most well known. This means that the entire military establishment is out of the equation. A solution to this is the appointment of a vice- president or two with a military background.

6. The election of Gamal Mubarak as the National Democratic Party's candidate for the presidency. Several days after President Mubarak announces his intention to resign, the NDP's Central Committee will convene to release a statement praising the move by president and leader Mubarak. In addition, the party secretariat will pronounce Gamal Mubarak, who will then be the party's secretary-general and head of the Committee for Political Affairs, to be its candidate for the presidency.

7. Ridiculous presidential elections. Presidential elections will be held with what is practically a sole candidate - the

NDP candidate - who will run against the al-Tagammu party's candidate... This will take place after candidates from al-Wafd and al-Ghad are prevented from running. "

Seven Obstacles to the Implementation of the Succession Plan

In his article, Ayman Nour outlined seven obstacles to Gamal Mubarak's inheriting his father's rule:

"1. The army: Gamal Mubarak's succession would mean that this would be the first time in Egypt's history, after three military republics, that there is president without a military background....

2. The parties: The disqualification of the large political parties, like al-Wafd and al-Ghad, the Nasserists, and al-Tagammu, poses a serious problem for the succession scenario. This problem can be sidestepped only by minimalizing the amendment of Article 76.

3. The Muslim Brotherhood: The Muslim Brotherhood's exit from the equation of the presidential elections, because they do not have a party. Independent Brotherhood activists will have difficulty collecting the required number of signatures from the Shura Council, and will also have difficulty collecting enough signatures from the local councils, and this could backfire against Gamal.

4. The Americans: The uncertainty surrounding the American position on Gamal's succession means that the scenario continues to be threatened by mines that could go off at any moment. This eventuality will be dealt with by feeding the outside world's perception that there is no other civilian

replacement for Mubarak aside from his son... or a new Hamas, as embodied by the Muslim Brotherhood. The authorities have made efforts to emphasize this throughout the last few months, by weakening liberal forces and sowing dissension among the largest and most prominent parties.

5. Public opinion: The public is not interested in handing over power to Gamal Mubarak. Gamal Mubarak can exercise his right to be the NDP candidate if it were, by chance, to elect him, as he is the party's secretary-general - but not as the president's son.

6. The pillars of the regime: The pillars of the regime in the reign of Mubarak Sr. will never agree to hand over all their powers to his son, who will of course bring in others to replace them...

7. Death: There are people who erroneously believe that the president's death would completely eliminate the idea of succession but this is not the case..."

Implementing the Plan

In conclusion, Nour lists a number of means that will help Gamal Mubarak implement the succession plan:

"- Money and businessmen: Gamal can use large sums of money to buy up everything, under the guise of donations from businessmen – who are actually Gamal's clique.

- America: Gamal Mubarak is interested in first presenting himself to America and knocking on its doors even before he knocks on the doors of his own homeland, and [those of] its citizens!

- The *Strike Force*: The *Strike Force* is a particular group of Gamal's associates, headed by Ahmad Ezz secretary of the al-

Manufia district of the NDP. This group includes businessmen, journalists, party hacks, and media people close to Gamal who can strike out forcefully at his rivals. This group will have centralized control over the district councils in the two weeks preceding the president's announcement of his resignation... and it will finance the local authorities so as to ensure that nothing whatsoever will go wrong with the implementation of Gamal's orders."

Then Nour adds more details to the assumed succession plan saying that other individuals will be included in that scheme:

"- A group of legal and constitutional authorities, which will write the special provisions in the constitutional amendment and will ensure... that they are implemented, in order to repel any real competition to Gamal. At their head stands Justice and Parliamentary Committees Minister Mufid Shihab, parliamentary head Fathi Srur, and al-Dakruri, Mubarak's attorney".

According to Nour, political assassination of Mubarak opponents will take place: "Among the illegitimate means to which that the group in charge of the succession scenario has resorted have been legal pressures and the ability to use any and all means to politically assassinate Gamal Mubarak's rivals, in hope of limiting their ability and freedom in the presidential race. The best proof of this is the Al-Ghad party"

Mubarak: Fin du Régime?

Forecasts of a *fin de siècle* fill the air, alternately breathless and reasoned. They point to the swiftly cascading natural and man-made disasters, terrorist bombings, political movement, recurring sectarian conflict, and economic malaise, all mingling in a portentous brew.

Murmurs abound that Mubarak's regime is in its final throes, that delaying local elections, swiftly renewing emergency law, and repeatedly cracking down on protest are signs of the beginning of the end. Predictably, current events are compared to the combustible final years of Sadat's tenure, when the tussle between an increasingly irrational president and an angry, organized society ended so abruptly, violently, and dramatically. (7)

There is an equally compelling view that such predictions are possible. Predicting anything as complex as regime change must bear a lot of assumptions. And even if change occurs, there's no way to determine precisely how it would happen and why. This precisely adds to the anxiety of the Egyptian people about the nearing end of the Mubarak's regime and what lies ahead. The Mubarak's regime has been dogged by crises and intensifying street protest since at least 2000, yet it totters on.

In spring 2003, as the American invasion of Iraq was imminent, the Mubarak government speedily secured the renewal of emergency law. Massive anti-war protests then shook the country, and biting anti-Mubarak slogans electrified the streets. Security forces viciously beat protestors and threatened the women among them with rape. Two opposition MPs were savagely attacked by hired thugs. Mubarak's huge visage over the NDP headquarters was torn off, and Gamal Mubarak led a hastily organized government anti-war protest in Cairo stadium, flanked by popular comedian Adel Imam and powerbroker Kamal el-Shazli.

Back then, opposition journalists Abdel-Halim Qandeel and

Abdellah al-Sennawi took turns criticizing the regime. They forecasted the impending doom of a spent regime devoid of any ounce of legitimacy, hastening its own ignominious demise.

When several presidential emissaries failed to tame the intrepid duo, Qandeel was plucked from a Cairo street in the dead of night and stuffed into a speeding car by four massive individuals in suits. They savagely beat him, demanded that he stop writing about the *Big People*, stripped him of all his clothes, and left him to fight for his life on a deserted highway on a frigid November night.

The incident led to an increase of Qandeel's popularity and fortified his resolve, earning him the respect of even those who opposed him before. As for Sennawi, he continues to tirelessly deliver weekly auguries of regime downfall. (8)

The enforcers of repression continue to follow orders and to smash dissidents. From governors to security directors at the top, to police chiefs, officers, and simple recruits at the bottom seem to be doing their share to run the coercion machine. Cairo Security Chief, Ismail al-Shaer, is considered more ruthless than his predecessor Nabil al-Ezabi. For his efforts in policing the numerous contentious episodes of 2005, Ezabi has been rewarded with a high level-position of governorship, claims Egyptian blogger Bahyia.

In order for the Mubarak regime to end, state security personnel must splinter and join the reform movement, even if secretly *à la Ukraine*. At the very least, a critical mass must shirk their duties and withhold their cooperation. The formidable capacities of the Egyptian state effectively contained that brief upsurge, and draconian new control mechanisms were instated to prevent any second acts. If the sinews of state control remain intact and loyal to the regime, it is difficult to imagine how the latter can be dislodged, adds Bahyia.

Some speculators seem to think that the military would step in at the right moment to prevent a handover of power to Gamal, or to save Egypt from other nightmarish prospects. If this logic holds, the military would have stepped in a long time ago. The most intriguing thesis is that the military no longer acts as a coherent, corporate entity. Since the expelling of the late Defense Minister abu-Ghazala, Mubarak has personally presided over the comprehensive depoliticization of the Egyptian military. Some speculators claim that the military can still act as the final arbiter and guardian of the republic, *Turkish-style*.

THE END DRAWS NEAR?

If there are very good reasons to doubt forecasts of imminent regime demise, there are equally good reasons not to uncritically accept assertions of regime stability. After all, no serious observer can dismiss the significant, perhaps seismic shifts over the past few years in how the regime interacts with its domestic and international interlocutors. A regime that was able to effectively quell a militant Islamist insurgency from 1992-1997 now seems unable to manage peaceful voters, peaceful judges, and peaceful street demonstrations, says Bahyia.

In September 2005, Mubarak was being pilloried and humiliated in public and private as he was putting himself up for *election*. The signs of decay are numerous and multiplying, two in particular stand out as indices of a potential cataclysmic upheaval. First is the extent to which Mubarak, and especially his family, has become the target of popular hatred, biting ridicule, or mild distaste. There is no disaster, policy decision, or daily inconvenience that is not popularly believed to originate at the doorstep of the presidential residence.

Whether these decisions are actually the work of the ruling family, it does not matter that much. What matters is the near-unanimous public perception, the incessant jokes, the rich rumors about the Mubarak family. *If Suzanne Mubarak is continuously presented to Egyptians as the First Lady of Virtue and Beneficence and her son is foisted upon the Egyptians through his father's media as the Visionary Young Modernizer with a Heart of Gold, it is no wonder that Egyptians believe the president's family runs the country,* wrote one blogger. Add other tangible facts such as the yawning succession vacuum, the marriage between business and power, and the never-missed opportunities to polish Gamal Mubarak.

If the Mubarak ruling family is increasingly viewed by the Egyptians as the problem, an unlikely sector is increasingly viewed as the solution. The second sign of regime decay is the Mubarak regime's unexpectedly drawn-out and now extremely public confrontation with judges who have received a highly unusual and intensifying public support as the only trustworthy, inspiring, and capable force in public life.

The outpouring of public support for judges took everyone by surprise, most of all the judges themselves. It surpassed the solidarity demonstrations of May 13, 14 August, and September 2, 2005, and it surpassed the turnout on March 17, 2006. As one judge reflected, "One amazing thing is that on our way from the Judges Club to the courthouse and back, the state security failed completely to prevent us from entering, and we were hugged by the masses. They knew us by name. They were singing for us. One of them kissed my hand. It was a huge day in the history of our country. I know that our days will be dearly remembered as part of our great history for years to come. Thank God I was part of it, no matter how small. And thank God I was on the right side."

The Mubarak regime wanted to dismiss the two *rebel judges*. Public support poured on the judges. MP Hamdeen Sabahy in front of throngs of judges, journalists, and lawyers said that if the two judges were dismissed, Egypt would have gained two candidates for president. The electrifying suggestion was met with enthusiastic applause.

The Judges' Club resolution in April 2, 2008 produced a powerfully worded document. Its last has a momentous ring to it: "Egypt's judges, while they represent one branch of state power, realize that the nation is the source of all powers, and that achieving security and stability has its source in the prosperity of the nation and the consent to its rulers, and that the rulers' esteem is in responding to the desires of citizens, not in haughtiness and intransigence. There is no way of achieving security and stability in the country merely through the repression of force and the control of power. Rather, the people's hope in justice must be preserved, as well as preserving their dignity and honor, and reviving their hope in reform, and establishing a true democratic life through fair elections and real transfer of power, and lifting all exceptional laws including ending the state of emergency, and unleashing freedom of expression, and the freedom to form parties, unions, and associations, without any restrictions, so that Egypt can regain its place among nations."

There are signs of impending implosion. Comparing current events to the twilight of Sadat's rule or Mubarak to Romania's Ceaușescu is good for dramatic effect. Egyptian politics have indeed arrived at a crossroads savoring the extraordinary uncertainties.

The United States could find itself faced with a dilemma should Gamal Mubarak ascend to the presidency. Committed to bringing democracy to the Middle East, the U.S. might find the creation of a new dynasty inconsistent with its intensions. It is not surprising that Gamal Mubarak may be seeking to garner American support and legitimacy by his frequent visits to the U.S. and by presenting himself both in private meetings and in public as a reliable friend to America and an element of both reform and stability. (9)

Gamal Mubarak spoke against America's war in Iraq. He led the largest orchestrated demonstration in Cairo in the 24-year history of the ruling party. (10) In an earlier statement, Gamal said that Egypt would not participate in any military action against Iraq. He called for solidarity with the Palestinian people, for the creation of a Palestinian state, and against the *Judaization of Jerusalem*. (11)

In spite of his anti-American stands, Gamal Mubarak has been received in Washington in a manner accorded to high government officials. On his first visit, he met with former President Bush. A *Washington Post* column describing his visit was titled: *Gorbachev on the Nile?* (12) In his visit in June 2005 to the U.S., Gamal had meetings with Vice President Cheney, Secretary of State Powell, Secretary of Defense Rumsfeld, and National Security Advisor Condoleezza Rice. Yet, the Obama administration stand towards the Mubarak regime and the possible succession of his son is yet to be determined.

"It is always the same splendid setting, and the same sad story. A senior American diplomat enters one of the grand presidential palaces in Heliopolis, the neighborhood of Cairo from which President Hosni Mubarak rules over Egypt. Walking through halls of marble and gilt, passing layers of security guards, he arrives at a formal drawing room where he is received with great courtesy by the Egyptian president. The two men talk amiably about U.S.-Egyptian relations, regional matters and the state of the peace process between Israel and the Palestinians. Then the American gently raises the issue of human rights and suggests that Egypt's government might ease up on political dissent, allow more press freedoms and stop jailing intellectuals. Mubarak tenses up and snaps... *If I were to do what you ask, the fundamentalists will take over Egypt. Is that what you want?* The diplomat demurs and the conversation moves back to the latest twist in the peace process".

- Newsweek columnist and editor, Fareed Zakaria

CONCLUSION

WHAT LIES AHEAD?

THE HAVES AND THE HAVE NOTS

"Egypt appears to be in the throes of an economic crisis. The macro-economic situation has deteriorated after the September 11. Egypt is undergoing a severe liquidity crisis caused by the loss of hard currency from few sources: The tourism was a key source of foreign exchange and the main engine of growth. Expected losses in the sector range from $2-3 billion. Airline and shipping: besides the decline of passengers, primarily tourists, the industry was hit by 50% increase in insurance premiums. Revenues from Suez Canal have also declined. Remittances from Egyptians working abroad have declined from $3.8 billion in 2000 to $3 billion in 2001, and further declines are projected", says economist Nimrod Raphaeli. (1)

Ahmad al-Wakil, the deputy chairman of the Egyptian chamber of commerce said in an economic symposium held in Alexandria on January 12, 2002, that the foreign exchange reserves have declined from $30 billion to $15 billion, between 1997-2001. He attributed the decline to the government's conflicting economic policies regarding the Egyptian pound which was devalued several times, and it is traded at a new low of 6.35 pounds to the dollar. (2)

Nabil Hashad, Director of the Arabic Center for Financial and Banking Studies, says that the rise of the dollar against the Egyptian pound is neither surprising nor unexpected. The reason is the inability of the commercial banks to fully meet the demand for foreign currency. As a result, those who have a legitimate need for dollars, e.g., importers and travelers, and those who wish to convert their savings into dollars for greater security, resort to the black market which is not bound by the ceiling on the exchange rate established periodically by the Central Bank of Egypt.

Foreign exchange reserves have declined to $14 billion which leave little flexibility for the central bank to intervene in the market. Recently, the Governor of Central Bank of Egypt, Mahmood Abu al-Eyoon, declared that there was no intention to devalue the Egyptian. (3) A few days later, it was revealed that the Abu al-Eyoon had asked Kuwait to deposit $150 million in the Egyptian central bank to bolster its foreign currency position. (4) It was also revealed that Egypt was seeking Kuwaiti buyers for some of its state-owned banks. (5)

The Senior Advisor in the Central Bank of Egypt, Muhammad al-Barbari indicated that additional devaluation of the pound in the near future was *generally conceivable*. He warned, however, against "some international organizations [conspiracy theory] that seek to ignite fire under the foreign exchange policy to force the Egyptian monetary authorities to decide on a large devaluation of the pound." (6) The Egyptian Minister of Finance, Midhat Hasanayn, informed members of the Egyptian parliament that the budget deficit for 2002, estimated at E£ 20 billion, and further stated that *none of them entails the issuing of new banknotes.*

The Egyptian government is to reschedule the internal debt to reduce interest and service charges from 23 to 20 billion Egyptian pounds ($5-4.4 billion) a year. [Egypt domestic debt is estimated at more than $160 billion equivalent, in addition to external debt of $26-27 billion.] *Al-Ahram* reported that prices have gone up to 60 percent.

According to former Egyptian Prime Minster Atef Ebid, the population of Egypt will reach 123 million in 2019. There are 800,000 new job seekers every year, and the number will rise together with the growth of population. He estimated the cost of creating one job in industry at E£ 100,000 ($20,000) and in agriculture 50,000 Egyptian pounds ($10,000). The total cost of job creation for 800,000 would be E£ 36 billion, or more than $7 billion.

Since there is no unemployment insurance in Egypt there was a tacit warning regarding social and political unrest if the problem of unemployment persists. (7) According to the Director General of the International Center for Agricultural Research in Dry Areas, Adel al-Biltagui, Egypt's increase in food consumption remains a big concern. (8)

IT'S THE ECONOMY... STUPID!

The International Labor Office (ILO) annual World Employment Report 2004-2005 found out that, the number of unemployed people in Egypt climbed to new heights in 2005. Young people aged 15 to 24 comprise almost half of the Egypt's unemployed and are more than three times as likely as adults to be out of work. The ILO called this figure *troublesome.* (9)

The Middle East and North Africa, MENA (10) stands out as the region with the highest rate of unemployment in the world. With an unemployment rate of 23.2 %, the Middle East is ahead of sub-Saharan Africa, the poorest region in the world, which has the second highest rate of unemployment, 19.7 %. The Arab League Economic Unity Council estimates unemployment in the Middle East (members of the Arab League only) at 20 percent. The number of unemployed people in MENA is particularly puzzling because the oil producing countries employ 7-8 million expatriate workers transmitting perhaps as much as $22 billion a year back to their home countries.

The employment to population ratio is a measure of the percentage of working-age population who are employed. Although MENA has registered a notable increase in this measurement, it has remained the lowest in the world, with 45.4 in 1993, and increasing only slightly to 46.4 a decade later. The latter figure contrasts with a ratio of 62.5 worldwide and a ratio of 57.0 in densely populated South Asia. (11)

The little increase in MENA reflects changes in women's employment. The ratio for women, which increased from 20.4 in

1993 to 23.5 in 2003, indicates fewer social and cultural restrictions on women's employment, although the ratio of 23.5 remains the lowest in the world. The figure for males, by contrast, has remained relatively constant (69.6 in 1993 and 68.6 in 2003).

The Have's and the Have-not's

The ILO developed the concept of *working poverty* to cover those who work, but do not earn enough to lift themselves and their families above the $1- or $2-a-day poverty line. The report does indicate, however, that the incidence of working poverty is much higher in the non-oil producing countries than in the oil-producing countries.

Nevertheless, to halve $1 a day working poverty by 2015, the GDP must grow at 4-5 percent a year. To halve the $2 a day working poverty by 2015, the GDP must grow by 8-10 percent a year. (12) This rate of growth will not be easy to achieve without profound structural reforms in both the economy and polity of most countries involved, in particular the non-oil producing countries.

MENA is the only region where productivity has not moved in tandem with GDP. The explanation for this unusual pattern is that the GDP growth was fueled primarily by the increases in oil revenues accompanied, according to the ILO report, by *stagnant productivity.* It is a perfect example, the ILO says, of why in the long term, "decent employment creation and productivity growth have to go hand in hand with GDP growth. Only then will economic growth lead to poverty reduction." (13) The report does make a distinction in the level of productivity between oil- and non-oil producing countries. (14)

The most significant feature is the structure of the population. MENA is characterized by its growing young population, with 37 percent below the age of 15 years in 2000, and 58 percent below the age of 25 years. (15) The working-age population is increasing by three percent a year. The biggest challenge facing policy-makers in the region is the high rate of youth unemployment, estimated at 25.6 percent in 2003, which is the highest in the world.

The unemployment rate of the MENA region has been hovering around the 23 per cent mark for the last decade. According to the ILO report this steady rate of unemployment reflects an average of 500,000 of additional unemployed per year. The increase in employment is not enough to absorb all those who enter the labor market annually.

In May 2005, Taleb Rifai, regional director of ILO, asserted that the high rate of unemployment in the Arab world, which at one estimate reached 20 percent, will ultimately result in a state of underemployment, as most people will be forced to take up jobs for low compensation packages that do not suit their qualifications, and will further result in increased poverty. (16)

Former Egyptian Minister Gowaili, and secretary-general of the Arab League Economic Unity Council, referred to an unemployment rate of 20 percent in the Arab countries. According to Gowaili, this percentage is translated into 22 million unemployed, of whom 60 percent are youth. This figure, he added, is likely to increase by three percent annually. He attributes the main cause of unemployment to the failure in most Arab countries to link educational orientation to the labor market requirements. (17)

It would be necessary to shift workers from a low productive employment, and from what the director-general of ILO called the ***urban alleyways*** of many cities in the region, into a more knowledge-based production of high value-added commodities. The shift to a more knowledge-based employment is also dictated by the limited prospects of increasing the scope of agriculture in most Arab countries. The Economic Unity Council of the Arab League points out that the Arab countries occupy 10 percent of the world territory, five percent of the world population, but only 0.5 percent of its water resources. (18)

In fact, the Arab countries already import food commodities worth $15 billion, and rising. (19) To reach a higher level of knowledge base, the Arab countries in the region would need to invest more in Research and Development (R&D). The Economic Unity Council of the Arab League estimates that the Arab countries spent 0.24 percent of their GNP on R&D. (20) Figures available elsewhere for individual countries show the big gap between the highest rated country in the world, Norway, with 1.6 percent of GNP in R&D, and Egypt, among the lowest, with 0.2 percent of GNP spent on R&D. In between are Israel with 0.9 percent; Qatar, 0.7 percent; and Jordan and Tunisia, 0.3 percent. (21)

The Arab countries in MENA would also need to attract foreign direct investment (FDI). These countries remain the least attractive to FDI, acquiring only between one to three percent of total FDI, because of inhospitable environment for foreign-dominated businesses, various restrictions on foreign exchange, inefficient labor market, absence of an adequate commercial code, corruption, oppression, bribes, and stifling bureaucracy.

Moreover, there is a psychological mindset in Arab countries that equates globalization with imperialism: Instead of seeking to bring its benefits to their countries, many Arab governments and even intellectuals treat it with suspicion and mistrust. Hence, the contrast has emerged whereby in 2005, China attracted $62 billion in FDI, against $6 billion in Arab countries.

THE ANGRY GENERATION

With a persistently high level of unemployment, many educated young Arabs are seeking opportunities outside their countries. In doing so, they seek to escape the obligation to accept jobs outside their specialization, inadequate scientific and technological infrastructure, low income opportunities for the highly skilled and political instability or political oppression in the native countries; and they seek to gain opportunities for entrepreneurship with minimal bureaucratic constraints. (22)

Among the lower skilled, migrations may be tied to the serious phenomena of human trafficking and grave physical risks. It is common nowadays to read about boats loaded with illegal workers sinking on the way from North Africa to southern Europe. Moreover, as a result of a high rate of unemployment, "different forms of passive and active violence are on the upswing reducing the spaces for dialogue, conflict resolution and consensus building," warns the report. (23)

In the words of ILO Director General Juan Somavia, "the world is facing a global jobs crisis of mammoth proportions, and a deficit in decent work that isn't going to go away by itself." Clearly, the statement is particularly pertinent to the situation in MENA, and especially to the Arab countries in that region.

Unemployment is a grave source of hopelessness, and hopelessness drives people to extremes. This was clearly demonstrated in the twentieth century in the rise of Nazism and Fascism. Unemployment has the great potential of being a source of political instability and even violence, and it is to no one's advantage to treat this economic dislocation with equanimity. Klaus Schwab, the president of the World Economic Forum, warned that unemployment in the Middle East is a *time bomb* that would require the creation of 100 million new jobs in the next 10 years to defuse it. (24)

The ticking bomb that the Egyptian government is oblivion to is the great number of young, unemployed, unmarried people that constitute a large segment of the population. Since the introduction of Sadat's Infitah policies in the late seventies, Egyptian society has faced an unprecedented crisis in housing. Young people seeking simply to marry and start a family can not find a place to live in. The sign *apartment for rent* has simply vanished from Egyptian society and has become a thing of the past.

In spite of the construction boom in real estate since the oil boom in the seventies due to the earnings of Egyptian expatriates working in Arab Gulf States, apartments are only available through purchase in tens of thousands of dollars that most average citizens cannot afford. Nevertheless, five star luxury complexes are being built for the super-rich and the well-to-do in the Egyptian society who can afford it; the five per centers!

A sense of frustration and hopelessness seem to be haunting Egyptian youth and the older people as well, who are struggling to make ends meet. The result has impacted Egyptian society in terms of the high rate of drug and alcohol use, divorce, domestic violence, road rage, sex crimes, prostitution, human trafficking, and corruption. Egyptian sociologists refer these waves of *uncommon behavior* to political oppression. In spite of the fact that Egypt has a number of opposition parties and one ruling party, yet most officials serving in the government are handpicked by the president from his own party.

Opposition parties are consumed fighting each other and the oppressive tactics of the government. The media is owned and run by Mubarak's government. The result is that there is a real political vacuum in Egypt in spite of all the façade. The average Egyptian citizen feels that his/her voice is not heard. Between a military dictatorship represented by Mubarak's regime and the fundamentalists who operate from under the ground; some Egyptians lean towards those who raise slogans like *Islam is the solution*.

In its report *Reforming Egypt: In Search of a Strategy*, the International Crisis Group, expressed its disappointment with the latest elections in Egypt that failed to bring any real change. "Egypt's first multi-candidate presidential election, a response to U.S. pressure, was a false start for reform". Formal pluralism has never seriously limited the dominance of Mubarak's NDP; extension to the presidential level is a token so long as the opposition is too weak to produce plausible candidates." Instead of permitting an orderly opening up of political space after years of authoritarian rule over a lifeless political environment, it confirmed the NDP's domination and determination to allow no serious opposition within the system. (25)

In a June 16, 2006 op-ed in the Lebanese *Daily Star*, Egyptian human rights activist Saad al-Din Ibrahim criticized Mubarak's ongoing attempt to stifle democracy through the government's continued implementation of its Emergency Law. The article was titled *Cairo Remains Restless… Government Fears another Outpouring of Support for Democracy.* In his article, Ibrahim asserts that Mubarak is now waging internal war against Egypt's judges, the Sinai Bedouins, and the Copt citizens of Egypt. (26)

"The Emergency Law has been in force since the assassination of President Sadat in 1981, and Mubarak claims that he needs another extension to combat terrorism. But, according to a recent human rights report, despite the Emergency Law, 89 people were killed and 236 wounded in terrorist attacks in Egypt during the previous 12 months. In neighboring Israel, which is still in the midst of a struggle with the Palestinians, only 18 were killed and 25 wounded in similar attacks during the same period. Yet Israelis do not live under an Emergency Law. Consider, moreover, that at the height of the Arab-Israeli conflict in 1973, Egypt's armed forces had one million troops. Now, only 350,000 serve in the military, while the internal security police recently hit the one-million mark." Ibrahim adds.

"The third recent war, this one over Christian Coptic citizenship rights, has been brewing for years. As Egypt was Arabized and Islamized, the Copts became a minority in their original homeland. In Mubarak's Egypt, citizens' equality, while stipulated in the

Constitution, is not respected or observed, especially with regard to the construction and protection of Coptic churches. There was even suspicion of an official hand in the attacks, in order to justify extending the Emergency Law."

"Mubarak's domestic wars are fuelled by Egypt's excluded, who are increasingly in rebellion against a regime that has long outlived its legitimate mandate. The battle with the judges may well prove to be Mubarak's Achilles' heel. Justice is a central value for Egyptians, and its absence is at the core of all protests. There could have been no more compelling evidence of this than the unprecedented numbers of people who rallied peacefully in solidarity with the judge," says Ibrahim.

A FINAL NOTE

In his widely read article post 9/11, *How to Save the Arab World, Newsweek* columnist Fareed Zakaria, diagnosed some of the chronic ailment that Egypt and the Arab world have been suffering from. He eloquently describes the relationship between the U.S. and Egypt in the following: "It is always the same splendid setting, and the same sad story. A senior American diplomat enters one of the grand presidential palaces in Heliopolis, the neighborhood of Cairo from which President Hosni Mubarak rules over Egypt. Walking through halls of marble and gilt, passing layers of security guards, he arrives at a formal drawing room where he is received with great courtesy by the Egyptian president. The two men talk amiably about U.S.-Egyptian relations, regional matters and the state of the peace process between Israel and the Palestinians.

Then the American gently raises the issue of human rights and suggests that Egypt's government might ease up on political dissent, allow more press freedoms and stop jailing intellectuals. Mubarak tenses up and snaps; *If I were to do what you ask, the fundamentalists will take over Egypt. Is that what you want?* The diplomat demurs and the conversation moves back to the latest twist in the peace process", says Zakaria. (27)

"The rulers of the Middle East are not democratic politicians with finely tuned senses of what their publics want. They are dictators. After all, if Mubarak were so close to his people, why would he need to arrest, torture and murder hundreds to stay in power? These men fear a public that they barely know. In the Middle East, the democrats are the first to seek refuge in fantasy, denial and delusion. The state-owned media do not need to promote crazed conspiracy theories about the Mossad's secret role in bombing the World Trade Center or the CIA's fabrication of the bin-Laden videotape... The *free* television station, *al-Jazeera*, does it voluntarily, and the public laps it up. America's allies in the Middle East are autocratic, corrupt and heavy-handed... The monarchs and dictators are quick to remind us always that for all their faults, they are better than the alternative." Zakaria explains. (28)

"They [terrorist acts] are a response to living under wretched, repressive regimes with few economic opportunities and no political voice. And they blame America for supporting these regimes. The reasons were the same; people disliked the regimes that ruled them and they saw America as the benefactor of those regimes. Perhaps the Middle East will move on a similar path;

violence, religious extremism and terrorism will be drained out of the political culture and, instead, its people can join the rest of the world in worrying about the threat from *McDonald's* and *Baywatch*." Zakaria said. (29)

In January 1979, the Pehlevi regime fell to the angry masses in Tehran. Shah Riza Pehlevi had to flee Iran with his family after ignoring cries of corruption and repression. In his reign, the gap between the poor and rich increased tremendously. Instead of implementing reform, he set his secret police, the SAVAK on his people.

Political opponents to the Shah led the angry masses to the arms of the Mullahs (the Ayatollahs). America soon found itself called the *Great Satan*. Before that, U.S. ambassador to Iran William Sullivan reported to Washington that *the Shah was in full control of the country and the opposition was no match for the well-fortified regime*.

A few weeks before the Shah went into exile, Sullivan still reported that it was *unimaginable that the regime would fall*. A similar scenario repeated itself with Ferdinand Marcos in the Philippines and Suharto in Indonesia. (30)

Anti-Western nationalism seems to be the predecessor of anti-Western Islamism, as was the case in Iran. As author Rouleau points out, the rise of political Islam is not surprising recently in Egypt, "given the social ills engendered by extended unemployment, especially among the qualified young; aggravated social polarization in which ill gained wealth, insolently displayed, stood out against the growing misery of the rural and urban population; and generalized corruption spreading right up to the highest levels of society and state" (31)

The Arab world has no institutions evolved by common consent for common purposes, under guarantee of law, and consequently there is nothing that can be agreed upon as the general good, says author David Pryce-Jones.

"No mechanism exists so that people may participate in whatever is being decided and performed in their name, a handful of absolute despots oppress and attack with every available stratagem all those within reach. The rich and strong mercilessly bully and exploit their inferiors... from the proudest power holder down to the humblest family, all are engaged in pillaging whatever they can for themselves, or at best for their tribe and religion, rather than considering the public interest and constructing a common wealth. Politics in practice is reduced to the black arts of applied force, and in any emergency, of terror, in all relationships, domestic, private and public, internal and external, violence is therefore not only customary but also systematic and utterly impervious to piecemeal reform or amelioration", Pryce-Jones explains. (32)

Pryce-Jones believes that Arabs are excluded from contractual relationships of this kind amongst themselves, and this in turn prejudices and handicaps their dealings with outsiders. Foreign affairs, commerce, even acquaintanceships are not conducted as between equals, but as probes conducive to victory or defeat, as though in an extension of feuding. So there is nothing that can yet be properly called the *Arab Society*, but only the inherited collectivity. (33)

Commenting on sectarian conflicts sweeping the Arab world,

and in Egypt, Pryce-Jones contends that "whether Sunni or Shia, ambitious men in all centuries abused the *Holy Law* they were supposed to be upholding, in sectarian wars and challenges to advance themselves. Religious beliefs cannot be conjured in protection…since the days of Selim III and Muhammad Ali, apparent modernization of this type has only been a façade, for in reality the absolute despot thereby acquires ever more efficient means of control and power holding on the one hand, and on the other of circumventing challengers and the mob. (34) Conspiracy, manipulation, and deception of opinion at home and abroad are still the requisite skills of pretenders to power, with exile and death as the fate of losers. With the lack of real opposition and oversight, there can be no conception of loyal opposition. To compromise is only to search for advantage by other means. Entire countries are as erratic as their rulers. But thanks to imported arms and communications, the price paid by the masses for these practices is each time costlier and bloodier, ripping away and canceling material progress that has been made... Military despotism, pure and simple, is the looming prospect or the rule of whoever is brutal enough to put a final stop to all ambitions, except for his own". Pryce-Jones further explains. (35)

May Kasem, political scientist at the American University in Cairo says that: "Political stability, peace, and development in the Middle East, like anywhere else, can best be achieved through reform rather than revolution ... Foreign support may protect and prolong the lifespan of an authoritarian regime, but it cannot maintain such a regime indefinitely. It is in the interest of all parties concerned, including authoritarian regimes and their international patrons, to opt for political reform rather than risk the imposed and unpredictable transformation of dissent. The U.S. ...should recognize that it should pressure friends into genuine reforms". (36)

"If we could choose one place to press hardest to reform, it should be Egypt.... In Egypt, we must ask President Mubarak to insist that the state-owned press drop its anti-American and anti-Semitic rants, end the glorification of suicide bombers and begin opening itself up to other voices in the country. Egypt is the intellectual soul of the Arab world. If it were to progress economically and politically, it would demonstrate more powerfully than any essay or speech that Islam is compatible with modernity and that Arabs can thrive in today's world", Zakaria warns. (37)

[illegible] groups [illegible] for political activity [illegible] that risk the [illegible] and [illegible] include [illegible] [illegible] should recognize that it should [illegible] forms."[illegible]

[illegible] could choose on [illegible] In Egypt we must [illegible] [illegible] the [illegible] owned [illegible] and [illegible] raise [illegible] [illegible] opening itself [illegible] voices [illegible] [illegible] work [illegible] political [illegible] more power [illegible] [illegible] Islam is compatible with modernity and that [illegible] can thrive in today's world," [illegible]

EPILOGUE

Today, Egypt is at dangerous crossroads. As president Mubarak enters his twenty-eighth year in power, Egypt's future is more uncertain than ever. Egyptian society is stagnant. Egyptians are pessimistic about the future of their country, unsure whether Egypt can weather peacefully an economic downturn and a troubled transition upon the incapacitation or death of its octogenarian leader. Indeed, at a time when the Obama administration is once again basing U.S. policy toward the Middle East on the assumption of the Egyptian government's durability, many Egyptians argue that Mubarak's regime is on the verge of collapse. (1)

A FAILING ECONOMY?

The Egyptian economy is in trouble. Egyptian unemployment hovers above 20-30 percent, almost twice the official Egyptian government estimate;(2) under-employment is epidemic.

Transparency International ranks Egypt in the bottom tier of Arab states for high levels of corruption. (3) The inflation rate continues to increase, (4) increasing pressure on the unemployed, poor and elderly. Food riots erupted in April 2008 as the annual rise in food prices topped 25 percent. (5) The gap between rich and poor is also growing. Perhaps three million Egyptians live in swank upper class villas in neighborhoods such as Ar-Rihab, Ash-Shruq, Sharm el-Sheikh, Marina, and Mukatam Heights while 44 percent of the country subsists on less than $2 per day. (6) Less than 10 percent of Egyptians own nearly 80 percent of the country's wealth. (7)

Mubarak and his party cannot shirk accountability as they have been in sole control of the economy for more than a quarter century. (8)

When Mubarak took power, the Egyptian economy was in a much better shape. Government public revenues were 8.3 billion Egyptian pounds (E£) in 1981. From 1986 to 1987, expenditures nearly doubled, from E£ 13.2 billion to E£ 22.2 billion. Budget deficits increased from E£ 4.9 billion in 1985-86 to E£ 8.7 billion in 1986-87. American economist Ibrahim M. Oweiss, an expert on the Egyptian economy, concluded that since the mid-1980s "the Egyptian economy has essentially stagnated." (8)

The growth rate of gross domestic product per capita has been approximately zero. (9) Mubarak has been unable to make the reforms necessary to address unemployment, inflation, housing, food crises, and Egyptians' other urgent needs.

Over the past decade, the Egyptian pound has lost almost half its value against the U.S. dollar. A recent report by Goldman Sachs suggests a greater devaluation may be on the horizon. "Without a further depreciation in the Egyptian pound, the Central Bank of Egypt would risk further big losses in the foreign exchange reserves and only delay the inevitable adjustment that is needed," the report found. (10) Should devaluation occur, cost-of-living would increase because of Egypt's dependence on imports for many goods and services? This in turn would drive below the poverty line the many million Egyptians either struggling to keep their families afloat.

Cairo should also be concerned over its foreign exchange reserve, which has fluctuated significantly. Between 1997 and 2001, it declined by half from $30 billion to $15 billion before recovering to $31 billion in 2008. (11) However, after the bread riots in April 2008, (12) the Egyptian government may not have the political will power to devalue its currency and so risks depleting its foreign exchange reserves, which, in turn, could constrain its ability to stabilize its own currency.

There is very little indication that the Egyptian government can turn the situation around. Annual growth is not enough to absorb new entrants into the labor market. (13) According to former Egyptian trade minister Ahmad Guwaili, the Egyptian education system does not prepare students adequately for the needs of the labor market. (14) Those who do succeed often leave the country to pursue more lucrative opportunities abroad.

According to the ILO, to halve the $1-a-day working poverty by 2015, GDP must grow at 4-5 percent a year, and to halve the $2-a-day working poverty by 2015, GDP must grow by 8-10 percent a year. Egypt's growth rate is closer to 3 percent for this year and will contract to 2.4 percent in 2010. (15) Nor has Egypt's productivity moved in tandem with GDP, an unusual pattern, which the International Labor Organization attributes to increase in oil revenue accompanied by stagnant productivity. (16)

Egypt has an overwhelmingly young population: 37 percent of the population is below fifteen-years-old, and 58 percent is younger than twenty-five, (17) and the working-age population is increasing by 3 percent per year. A quarter of young men and a whopping 59 percent of young women are unemployed. (18)

The Mubarak regime has done little to increase employment, especially among youth. Ninety percent of the unemployed are between fifteen and twenty-four. (19) One writer in the Egyptian weekly al-Ahram expressed his frustration with the current labor situation: "The drowning of 184 young Egyptian men off Italian coasts didn't make waves in this country. It happened off Libya. It happened off Greece. And it keeps happening. Over and over, our young men brave death to get away ... there is a reason. There is a well of poverty and despair so deep that impels them to act so insanely" (20).

The problem transcends the economic and can have profound social ramifications since many Egyptian men can neither afford to rent nor purchase an apartment, let alone marry, (21) a dangerous phenomenon in a country that, in the recent past, has had to battle an insurgency of young men recruited by violent Islamist groups. Amidst this affordable housing crisis, developers have constructed luxury complexes for the affluent, a jarring irritant to the dispossessed.

Even if the young and unemployed do not turn to Islamism, either for lack of conviction or because of the effectiveness of the state security apparatus, their despair and frustration can manifest itself in a high rate of drug and alcohol use, divorce, domestic violence, sex crimes, and prostitution, all of which compound Egyptian social and economic problems. (22)

THE OPPOSITION?

Mubarak handpicks high level officials from within the NDP to serve in all high level posts, and most mid-level posts. After decades of democratic drought, opposition parties are ineffective and have little organization capacity. When they do organize, they face a lack of resources and oppressive government tactics. As Mubarak's government owns the media even the best organized opposition receives little public exposure.

When the ruling party does abuse its power or flout the constitution, Egyptians have little recourse. According to the U.S. State Department's 2008 Country Report, the Egyptian executive branch interferes with the judiciary. Senior officials can operate with impunity regardless of the law. Nowhere is this more apparent than with regard to judicial oversight of elections. By law, the judiciary in Egypt is required to supervise elections, but many judges report government pressure to legitimize fraud. Since the 2005 presidential elections, judges have led protests and sit-ins protesting against the government's decision to prosecute two senior colleagues: Hisham Bastawisi and Mahmud Mekki, members of the Court of Cassation, Egypt's highest appellate court, who sought an inquiry into fraud in the presidential elections and have asked for electoral and political reform. (23) Egyptian-American sociologist Saad Eddin Ibrahim, an increasingly strident critic of the regime, suggested that the battle with the judges may well prove to be Mubarak's Achilles' heel. (24)

Ibrahim criticized Mubarak's use of the Emergency Law, first imposed in 1981 which gave the security forces broad powers to search without warrants and detain indefinitely without charge. While Mubarak promised an end to the Emergency regime, the NDP-dominated parliament simply wrote its provisions into reformed anti-terror legislation. (25)

As the Bush administration abandoned its freedom agenda after the Hamas victory in Palestinian elections and with Secretary of State Hilary Clinton acknowledging openly in the context of China that the Obama administration would prioritize human rights concerns even less, the Mubarak regime appears to feel itself having carte blanche to curtail civil liberties.

The State Department's 2008 human rights report found that Cairo's respect for freedoms of press, association, and religion all declined over the year. The Egyptian government continues to restrict other civil liberties, particularly freedom of speech, access to the Internet, and freedom of assembly, as well as crackdown on the activities of nongovernmental organizations. (26)

As a result, there is a dangerous political void in Egypt. The average Egyptian citizen feels that his voice is not heard. (27) While Egypt nominally allows multiparty elections, polling brings no change. The International Crisis Group called the 2005 elections "a false start for reform" and noted "presidential elections are merely symbolic so long as the opposition is too weak to produce plausible candidates." (28)

U.S. abandonment of demands to reform and the Rice and Clinton State Department's embrace of Mubarak and his son Gamal has both encouraged the Egyptian leadership to accelerate its crackdown on dissent and raised the Egyptian public's cynicism toward the United States.

Such cynicism was compounded by the long-delayed 2008 municipal elections considered sham by both Egyptian and outside observers. Not only independent candidates close to the outlawed Muslim Brotherhood, but also politicians from registered opposition parties reported difficulties registering in an apparent government campaign to prevent opposition candidates from participating in the elections. More than 3,000 candidates, whose registration the government prevented, sued the government. Although the courts ruled in favor of the candidates in 2,664 cases, the government refused to implement the rulings.

On March 30, 2009, Human Rights Watch issued a statement questioning the legitimacy of the elections in which, subsequently, NDP candidates won 92 percent of the seats. There were only nine women in the People's Assembly (out of 454 total seats) and twenty-one in the upper-level Shura Council (out of 264). Only three women received portfolios in the thirty-two member cabinet. Christians are as under-represented as women. Copts may represent 8 to 12 percent of the population, but received less than 2 percent of the seats in the People's Assembly and Shura Council. (29) The Carnegie Endowment for International Peace described the elections as "a step backwards for Egyptian politics," and the Egyptian Organization for Human Rights (EOHR) did not monitor the elections because of citizens' reluctance to participate and the elections' lack of competitiveness. (30)

A Challenge to Obama?

The danger for the West is that dissatisfaction which already manifests itself in general anti-Western and very specific anti-American sentiment could be the precursor to even more virulent anti-Western Islamism. It is possible to find parallels in Egypt to pre-revolutionary Iran. Years before the Islamic Revolution in Iran, young Iranians were applauding Jalal al-e Ahmad's Westoxification, a strident condemnation of Western influence on society. (31)

As former French diplomat Eric Rouleau noted more than a decade ago, the rise of political Islam should not surprise in Egypt, given the social ills engendered by extended unemployment, especially among the qualified young; aggravated social polarization in which ill gained wealth, insolently displayed, stood out against the growing misery of the rural and urban population; and generalized corruption spreading right up to the highest levels of society and state.(32) Unlike Nasser and Sadat, Mubarak has never appointed a vice-president and polishing his son Gamal to be his successor, a mockery of Egyptian republicanism and democracy. (33) Egyptians are enraged that they appear ready to follow the path of Syria, in which a president, who came to power in a military coup, installed his own son as successor.

If Gamal takes power, Egyptians fear he would continue his father's policy of enriching the elite, suppressing the poor, all while ignoring effective reform. Mubarak turned Egypt into a police state rivaling Syria's or Tunisia's with a security force infrastructure that numbers nearly two million.(34)

Indeed, many U.S. analysts acknowledge Egypt's instability. "It will rock the world," wrote Michelle Dunne, a Carnegie Endowment for International Peace scholar. "Octogenarian Mubarak, will leave office, either by his own decision or that of providence, probably within the next three years." (35)

Instability in Egypt after Mubarak's incapacitation or death may become an international security concern. There is no clear chain of command or civil society base to facilitate the transfer of power to the next president.

According to Thomas Barnett, a national security analyst and former professor at the U.S. Naval War College, the insecure succession could create a vacuum in which the Muslim Brotherhood could rise: "the Brotherhood is retracing the electoral pathway to power blazed by Hamas in Palestine and Hezbollah in Lebanon: hearts and minds first, blood and guts later".(36)

Meanwhile, there are already signs of discord between Washington and Cairo. Robert Satloff of the Washington Institute for Near East Policy told the U.S. Congress, "The foundation of the bilateral relationship has eroded. Divergences have emerged over a wide range of Egyptian policies." (37)

President Obama will find himself facing a difficult choice when instability strikes the largest Arab country. Every Egyptian leader since Nasser has arisen from the military. Would an ambitious general stage another coup? Perhaps under populist pressure, would a new regime or junta scrap the Camp David accords as some judges demanded during the July 2006 Israel-Hezbollah war? (38)

Or is it possible that the Muslim Brotherhood may gain strength, even paramount control? Populism—Islamist or otherwise—should be a concern given a moribund economy and growing disparity between classes and the amount of military equipment and even nuclear technology which the U.S. government has provided Egypt.

American policymakers could soon face the same tough choice on Egypt that they once suffered with Iran's faltering Shah, says Barnett giving his advice to the Obama adminstration:

"Step in with maximum effort during a succession crisis or let the chips fall where they may. Washington's soft peddling of democracy hasn't moved the highly corrupt government toward any serious political reform, as the Mubaraks prefer Beijing's blueprint over anything we might offer. And, as the regime resorts to stoking anti-Western and anti-Semitic popular sentiment, it gets harder to imagine a path forward for U.S.-Egyptian relations as this global recession advances. All I can say, Mr. President, is that when you decide which major Islamic capital will be the venue for your much-anticipated address to the Muslim world, do yourself a favor and pass on restive Cairo, because you just might trigger more response than your administration can afford right now." (39)

Former and last King of Egypt, Farouk with his wife Queen Nareeman and their baby son Ahmed Fouad before being deposed and exiled to Italy where he was poisoned by one of Nasser's henchmen.

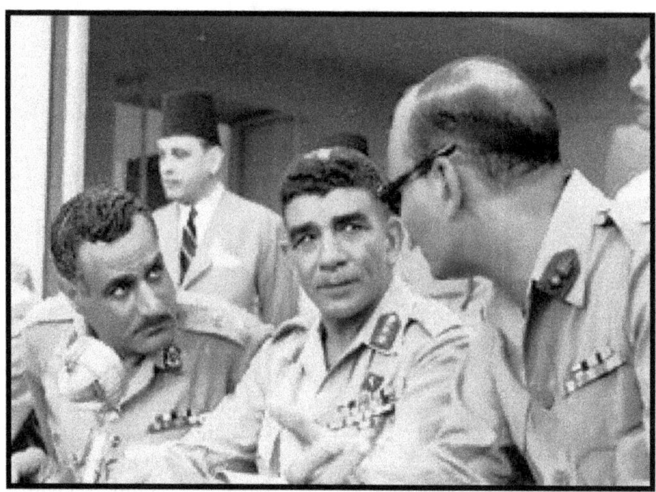

Colonel Nasser, left, General Naguib, middle, and Salah Salem, right, were members of the Free Officers who staged a military coup and deposed King Farouk on July 1952. Naguib, a figure head, was put under house arrest by Nasser.

The Mufti (Grand Sheikh) of Jerusalem, Hajj Amin al-Hussaini saluting Nazi troops. Al-Hussaini allied himself with Hitler and Mussolini and spread Fascist and Nazi ideas and movements in the Arab world. After the fall of the Third Reich, the Mufti was sought as a war criminal. He was given refuge by Nasser in Egypt along with many ex-Nazis.

رحلة بدون رجعة !

تبرعات للأعداء .. وتجميد للأموال .. وتخريب اقتصاد

غادر الخطرون ممن لا جنسية لهم ميناء الاسكندرية .. حملتهم باخرة الى خارج المياه الاقليمية .. الى بلادهم .. او الى اى مكان على الارض يشاءون .. وكانت التأشيرة المختومة على جواز سفر كل واحد منهم تشى بالخط العريض على انهم مسافرون فى « رحلة بدون رجعة » !

The massive exodus of Egyptian Jews was hailed by Nasser's media as a "One Way Trip without Return" claiming that Jews were *"aiding the enemy and ruining the economy"*.

The Ben Ezra synagogue in downtown cairo is one the few temples remaining after the Egyptian Jewish community dwindled from more than 100,000 to less than a hundred.

Nasser (middle) with Nikita Khrushchev during his honeymoon days with the former Soviet Union. Right to Nasser was Marshal Amer, Nasser's Minister of Defense who committed suicide after the Six Days War.

Sadat admiring the mummy of King Ramses II that he emulated himself after. To his right, stood Mubarak, considered also a Pharaoh for his autocratic and authoritarian style of ruling.

Mubarak (left) next to Sadat laughing few minutes before the assassination of Sadat on October1973 while watching the military parade.

The assassination of Sadat on October 1973.

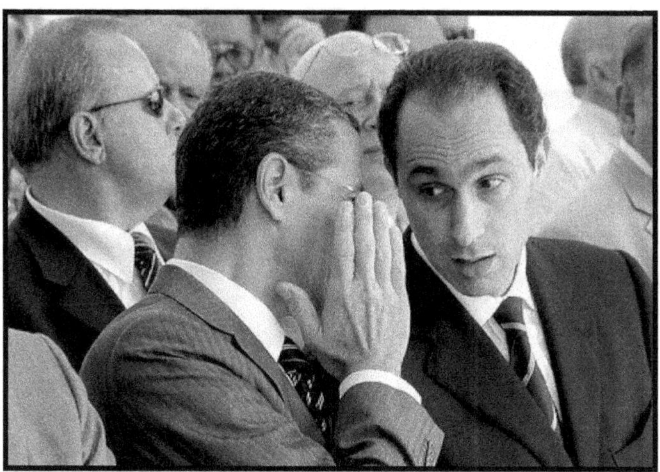

Gamal Sadat, son of late President Sadat, whispering to Gamal Mubarak during the 25th anniversary ceremonies of Sadat's assassination.

Gamal and Alaa Mubarak, President Mubarak's sons, while attending the 25th anniversary of Sadat's assassination.

First Lady Suzanne Mubarak sits on the board of almost every NGO in Egypt.

Cartoonists have predicted that the days of Mubarak's regime are numbered.

Indonesia's late dictator Suharto. His family and small elite monopolized the economy and garnered unimaginable amounts of wealth. His fall was another shock to Western observers.

Former president of the Philippines Ferdinand Marcos and wife Emelda had to flee their country after decades of corrupt rule that only the elite and cronies benefited from.

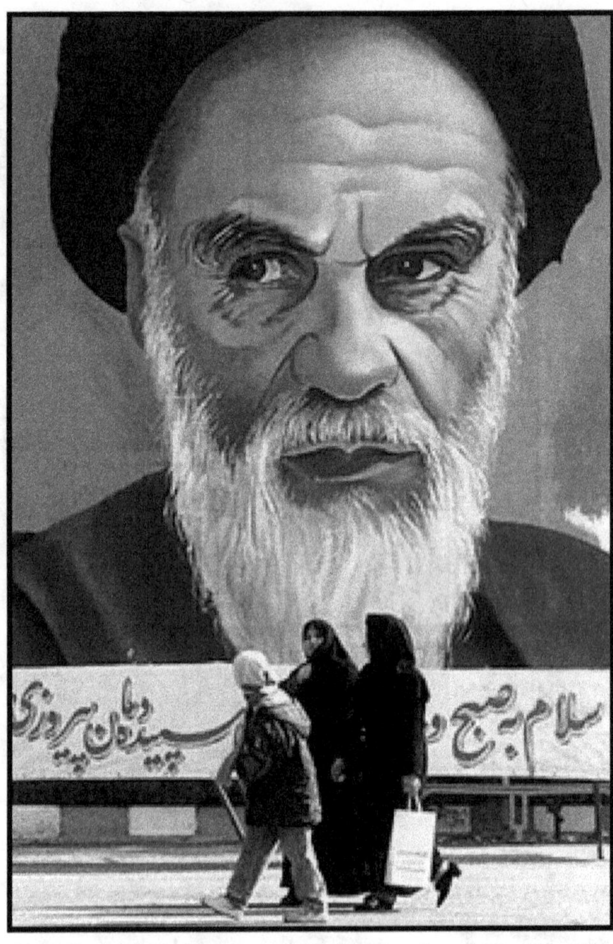

The fall of the Shah of Iran was considered unthinkable. The Shah's lavish life style, corruption of his government, and its brutality dealing with dissidents, led to the takeover by the fanatic Ayatollahs.

Pope Shenouda, Patriarch of the Egyptian Coptic Church, was one of the thousands of political dissidents rounded up and arrested shortly before Sadat's assassination in 1981.

Members of the Egyptian political movement Kifaya demonstrating and exposing the corruption of the Mubarak regime.

Egyptian police forces beating a demonstrator in Cairo. Torture has been routinely practiced and many videos were leaked to the media leading to the arrest and trial of few Egyptian police officers.

Egyptian journalists demonstrate in Cairo protesting the lack of freedom under the Mubarak regime while anti-rioting forces trying to break up the protest.

Egyptian factory workers rioting and stumping on a big picture of Mubarak. A similar scene to what Iraqis did after the fall of Baghdad.

The Central Security Forces are a familiar scene around Egypt anticipating and clamping on any sign of protest using extreme violent means, tear gas and water cannons.

American businesses are usually a favorite target for rioters as seen in the damages done to a KFC and a McDonald's branches in Cairo.

Leaflets have been circulating in Egypt calling for an uprising against the Mubarak regime with images of Egyptian youth throwing stones at police forces, similar to images of children in Gaza.

NOTES

PREFACE

1. *The Country to Watch: Egypt*, By Thomas P. M. Barnett, Esquire, October 2006, Volume 146, Issue 4.

INTRODUCTION

1. *Egypt-United States Relations*, Congressional Research Service, Foreign Affairs, Defense, and Trade Division, Library of Congress, June 15, 2005.
2. Ibid
3. Al-Ahram Weekly (Egypt), October 11- 17, 2001 http://www.ahram.org.eg/weekly/2001/555/letters.htm.
4. Al-Ahram Weekly, November 8-14, 2001.
5. Al-Ahram Weekly (Egypt), October 11-17, 2001 http://www.ahram.org.eg/weekly/2001/555/letters.htm.
6. Al-Ahram Weekly, October 18-24, 2001 http://www.ahram.org.eg/weekly/2001/556/letters.htm.

PART I: THE LEGACY OF THE PHARAOH CONTINUES

1. Chehabi, H. E., and Juan Linz, *Sultanistic Regimes*, eds. Sultanistic Regimes. Baltimore: Johns Hopkins University Press, 1998. p.7.
2. Joyce Tyldesley, Ramses: Egypt's Greatest Pharaoh, Viking/ Penguin Books (2000), p.73
3. Tyldesley, Ramses, p.73
4. Exodus 14.
5. Exodus 1:11
6. Tyldesley, Ramesses, p.82
7. Kitchen, On the Reliability of the Old Testament, William B. Eerdmans Publishing Company (2003), p.662.
8. Mohamed Heikal, *The Autumn of Fury*, Random House, 1983, p.74.
9. Ibid
10. David Pryce-Jones, *The Closed Circuit, An interpretation of the Arabs*, Harper & Row, 2002, p. 249.
11. Amy Chua, *World on Fire*, Doubleday, 2003, p. 224.
12. Maye Kassem, *Egyptian Politics; The dynamics of Authoritarian Rule*, Lynne Eiener Publishers, 2004, p. 29.
13. Ibid, p. 28.
14. Springborg, Robert. *Mubarak's Egypt: Fragmentation of Political Order*. Boulder: Westview, 1989, p. 124.
15. Kassem, p. 29.
16. Ibid, p. 29.
17. Hinnebusch, Raymond A. "Formation of Contemporary Egyptian State from Nasser to Mubarak", In the *Political Economy of Contemporary Egypt*, ed. Ibrahim M. 'Oweiss. Washington, D.C.: Center

for Contemporary Arab Studies, Georgetown University, 1990, p. 86.

2 CHEERLEADERS, STARMAKERS, AND YES-MEN: MUBARAK'S POLITICAL MACHINE

1. Al-Gumhuriya (Egypt), October 14, 2001.
2. Al-Akhbar (Egypt), October 15, 2001.
3. Al-Gumhuriya (Egypt), October 14, 2001.
4. October (Egypt), October 14, 2001.
5. Roz Al-Youssuf (Egypt), October 6, 2001.
6. Al-Akhbar (Egypt), October 15, 2001.
7. Al-Ahram (Egypt), October 13, 2001.
8. Al-Ahram (Egypt), October 15, 2001.
9. Al-Ahram (Egypt), October 26, 2001.
10. Al-Akhbar (Egypt), October 11, 2001.
11. Ibid
12. Roz Al-Youssuf (Egypt), October 26, 2001.
13. Al-Akhbar (Egypt), October 14, 2001.
14. Al-Ahram (Egypt), October 11, 2001.
15. Al-Akhbar (Egypt), October 14, 2001.
16. Al-Akhbar (Egypt), October 14, 2001.
17. Al-Gumhuriya (Egypt), October 15, 2001.
18. Al-Ahram (Egypt), October 18, 2001.
19. Al-Ahram (Egypt), October 13, 2001.
20. Al-Akhbar (Egypt), October 12, 2001.
21. Al-Mussawar (Egypt), October 19, 2001.
22. Akher Sa'a (Egypt), October 24, 2001.

3 THE BENEFICIARIES: WHO REALLY RULES EGYPT?

1. Corruption in Egypt, Colonel Muhammad Al-Ghanam, Former director of legal research, Egyptian Interior Ministry, Pravda, Retrieved from http://english.pravda.ru/opinion/columnists/17-05-2004/5612-egypt-0 Posted on 17.05.2004.
2. Ibid
3. EGYPT: Corruption hampering development, says opposition report, by Ben Hubbard/IRIN. Retrieved on 11/10/2006 http://www.irinnews.org/report.asp?ReportID=54398&SelectRegion=Middle_East&SelectCountry=EGYPT
4. Ibid
5. Ibid
6. Ibid
7. Kefaya, Judicial and Documentary File, *Corruption in Egypt…A dark cloud that does not vanish*. Retrieved on 6/6/2006
8. Ibid
9. Ibid
10. Al-Ahaly, March 3rd, 1995.
11. Rose Al-Yousef, Feb. 2nd, 1987, p. 23.
12. Kefaya, *Corruption in Egypt…A dark cloud that does not vanish*".
13. Ibid

14. Ibid
15. Ibid
16. Al-Ahram daily newspaper, October 25th, 2004.
17. Nahdhat Masr newspaper, Dec. 25th, 2004.
18. Al-Ahram, Dec. 24th, 2004.

4 Corruptistan: the Party, the Bureaucracy, Business Moguls and the Military

1. Robert H. Jackson and Carl G. Rosberg, *Personal Rule in Black Africa*: Prince, Autocrat, Prophet, Tyrant. University of California Press; New Ed edition (November 13, 1982), p. 23.
2. Ibid
3. Ouda, El-Borai, and Sa'ada, *A Door into the Desert*, p. 24.
4. Ibid
5. Al-Kabbani, *Behind the Walls of Oblivion*, p. 5.
6. Cassandra, *The Impending Crisis in Egypt*, p. 23.
7. Al-Masri Al-Yawom, 4 March, 2006, issue 629.
8. Al-Arabi Al-Nasseri, 8 January, 2006, issue 992.
9. Al-Usboa, 23 January, 2006, issue 461.
10. Ibid

5 For God, Pharaoh and Country: Nationalism, Egyptian style

1. David Price-Jones, *The Closed Circuit*, Ivan R. Dee publisher, 2002, p. 248.
2. Ibid, p. 252.
3. Ibid.
4. Ibid, p. 250.
5. Ibid, p. 249
6. Ibid.
7. Ibid, p. 97.
8. Fouad Ajami, *A Dream Palace of the Arabs*, Pantheon Books, 1998.
9. Ibid, p. 379.
10. Bernard Lewis, *Semites and Anti-Semites*, W. W. Norton and Company, 1999, p. 140.
11. Ibid, p. 147.
12. Ibid, p. 148.
13. Ibid, p. 131.
14. Ajami, p. 207. Also see Heikal, Mohamed, *The Autumn of Fury*, Random House, 1983, and Kassem, Maye, Egyptian Politics; The dynamics of Authoritarian Rule, Lynne Eiener Publishers, 2004.
15. Kepel, Gilles, *Muslim extremism in Egypt: The Prophet and pharaoh*. Translated from French by Jon Rothschild. Berkeley & Los Angeles: University of California Press, 2003. See p. 194-199.
16. Sayyid Qutb, Hadha al-Din, Cairo: Dar Al-Qalam, 1962, p.85. In Qutb's book Al-'Adala Al-Ijtima'iyya fi al-Islam (Social Justice in Islam). Also see Sivan, Emmanuel, Radical Islam: Medieval

theology and modern politics. New Haven & London: Yale University Press, 1990. See p. 94-107. also mentioned in www.alneda.com.
17. Ibid.
18. www.alminbar.cc/alkhutab/khutbaa.asp?mediaURL=1220.
19. www.alminbar.cc/alkhutab/khutbaa.asp?mediaURL=4141, May 11, 2001.
20. http://www.almaqdese.com/c?c=1.1.
21. http://www.islamonline.net/iol-arabic/dowalia/alhadath-17-11/alhadath2.asp, November 17, 1999. For more on this conference, see MEMRI Special Dispatch No. 59, http://memri.org/bin/articles.cgi?Page=archives&Area=sd&ID=SP5999, November 19, 1999.
22. Al-Jazeera television (Qatar), July 10, 2002.
23. Roz Al-Yousef (Egypt), May 31, 2003. Special Dispatch Series - No. 526, June 20, 2003, No.526
24. Roz Al-Yousef (Egypt), May 17, 2003, as cited in Al-Quds Al-Arabi (London), May 19, 2003.
25. Roz Al-Yousef (Egypt), May 24, 2003, as cited in Al-Quds Al-Arabi (London), May 26, 2003.
26. Al-Watan (Saudi Arabia), December 12, 2003.
27. Al-Sharq Al-Awsat (London), September 23, 2004.
28. See: Al-Jabri, Mohamed Abed, *The Arab Political Reason: Determinants and Manifestations* [Al-'Aql as-Siyasi al-'Arabi: Muhaddidatuh wa Tajaliyatuh]. Casablanca & Beyrouth, 1990. Also see: Al-Jabri, Mohamed Abed, Naqd al'Aql al-'Arabi. Vol. I: « The Formation of the Arab Reason » [Takwin al-'Aql al-'Arabi]. Casablanca & Beyrouth, 1984. Vol II: The Structure of the Arab Reason [Binyat al-'Aql al-'Arabi]. Casablanca & Beyrouth, 1986. Vol III: and Al-Jabri, Mohamed Abed, The Arab Political Reason: Determinants and Manifestations, [Al-'Aql as-Siyasi al-'Arabi: Muhaddidatuh wa Tajaliyatuh].Casablanca & Beyrouth, 1990
29. Ibid
30. A similar political climate prevailed during the Dark Ages in Europe. Accusations of being infidel or a heretic were rampant. Religious wars were declared by the whims of the nobility and the Vatican. The First Crusade was launched in 1095 by Pope Urban II with the stated goal of capturing the sacred city of Jerusalem and the Holy Land from Muslims. He helped mobilized the peasants from round Europe by his speech in which he described Muslims as pagans and infidels by saying: "God himself will lead them, for they will be doing His work. There will be absolution and remission of sins for all who die in the service of Christ. Here they are poor and miserable sinners; there they will be rich and happy. Let none hesitate; they must march next summer. God wills it! All who die by the way, whether by land or by sea, or in battle against the pagans, shall have immediate remission of sins. This I grant them through the power of God with which I am

invested. Oh, what a disgrace if such a despised and base race, which worships demons, should conquer a people which has the faith of omnipotent God and is made glorious with the name of Christ!"
Once the Crusaders had entered the city of Jerusalem almost every inhabitant of Jerusalem was killed over the course of that afternoon, evening and next morning. Muslims, Jews, and even a few of the Christians were all massacred with indiscriminate violence. Many Muslims sought shelter in the Al-Aqsa Mosque, where, according to one famous account in Gesta, "the slaughter was so great that our men waded in blood up to their ankles..." According to Raymond of Aguilers; "men rode in blood up to their knees and bridle reins." Tancred claimed the Temple quarter for himself and offered protection to some of the Muslims there, but he could not prevent their deaths at the hands of his fellow crusaders.

6 The Old Guard, Cultists and the Underground: The Opposition

1. *Civil Society and Democratization in the Arab World,* the Ibn Khaldun Center for Development Studies' Annual Report. 2004, Published July 2005
2. Ibid.
3. *Egypt: Police Severely Beat Pro-Democracy Activists, One Activist Also Sexually Assaulted, In Cairo,* on May 31, 2006, by Human Rights Watch http://hrw.org/english/docs/2005/12/07/egypt12161.htm
4. Norton, Augustus Richard, *Civil Society in the Middle East,* (Social, Economic and Political Studies of the Middle East, Vol 1), p. 7.
5. Sa'ad Eddine Ibrahim, *Democratization in the Arab World,* p. 28.
6. Kasem, *Egyptian Politics, the Dynamics of Authoritarian Rule,* Lynne Eiener Publishers, 2004, p. 87.
7. Vatikiotis, P.J. *The History of Modern Egypt: From Muhammad Ali to Mubarak,* The Johns Hopkins University Press; 3rd edition (May, 1986) p. 401.
8. Kasem, *Egyptian Politics, the Dynamics of Authoritarian Rule,* p. 90.
9. Waterbury, John, *The Egypt of Nasser and Sadat*: The Political Economy of Two Regimes. Princeton Studies on the Near East, (Paperback - May 1983), p. 78.
10. El-Shafi'e, *Trade Unions and State in Egypt,* p. 34.
11. Egypt, Country Reports on Human Rights Practices - 2005, Released by the Bureau of Democracy, Human Rights, and Labor, March 8, 2006. Retrieved from http://www.state.gov/g/drl/rls/hrrpt/2005/61687.htm
12. Khalil, *Out of Mind* – Emamarni, 180 Degrees, quoted in Kasem's, *Egyptian Politics, the Dynamics of Authoritarian Rule,* Lynne

Eiener Publishers, 2004.

13. Kasem, *Egyptian Politics, the Dynamics of Authoritarian Rule*, p. 109.
14. Jackson and Roseberg, *Personal Rule in Black Africa*, in Social Problems in Africa: New Visions, Praeger Publishers (July 30, 2001), p. 267.
15. Springborg, *Patterns of Association in the Egyptian Political Elite," In the Political Elites in the Middle East*, ed. George Lenczowki. Washington, D.C.: American Enterprise Institute for Public Policy Research, 1975, p.171.
16. Zakaria, Terrorism, quoted in Kasem's, *Egyptian Politics, the Dynamics of Authoritarian Rule*, Lynne Eiener Publishers, 2004.

PART II: DEMAGOGUES, ZEALOTS AND ANTI-SEMITES

1. http://www.adl.org
2 http://www.adl.org/Anti_semitism/arab/as_egypt_03_2004/default.asp
3. Al- Ahram, "Anti-Semitism: Zionist Creation of the Semantic Terror" by Dr. Fathi al- Baradi'i, February 19, 2004.
4. The address was given at the 20th anniversary of the National Endowment for Democracy, Washington, D.C. on November 6, 2003. http://www.ned.org/events/anniversary/oct1603-Bush.html, United States' Chamber of Commerce, Washington, D.C.
5. Al-Quds Al-Arabi (London), November 12, 2003, as cited in Akidati (Egypt), November 11, 2003.
6. Al-Ahram (Egypt), November 10, 2003.
7. Al-Gumhouriyya (Egypt), November 12, 2003.
8. Al-Wafd (Egypt), November 11, 2003.
9. Al-Arabi (Egypt), November 9, 2003.
10. Al-Ayyam (Palestinian Authority), November 12, 2003.
11. Teshreen (Syria), November 12, 2003.
12. Teshreen (Syria), November 8, 2003.
13. http://memri.org/bin/articles.cgi?Page=archives&Area=sd&ID=SP60203, Special Dispatch Series - No. 602, November 4, 2003 No.602
14. Al-Ahram (Egypt), September 20, 2002.
15. See MEMRI Special Dispatch No. 559, August 28, 2003.
16. See Ambassador Welch's lecture at http://www.usembassy.egnet.net/ambassador/sp102003.htm
17. See MEMRI Special Dispatch No. 562, September 1, 2003.
18. Al-Gumhuriya (Egypt), October 3, 2003.
19. Al-Arabi (Egypt), October 26, 2003.
20. Al-Gumhuriya (Egypt), October 26, 2003.
21. Aqidati (Egypt), October 26, 2003.
22. Al-Gumhuriya (Egypt), October 25, 2003.

8 THE AMERICANS: CO-CONSPIRATORS AND ACCOMPLICES?

1. PA Chairman Arafat's National Security Advisor Jibril Rajoub said in an October 10 interview on the Lebanese TV channel LBC: "Who has profited from the events in Taba? "In my opinion, the first to profit is Sharon and the second is Bush. Sharon, in his continuous and unprecedented aggression against the Palestinian people in Gaza and elsewhere, will try to use what happened in Taba as a pretext to continue his war under the title of 'fighting terrorism,' although we are subjected to Sharon's official and international terrorism." See MEMRI.org - Special Dispatch Series - No. 801, October 15, 2004 No.801 http://memritv.org/Search.asp?ACT=S9&P1=281
2. Al-Gumhuriya (Egypt), October 12, 2004.
3. Al-Quds Al-Arabi (London), October 15, 2004.
4. Aqidati (Egypt), October 12, 2004.
5. http://www.islamonline.net/Arabic/politics/2004/10/article07.shtml
6. Nahdat Misr (Egypt), October 9, 2004.
7. Nahdat Misr (Egypt), October 9, 2004.
8 http://www.islamonline.net/Arabic/politics/2004/10/article07.shtml
9. Al-Rai Al-Aam (Kuwait), October 9, 2004. http://www.alraialaam.com/09-10-2004/ie5/international.htm
10. Al-Usbu' (Egypt), October 11, 2004.
11. http://www.ikhwanonline.com/Article.asp?ID=8890&SectionID=356, October 9, 2004.
12. Al-'Alam TV (Iran), October 12, 2004.
13. Al-Sharq Al-Awsat (London), October 10, 2004.
14. For more information read MEMRI Special Reports No. 7: The Events of September 11 and the Arab Media: The New Anti-Semitic Myth and No. 6: A New Anti-Semitic Myth in the Middle East Media: The September 11 Attacks Were Perpetrated by the Jews.
    Also mentioned in Special Dispatch Series - No. 423, October 1, 2002 No.423
15. Al-Ahram (Egypt), September 20, 2002.
16. Taken from the original English version entitled „Time to Get the Facts Right," on the United States Embassy in Egypt Web site, http://www.usembassy.egnet.net/newsa.htm
17. Al-Usbu'(Egypt), September 23, 2002.
18. Al-Gumhuriya (Egypt), September 22, 2002.
19. Al-Usbu' (Egypt), September 23, 2002.
20. Al-Gumhuriya (Egypt), September 24, 2002.
21. Al-Ahram (Egypt), September 24, 2002.
22. Al-Quds Al-Arabi (London), September 26, 2002.
23. Al-Ahram (Egypt), April 11, 2005. Also mentioned in Special Dispatch Series - No. 902, May 3, 2005 No.902

9 A Knight without a Horse: Propagandists and Spin Doctors in al-Jazeera Age

1. See MEMRI's Inquiry and Analysis Series Nos. 109, 113 and 114 (Nov. 8, Dec. 10 and Dec. 20, 2002, respectively).
2. Ibid
3. A group of Damascene Jews were accused of the ritual murder of an Italian Capuchin friar, Thomas, and his Muslim servant. The incident reflected the manipulation of Christian anti-Semitism and popular Muslim anti-Jewish sentiment aggravated by the struggles of the European powers that were vying at that time for influence in the Ottoman Empire, as counted by Menahem Milson, Professor of Arabic Literature at the Hebrew University of Jerusalem and MEMRI's academic advisor. This account is quoted from his article on a February 20, 2003 lecture at the Vidal Sassoon International Center for the Study of Anti-Semitism.
4. A New Anti-Semitic Myth in the Middle East Media: The September 11 Attacks Were Perpetrated by the Jews (Washington, DC: MEMRI, 2002).
5. Yigal Carmon, "Harbingers of Change in the Anti-Semitic Discourse in the Arab World" (MEMRI, Inquiry and Analysis Series, No. 135, April 23, 2003).
6. Qur'an, 2:65, 5:60, 7:166. Two of these texts (2:65 and 7:166) specify that violation of the Sabbath was the cause of the transmogrification.
7. See MEMRI Special Report No. 11 (November 1, 2002), by Aluma Solnick, 'Based on Koranic Verses, Interpretations, and Traditions, Muslim Clerics State: The Jews Are the Descendants of Apes, Pigs, And Other Animals'.
8. See MEMRI's Inquiry and Analysis Series Nos. 109, 113 and 114, Special Report - No. 26 February 27, 2004 No.26, and Nov. 8, Dec. 10 and Dec. 20, 2002, respectively.
9. See Yael Yehoshua, "Abu Mazen: A Political Profile" (MEMRI, Special Report No. 15, April 29, 2003) chapter V (Zionism and Holocaust Denial).

10 The Jews of Egypt: Rounding up the Usual Suspects

1. Genesis. xiii. 10; Ex. xvi. 3; Numbers xi. 5, Retrieved from http://en.wikipedia.org/wiki/History_of_the_Jews_in_Egypt
2. *Annuaire des Juifs d'Egypte et du Proche-Orient*, 1942, ed. Maurice Fargeon (Cairo: La *Société des Editions Historiques Juives d'Egypte*, 1943) 117
3. *«Rapport présenté à l'Agence Juive Département du Moyen Orient sur la situation actuelle des Juifs en Egypte par un Juif d'Egypte ayant quitté l'Egypte vers la fin de l'année 1949,»* 13.

Central Zionist Archives (Jerusalem) S20/552, Jewish Agency, Department for Middle Eastern Jews, Matzav ha-yehudim be-mitzrayim, 1948-1952/no subdivision (Henceforth CZA).

4. Joel Beinin, *Egyptian Jewish identities, communitarianisms, nationalisms, nostalgias*, SEHR, volume 5, issue 1: Contested Polities, 27 February 1996. Also mentioned in his article "*Rethinking Nationalisms in the Arab World*" read at the University of Colorado, Boulder, Colorado on September 21-24, 1994 and sponsored by the National Endowment for the Humanities. The research was assisted by a grant from the Joint Committee on the Near and Middle East of the Social Science Research Council and the American Council of Learned Societies with funds provided by the National Endowment for the Humanities and the Ford Foundation. Retrieved from: http://www.stanford.edu/group/SHR/5-1/text/beinin.html
5. Eric Davis, *Challenging Colonialism: Bank Misr and Egyptian Industrialization*, 1920-1941 (Princeton: Princeton UP, 1983) 93-97 and L'Annuaire des Juifs d'Egypte et du Proche-Orient, 1942: 248.
6. Ibid
7. Israël, Nov. 18 1937, qtd. in Bat Ye'or, "*Zionism in Islamic Lands: The Case of Egypt,*" Wiener Library Bulletin 30.43-44 (1977): 27.
8. Joel Beinin, *Egyptian Jewish identities, communitarianisms, nationalisms, nostalgias*. SEHR, volume 5, issue 1: Contested Polities, 27 February 1996.
9. CZA S25/5218, R. Cattaoui et E. N. Goar, "*Le point de vue des communautés Juives d'Egypte: Note sur la question juive.*»
10. Benin, *Egyptian Jewish identities, communitarianisms, nationalisms, nostalgias.*
11. Edna Bonacich and John Modell, *The Economic Basis of Ethnic Solidarity,* (Berkeley: University of California Press, 1980) 110.
12. On the Cicurel family, see Krämer 44-45, 101, 107, 213; Robert Tignor, *State, Private Enterprise, and Economic Change in Egypt,* (Princeton: Princeton UP, 1984) 60, 66, 102; Mizrahi 64-65; *L'Annuaire des Juifs*, 1942 250; Nabil `Abd al-Hamid Sayyid Ahmad, *al-Hayat al-iqtisadiyya wa'l-ijtima`iyya li'l-yahud fi misr*, 1947-1956 (Cairo: Maktabat Madbuli, 1991) 38-40.
13. Nabil Abd al-Hamid Sayyid Ahmad, *al-Hayat al-iqtisadiyya wa'l-ijtima`iyya li'l-yahud fi misr*, 1947-1956 (Cairo: Maktabat Madbuli, 1991), 39.
14. Albert D. Mosseri, "L'espoir d'un vieux sioniste," Israël 6.12 (20 mars 1925):1, qtd. in Michael Laskier, The Jews of Egypt, 1920-1970 (New York: New York UP, 1992) 51.
15. See Israel Gershoni and James Jankowski, Beyond the Nile Valley (Cambridge: Cambridge UP, 1995).
16. Maurice Mizrahi, *L'Egypte et ses Juifs: Le temps révolu*, xixe et xxe siècle (Geneva: Imprimerie Avenir, 1977) 37-44; Gudrun Krämer, *The Jews in Modern Egypt*, 1914-1952 (Seattle: U of Washington P, 1989) 126, 128.
17. Benin, *Egyptian Jewish identities, communitarianisms,*

nationalisms, nostalgias. http://www.stanford.edu/group/SHR/5-1/text/beinin.html

18. Shimon Shamir, "*The Evolution of the Egyptian Nationality Laws and Their Application to the Jews in the Monarchy Period," The Jews of Egypt: A Mediterranean Society in Modern Times*, ed. Shimon Shamir (Boulder: Westview, 1987), p.41, 58.
19. Shamir, p. 34.
20. Arkhion ha-Haganah (Tel Aviv) 14/1024, "*Pe`ulot ha-haganah be-mitzrayim, 1947,"* Avigdor (Levi Avrahami) le-ha-ramah, Sept.1st , 1947.
21. Mourad El-Kodsi, *The Karaite Jews of Egypt*, 1882-1986 (Lyons, NY: Wilprint, 1987) and Yosef Algamil, Hayahadut hakara'it be-mitzrayim be`et he-hadashah (Ramla: Ha-Mo'etzah ha-'Artzit shel ha-yehudim ha-kara'im be-yisra'el, 1985).
22. Thomas Philipp, *The Syrians in Egypt*, 1725-1975 (Stuttgart: Franz Steiner Verlag, 1985) 137.
23. E. J. Blattner, ed., *Le Mondain égyptien: L'annuaire de l'élite d'Egypte* (The Egyptian Who's Who) [title varies] (Cairo: Imprimerie Française, 1947, 1952, 1954, 1956, 1959).
24. See the French novel by his daughter, Marcelle Fisher, Armando (Tel Aviv: Yeda Sela, 1982). See also Aviezer Golan's compiled an authorized collective memoir, Operation Susannah.
25. Al-Ahram, 6 Oct. 1954, also mentioned in Al-Musawwar, 15 Oct., 29 Oct., 17 Dec., 1954 and Hasan al-Husayni, «*Ma`a jawasis isra'il fi al-sijn,"* Jan. 7, 1955. *The Story of Zionist Espionage in Egypt,* (Cairo: Ministry of Information, 1955) 25, 61.
26. Joel Gordon, *Revolutionary Melodrama; Popular Film and Civic Identity in Nasser's Egypt,* Center for Middle Easter Studies, the University of Chicago, 2002.

11 Gatekeepers and Infidels: The Religious Right versus the Intelligentsia

1. For more on Ali Salem, see: MEMRI Special Dispatch No. 728, "*Satirist Ali Salem to Arab League: There's Light at the End of the Tunnel,*" June 8, 2004, http://memri.org/bin/articles.cgi?Page=archives&Area=sd&ID=SP72804 ; MEMRI TV Clip No. 696, "*Egyptian Playwright Ali Salem Argues With Egyptian Nationalists Over Visits to Israel,*" May 29, 2005, http://www.memritv.org/search.asp?ACT=S9&P1=696; MEMRI TV Clip No. 296, "Egyptian Playwright Ali Salem: *The Arab World is Threatened by the Terror Groups, Not by Israel and the U.S.,*" October 18, 2004, http://www.memritv.org/search.asp?ACT=S9&P1=296
   Special Dispatch Series - No. 93, May 12, 2000 No.93. Also see Salem's interview in Al-Sharq Al-Awsat (London), in June 2006,
2. "The New Call" was established in the early 90's to promote classical liberal values in Egypt.
3. Al-Usbu, (Egypt), April 10, 2000.
4. Al-Usbu, (Egypt), April 10, 2000.

5. 'Muasasat Ibn Khaldoun' is a research institute established in Cairo in the early 1990's. The institute produces a publication called "Al-Mujtama' Al-Madani" ("Civil Society").
6. In 1998 some of the Egyptian participants in the Copenhagen Conference (1997) formed an NGO supported by the Egyptian Foreign Ministry, in order to bring to bring about Netanyahu's defeat. This movement, aka, "The Peace Movement", was headed by Salah Basyuni, former Egyptian ambassador in the USSR, before its collapse.
7. Al-Usbu (Egypt), April 10, 2000.
8. In January 1997 the Danish government sponsored an international conference called "The International Alliance for Peace." Its participants were Egyptians, Israelis, Jordanians and Palestinians. The conference formed a steering committee, headed by the late Lutfi Al-Khuli, an Egyptian communist intellectual.
9. Al-Ahrar (Egypt), April 9, 2000.
10 - IRNA (Iran), February 12, 2005.
11 - Aluma Dankowitz, *Accusing Muslim Intellectuals of Apostasy*, MEMRI.org
12. See article by liberal Tunisian intellectual Lafif Lakhdar, http://www.rezgar.com/debat/show.art.asp?t=2&aid=8336, July 1, 2003.
13. Al-Ahram Al-Arabi (Egypt), July 3, 2004.
14. Roz Al-Yusouf (Egypt), September 17, 2004.
15. Al-Sharq Al-Awsat (London), October 19, 2004.
16. Al-Hayat, London, September 9, 2004.
17. Khawarij, the first religious opposition in Islam, was formed when a group of Muslims left the camp of the Fourth Caliph ,Ali bin Abi-Taleb at the Battle of Sifin in 657.
18. Mu'tazila, a theoretical rationalistic stream of the 9th and 10th centuries, sought to set out the principles of religious faith in logical and rational formulae.
19. http://mojahid.net/ib/index.php?s=880b3a65504793196a9941ae4 72f7bf5&showtopic=4332&st
20. Al-Masri Al-Yawm (Egypt), October 25, 2004, as cited in Al-Quds Al-Arabi (London), October 26, 2004.
21. Ijtihad, or using individual judgment, was suspended in the 10th century by a consensus of ulema (Islamic clerics), and its resumption has not been permitted since. For the full text of the recommendations, see http://www.mengos.net/events/04newsevents/egypt/october/ibnkhaldun-English.htm
22. Al-Rai Al-Aam (Kuwait), October 8, 2004.
23. http://www.hrinfo.net/egypt/makal/pr041010.shtml
24. Al-Sharq Al-Awsat, London, November 7, 2004.
25. Al-Jazeera TV, Qatar, October 5, 2004.
26. Roz Al-Yousuf (Egypt), April29, 2005.
27. Fakhr Al-Din Al-Razi, d. 1209.
28. The bombing at the Khan Al-Halili, on April 7, 2005.
29. These two concepts – shumuliyya and hakimiyya – are closely related. Shumuliyya states that all aspects of life fall under

the jurisdiction of Islamic law. Hakimiyya states that the only legitimate government is Allah's government, which in practical terms means government according to Islamic law.

30. The specific mention of the schools is probably a reference to Egypt's two-track educational system

12 The Copts: Strangers in their Native Land!

1. MERI.org, Special Dispatch Series, November 16, 2005 No.1023
2. Special Dispatch Series - No. 352, March 8, 2002 No.352
3. Al-Quds Al-Arabi (London), March 7, 2002.
4. http://www.elaph.com/ElaphWeb/ElaphWriter/2006/7/161549.htm, July 9, 2006. Also mentioned in MERI.org, Special Dispatch Series - No. 1306, October 5, 2006 No.1306
5. The reference here is to the events of October 2005, which followed the performance at a church of a play that was perceived by the Muslims as defaming Islam and Muslims. Four people were killed and dozens injured in the subsequent rioting in the city.

Part III: The Beginning of the End

1. Wikipedia
2. Ibid
3. Dr. Nimrod Raphaeli, Senior Analyst of MEMRI's Middle East Economic Studies Program, *The Grooming of Gamal Mubarak.* http://www.memri.org/bin/articles.cgi?Area=ia&ID=IA14103
4. Magdi Abdelhadi, BBC regional analyst, *Moubarak son raises public profile*. http://news.bbc.co.uk/2/hi/middle_east/3646026.stm
   Inquiry and Analysis Series - No. 141
   July 8, 2003 No.141
5. http://hrw.org/english/docs/2005/12/07/egypt12161.htm July 4, 2006 No.1196.
6. April 4, 2006, article by Ayman Nour, Al-Ghad party website http://www.elghad.org/modules.php?name=News&file=article&sid=146
7. Mubarak: Fin du Régime?
   http://72.14.253.104/search?q=cache:
   nYGjVEIIQp0J:baheyya.blogspot.com/
   +%22+political+corruption+in+Egypt%22&hl=en&gl=us&ct=clnk&cd=2, May 02, 2006
8. Nimrod Raphaeli, *The Grooming of Gamal Mubarak* http://www.memri.org/bin/articles.cgi?Area=ia&ID=IA14103
9. Al-Hayat (London), March 6, 2003.
10. Al-Hayat (London), March 6, 2003.
11. Al-Hayat (London), March 19, 2003.
12. The Washington Post, February 10, 2003.

Conclusion

1. Dr. Nimrod Raphaeli, *Economic Crisis in Egypt*, Middle East Economic News Report - No. 20, January 21, 2002 No.20.
2. Al-Sharq Al-Awsat, January 14, 2002.
3. Al-Hayat, January 15, 2002.
4. Al-Sharq Al-Awsat, January 10, 2002.
5. Al-Hayat, January 11, 2002.
6. Al-Hayat, January 16, 2002.
7. Akhbar Al-yom, January 14, 2002; Al-Ahram On Line, 17-23 January, 2002.
8. Al-Hayat, January 10, 2002.
9. A statement by ILO director-general at the World Economic Forum in Davos, Switzerland, January 25, 2006.
10. The Middle Eastern and North African countries covered in the report are: Bahrain, Djibouti, Islamic Republic of Iran, Iraq, Israel, Jordan, Kuwait, Lebanon, Oman, Qatar, Saudi Arabia, Somalia, Syrian Arab Republic, United Arab Emirates, West Bank and Gaza Strip, and Yemen; the North African countries include Algeria, Egypt, Libyan Arab Jamahiriya, Morocco, Sudan, Tunisia.
11. ILO Report, Table 1.3, p.27.
12. Ibid., p.32, table 1.4.
13. Ibid., p.30.
14. Ibid. pp. 57-58.
15. According to the study by UNDP, the percentage of population under 15 in 1999 stood as follows in selected countries: UAE (26.7); Libya (34.7); Egypt (36.0); Iran (38.7); Jordan (40.2); Syria (41.7); and Saudi Arabia (43.4).
16. People's Daily Online, May 8, 2005. The unemployment rate of 20 percent in the Arab countries was stated by Ahmed Gowaili, secretary-general of the Arab League Economic Unity Council. Al-Ahram (Egypt), January 26, 2006
17. World Tribune.com (February 10, 2003) and Al-Ahram (Egypt), January 26, 2006.
18. Al-Ahram (Egypt), January 26, 2006.
19. Dr. Nimrod Raphacli is Senior Analyst of MEMRI's Middle East Economic Studies Program.
20. Ibid
21. UNDP, pp.52-53.
22. ILO Report, p.61.
23. *"Dealing with the Global Jobs Crisis,"* opinion piece by Juan Somavia, director-general of International Labor Office, January 25, 2006.
24. Al-Hayat (London), February 10, 2006.
25. Crisis Group, Reforming Egypt: In Search of a Strategy, Middle

East/North Africa Report N°46, 4 October 2005.
26. The Daily Star (Lebanon), June 16, 2006. Special Dispatch Series - No. 1191, June 22, 2006 No.1191.
27. Fareed Zakaria, *How to Save the Arab World: Washington's hands-off approach must go. The first step to undermining extremism is to prod regimes into economic reform*, Newsweek, December 24, 2001.
28. Ibid.
29. Ibid.
30. Milani, Mohsen, *The Making of Iran's Islamic Revolution*, pp. 111-112.
31. Rouleau, *Egypt's Islamists Caught in a Bind.*
32. David Pryce-Jones, *The Closed Circuit, An interpretation of the Arabs*, Harper & Row, 2002, p.402.
33. Ibid, p. 403.
34. Ibid, p. 404.
35. Ibid, p. 405.
36. Kasem.
37. Zakaria.

EPILOGUE

1. Abdelhalim Qandeel, Al-Ayam al-Akhira [The Final Days] (Cairo: Dar Ath-Thaqafa al-Jadida, 2008), "Introduction."
2. *Daily News Egypt* (Giza), Feb. 15, 2009.
3. "2008 Corruption Perceptions Index," Transparency International, Berlin.
4. Market Watch (Dow Jones & Company, Inc., New York), Apr. 11, 2008.
5. International Herald Tribune (Paris), Apr. 6, 2008.
6. "Human and Income Poverty: Developing Countries," Human Development Report 2007/8. (New York: UNDP, 2007), p. 240.
7. Khalil al-Anani, "Union of Dictatorships," Islamists Today, Aug. 20, 2008; Daily News Egypt, Aug. 26, 200.
8. Ibrahim M. Oweiss, "Egypt's Economy: The Pressing Issues," Georgetown University, accessed Mar. 13. 2009.
9. Alan Richards, "Economic Roots of Instability in the Middle East," Middle East Policy Sept. 1995, pp. 175-87.
10. Bloomberg.com, Feb. 18, 2009.
11. Asharq al-Awsat (London), Jan. 14, 2002.
12. Associated Press, Apr. 10, 2008; ABC News, Apr. 10, 2008.
13. *Al-Ahram* (Cairo), Jan. 26, 2006; Al-Hayat (London), Jan. 16, 2008.
14. Nimrod Raphaeli, "Unemployment in the Middle East: Causes and Consequences," Inquiry and Analysis, no. 265, Middle East Media Research Institute (MEMRI), Feb. 10, 2006.

15. International Herald Tribune, Feb. 24, 2009.
16. World Employment Report 2004-2005 (Geneva: U.N. International Labor Organization, 2004), p. 30.
17. Michelle Dunne, "A Post-Pharaonic Egypt?" The American Interest, Sept. /Oct. 2008.
18. BBC News.com, Feb. 16, 2005.
19. "Egypt," U.N. International Labor Organization, May 22, 2006.
20. Al-Ahram Weekly (Cairo), Nov. 8-14, 2007; Ash-Sharq (Doha), Nov. 9, 2007, in the MEMRI Economic Blog, Nov. 9, 2007.
21. Egyptian Gazette (Cairo), Oct. 20, 2007.
22. Agence France Presse, Oct. 3, 2007; Mohamed Talaat el-Harawi, "U.S. State Department: Egypt Is a Transit Country for Human Trafficking," U.S. Copt Association, Jan 20, 2009; "Country Narratives: Egypt," Trafficking in Persons, 2008 (Washington, D.C.: U.S. State Department, 2008), pp. 111-2.
23. BBC News, Apr. 20, 2006.
24. The Daily Star (Beirut), June 16, 2005.
25. The Daily Star, June 16, 2005; BBC News, May 26, 2008.
26. "2008 Human Rights Report: Egypt," 2008 Country Reports on Human Rights Practices (Washington, D.C.: United States State Department, Bureau of Democracy, Human Rights, and Labor, Feb. 25, 2009).
27. Maye Kassem, Egyptian Politics, the Dynamics of Authoritarian Rule (Boulder: Lynne Rienner Publishers, 2004), pp. 87, 90, 109.
28. "Reforming Egypt: In Search of a Strategy," International Crisis Group, Oct. 4, 2005.
29. "2008 Human Rights Report: Egypt."
30. Cited in "2008 Human Rights Report: Egypt."
31. Jalal al-Ahmad, Gharbzadagi [Westoxification] (Tehran: 1962).
32. Le Monde Diplomatique (Paris), Jan. 8, 1998.
33. Daniel Sobelman, "Gamal Mubarak, President of Egypt?" Middle East Quarterly Spring 2001, pp. 31-40; Gamal Mubarak, "We Need Audacious Leaders," interview, Middle East Quarterly, Winter 2009, pp. 67-73.
34. The Daily Star, June 16, 2005.
35. Dunne, "A Post-Pharaonic Egypt?"
36. Thomas P. M. Barnett, "The Country to Watch: Egypt," Esquire, Oct. 2006.
37. Robert Satloff, "U.S. Policy towards Egypt," testimony to the U.S. House Committee on International Relations, Apr. 10, 1997.
38. YNetNews.com, Aug. 4, 2006 .

39 Barnett, Thomas P.M., Egypt's future looks scary , Monday, December 29, 2008. http://www.knoxnews.com/news/2008/dec/28/four-scary words-egypt-after-h osni-mubarek/

GLOSSARY

Ablution (Wudu): The ritual of washing one's body in preparation for prayer.

Adhan: The call to prayer by muezzin.

Allah: The Arabic word for God is Allah, whether the Arabic speaker is referring to the Christian or the Muslim God. Some Muslims believe that the word Allah cannot be translated into other languages and maintain its identification with the one true God. Allah has ninety-nine other sacred names. Allah is simply the Arabic world for God, related to the Hebrew Elohim; it can be seen as analogous to the German word Gott, the French Dieu, or the Spanish Dios. It's not the personal name of a deity within a pantheon, like Thor, Aphrodite or Siva.

Akhenaton: Founder of the first monotheistic religion, Atonism.

Arab: One who speaks Arabic and shares the heritage of Arabic culture is an Arab. An estimated 95% of Arabs are Muslim; the remainder is primarily Christian. However only 20% of Muslims worldwide are Arabs (the largest Muslim country is Indonesia).

As-salaam alaikum: The usual English transliteration of the traditional Arabic greeting, which is translated "peace be upon you." The one being greeted reverses the blessing in response with "and upon you, peace," or wah alaikum as-salaam.

Asr: In Arabic, this word meaning "afternoon" is also the name of the afternoon prayer that is among the five obligatory daily prayers for Muslims.

Bismillah: The usual English transliteration of the first word of the first line of the Koran. Translated as "in the name of God," it is used frequently as an invocation at the start of an action no matter how trivial.

Fardh: Obligatory deeds to be observed by a Muslim, like Salat, Fasting, and other duties.

Fasting, siyam: Abstaining from eating, drinking, smoking, sexual encounters from sunrise to sunset during the holy month of Ramadan.

Fatwa: Religious ruling

Hafez: The person capable of memorizing the whole Quran.

Hajj: Performing the pilgrimage to Makkah (Mecca) and Medinah by those who are capable of doing it physically and financially once in a lifetime. It is the fifth pillar of Islam.

Halal: The English transliteration of the Arabic term referring to something that is permitted. For example, halal meat has been slaughtered and prepared according to Muslim standards.

Haram: The English transliteration of the Arabic term with two core meanings. One means a sacred precinct or area set aside from the world (for example, Mecca). In English, it became harem and referred only to the Ottoman custom of sequestering women of nobility in separate living quarters. The second refers to that which is proscribed by Muslim law and tradition and forbidden to the faithful, such as the eating of pork.

Hijra: The Arabic word for the migration of Muhammad from Mecca to Medina in 622 A.D. The Muslim calendar dates from this year.

'Id al-Fitr: One English transliteration of the Arabic name for the feast that celebrates the end of the month-long Ramadan daylight fast (also called Eid al-Fitr).

Imam: This term has different meanings for the Sunni and Shi'a branches of Islam. For the Sunni, the term refers to the prayer leader at a mosque. As there is no priesthood in Islam, this person is not equivalent to priest or pastor. He is merely conversant in the Koran and chosen by consensus. For the Shi'a, the term is reserved for the successors to the sons of 'Ali (Muhammad's son-in-law) and their spiritual and political leaders.

Isha: The Arabic word for evening, this is the closing prayer of the day (about 1-1/2 hours after sunset), one of five obligatory prayers for Muslims.

Islam: Literally, the Arabic word Islam means submission. For a Muslim (one who submits), Islam is peace through submission to the will of Allah.

Masjid: Mosque, the place for prayer.

Isma'ilis: A sectarian offshoot of Shi'a Islam. The leader of the Nizari branch holds the title Aga Khan. The current one is 49th in an unbroken line of descent. There are perhaps 2 million Isma'ilis worldwide.

Jihad: The English transliteration of the Arabic word for "struggle." When used to mean a fight in defense of Islam, it has taken the connotation of "Holy War."

Jum'ah: One English transliteration of the Arabic term for the mid-day Friday congregational prayer service, usually in a mosque (others are juma and jumu'a).

Koran: The traditional English spelling for the book containing Allah's revelations in Arabic to Muhammad through the angel Gabriel is Koran. It also is transliterated from the Arabic as Qur'an, or Quran. The language of the Koran, as the spoken word of God, became the basis of formal or classical Arabic.

Maghrib or Maghreb: The Arabic word for sunset. Maghrib is one of five obligatory daily prayers for Muslims. The term also denotes, collectively, the Muslim countries of North Africa, the "land of the setting sun" west of Arabia.

Mahdi: Part of a collection of words meaning variously messiah, prophet, anointed one. Mahdism is the belief that a divinely guided restorer of Islam will establish a prophetic kingdom at the end of history. The best-known person claiming the title of Mahdi was the Muslim warrior who fought the British in the Sudan in the 1880s, defeating Gen. Gordon at Khartoum.

Medinah: The second holy city in Islam, where Prophet Muhammad and his successors were buried, and were he migrated to and lived in till the end of his life.

Mihrab: The niche in the center of the front wall inside a mosque noting the direction of the Ka'aba in Mecca, the direction Muslims face for prayer.

Muslim: One who practices Islam is Muslim (the now out-of-favor English transliteration is Moslem).

Omrah: The journey to Mekkah at any time of year to perform a ritual similar to Hajj. Some people prefer to it as "smaller Hajj".

Peace Be Upon Him: Sometimes abbreviated in print as PBUH, this exclamation often is used by Muslims after mentioning the name of one of the prophets, especially Muhammad. Native speakers of Arabic sometimes use the English transliteration of the Arabic text, "sala Allah alayhi wa salaam", (which also can be translated "God's blessings and peace be upon him"). Some Muslims also add "subanna watallah" (or "Glory be upon him") following mention of the name Allah.

Pillars of Islam: The five essentials of Islam are the profession of faith (shahadah), performing the prayers (salat), the giving of 2.5% of one's net income to charity (zakat), pilgrimage to Mecca (hajj) and fasting during Ramadan (saum).

Ramadan: The ninth month of the Islamic year is spent fasting from sunrise to sunset.

Shahadah (or shahada): The public confession whereby one becomes a Muslim, hence one of the pillars of Islam. One English translation is, "There is no God but Allah and Muhammad is the Prophet of Allah."

Shari'ah or shari'a: The English transliteration of the Arabic term referring to Islamic law, which is based on the Koran and the hadith. There are four main schools of shari'a which disagree with each other on a variety of interpretations (named for their founders, they are

Hanafi, Hanbali, Maliki and Shafi'i).

Shi'ia Islam: About 10% of practicing Muslims are Shi'ite. The name derives from Shi'a, meaning partisans or followers, and refers to those who believe that the successors to Muhammad should come only from descendants of his family. The first Shi'ites were partisans of Ali ibn Abi Talib, Muhammad's son-in-law and husband of his favorite daughter, Fatima.

Sunnah or Sunna: The English transliteration of the Arabic term for the "true path" or example set by Muhammad, the way he behaved and acted during his life. Sunnah Acts and deeds observed by the prophet Muhammad, pbuh, but not considered Fardh (obligatory), more of a volunteer nature.

Sunni Islam: About 90% of practicing Muslims are Sunni, a term derived from Sunna and meaning people who follow the "true path".

Ulema: The English transliteration of the plural for the Arabic 'alim, which means a learned person. Ulema usually refers to "orthodox" Islamic theologians, scholars and teachers.

Ummah or Umma: The English transliteration of the Arabic word denoting at one level the religious community in which a Muslim participates and at another, the entire community of *believers* in Islam.

Qazi, kazi: Judge

Umrah: Paying a visit to Ka'bah, performing Tawaf around it, and walking between the mounts of Safa and Marwah seven times in the prescribed rituals.

Zakat ul-Fitr: Zakat ul-fitr is the charity or almsgiving, which must be paid by every Muslim, young and old, male and female, at the end of the month of fasting (Ramadan).

BIBLIOGRAPHY

Abd al-Hamid Sayyid Ahmad, Nabil, *al-Hayat al-iqtisadiyya wa'l-ijtima`iyya li'l-yahud fi misr*, 1947-1956 (Cairo: Maktabat Madbuli, 1991.

Adwan, Charles, *"Reform in Independent Lebanon: The Roller Coaster of Trial and Error,"* Beirut: The Lebanese Transparency Association, 2002.

Ajami, Fouad, *The Arab Predicament*, Cambridge University Press, 1981.
________, *Dream Palaces of the Arabs*, New York, Pantheon, 1998.

Al-Affendi, Abd al-wahab, *Rationality of Politics and Politics of Rationality*. In A. Tamimi and J. Esposito, eds., Islam and Secularism in the Middle East, New York University Press, 2002.

Al-Jabri, Mohamed Abed, *The Arab Political Reason: Determinants and Manifestations* [Al-'Aql as-Siyasi al-'Arabi : Muhaddidatuh wa Tajaliyatuh]. Casablanca & Beyrouth, 1990.
________, Naqd al'Aql al-'Arabi. Vol. I : « *The Formation of the Arab Reason* » [Takwin al-'Aql al-'Arabi]. Casablanca & Beyrouth, 1984. Vol II: The Structure of the Arab Reason [Binyat al-'Aql al-'Arabi]. Casablanca & Beyrouth, 1986. Vol III :
______________, *The Arab Political Reason: Determinants and Manifestations*, [Al-'Aql as-Siyasi al-'Arabi : Muhaddidatuh wa Tajaliyatuh].Casablanca & Beyrouth, 1990.
______________, *Ad-Dimuqratiyah wa Huquq al-Insan*. Beyrouth, 1994.
______________, *Ad-Din wa ad-Dawla wa Tatbiq ash-Shari'a*, Beyrouth, 1996.

Al-Kabbani, Niven. *Behind the Walls of Oblivion*, The Program for the Amelioration of Prizon Conditions. Cairo: Human Rights Center for the Assistance of prisoners Press, 2000.

Atwood, Brian, *"Corruption: A Persistent Development Challenge,"* in Economic Perspectives, November1998.

Ayubi, Nazih, *Overstating the Arab State: Politics and Society in the Middle East*. London: I. B. Tauris, 1996.
________. *Political Islam: Religion and Politics in the Arab World*. London: Routledge, 1991.
_______. *The State and Public Policies in Egypt since Sadat*. Reading, Mass.: Itasca Press, 1991.

Azzam, Maha. *"Egypt: Islamists and the State under Mubarak"*. In Islamic Fundamentalism, eds. Abdel-Salam Sidahmed and Anoushiravan Ehteshami. Boulder: Westview, 1996.
Baker, Raymond William. *Egypt's Uncertain Revolution under Nasser and Sadat*. Cambridge: Harvard University Press, 1978.
Bonacich, Edna, and John Modell, *The Economic Basis of Ethnic*

Solidarity. Berkeley: Uinversity of California

Bill, James A. and Robert Springborg. *Politics in the Middle East.* 4th ed. New York: HarperCollins Colledge Publishers, 1994.

Brooker, Paul. *Non-democratic Regimes: Theory, Government and Politics.* New York: St. Martin's Press, 2000.

Brownlee, Jason. *The Decline of Pluralism in Mubarak's Egypt.* Journal of Democracy 13, no. 4 (October 2002).

Cassandra. *The Impending Crisis in Egypt.* Middle East Journal 4949, no. 1(Winter 1995): 10-27.

Chehabi, H. E., and Juan Linz, eds. Sultanistic Regimes. Baltimore: Johns Hopkins University Press, 1998.

Chua, Amy, *World on Fire*, Doubleday, 2003.

Egypt: 2001. *The World Factbook.* Washinton, D.C.:U.S. Central Intelligence Agency, 2001.

El-Kodsi, Mourad, *The Karaite Jews of Egypt*, 1882-1986. Lyons, NY: Wilprint, 1987.

Eric Davis, *Challenging Colonialism: Bank Misr and Egyptian Industrialization*, 1920-1941 (Princeton: Princeton UP, 1983.

Gillies, David. *Between Principles and Practice: Human Rights in North-South Relations.* Montreal: McGill-Queens University Press, 1996.

Gordon, Joel, *Revolutionary Melodrama; Popular Film and Civic Identity in Nasser's Egypt,* Center for Middle Easter Studies, The University of Chicago, 2002.

Hadjaj, Djillali, *Campagne Gouvernementale Contre la Corruption et Violation des Droits de l-Homme:* l'Exemple de l'Algerie, Paper Presented at the 9th International Anti-Corruption Conference.

Heikal, Mohamed, *The Autumn of Fury*, Random House, 1983.
_____________, *The Cairo Documents*, Flammarion, 1972.
_____________, *The Road to Ramadan*, Collins, London, 1975.
______, *Le Sphinx et le Commissar*, Editions Jeune Afrique, Paris, 1980.

Hinnebusch, Raymond A. *"Formation of Contemporary Egyptian State from Nasser to Mubarak"*, In the *Political Economy of Contemporary Egypt*, ed. Ibrahim M. 'Oweiss. Washington, D.C.: Center for Contemporary Arab Studies, Georgetown University, 1990.
Hirst, David, *The Gun and the Olive Branch,* Faber and Faber, London, 1977.

Ibrahim, Sa'ad Eddine. "Democratization in the Arab World". In *Civil Society in the Middle East,* vol.1, ed. Augustus Richard Norton. New

York: E. J. Brill, 1995, pp. 27-54.

_______________, *Islam and Democracy.* Cairo. American University in Cairo Press, 1996.

Jackson and Roseberg, *Personal Rule in Black Africa*: Prince, Autocrat, Prophet, Tyrant, University of California Press, 1982.

Johnston, Michael, "*Corruption and Democracy: Threats to Development, Opportunities for Reform,*" Hamilton, New York: Colgate University, 2000.

Kassem, Maye, *Egyptian Politics; The Dynamics of Authoritarian Rule*, Lynne Eiener Publishers, 2004.

__________, *In the Guise of Democracy: Governance in Contemporary Egypt*, London: Itasca Press, 1999.

Kepel, Gilles, *Muslim extremism in Egypt: The Prophet and pharaoh.* Translated from French by Jon Rothschild. Berkeley & Los Angeles: University of California Press, 2003. See p. 194-199.

Kienle, Eberhard. *A Grand Delusion: Democracy Reform in Egypt*, London: I. B. Tauris, 2001.

Kitchen, *On the Reliability of the Old Testament*, William B. Eerdmans Publishing Company, 2003.

Krämer, Gudrun, *The Jews in Modern Egypt*, 1914-1952. Seattle: University of Washington Press, 1989.

Lacouture, Jean, *Nasser*, Seuil, Paris, 1971.

Lewis, Bernard, *Semites and Anti-Semites.* New York and London: W. W. Norton & Company, 1999.

Lynch, Marc, *Voices of the New Arab Public*, Iraq, Al-Jazeera, and the Middle East Politics Today, Columbia University press, 2006.

Military Courts in Egypt: Courts without Safeguards, Judges without Immunity, and Defendants without Rights. Center for Human Rights Legal Aid Report, Cairo, September, 1995.

Nielsen, Michael, and Jakob Haugaard, *"Democracy, Corruption and Human Development,"* Denmark: University of Aarhus, 2000.

Philipp, Thomas, *The Syrians in Egypt*, 1725-1975. Stuttgart: Franz Steiner Verlag, 1985.

Pryce-Jones, David, *The Closed Circuit, An interpretation of the Arabs*, Harper & Row, 2002.

Rugh, William A., *Arab Mass Media, Newspapers, Radio, and Television in Arab Politics, Praeger*, Westport, Connecticut, London, 2004.

Sadat, Anwar, *The Full Story of the Revolution* (Arabic). Dar al-Hila, Cairo, n.d.

___________, *My Son, This is Your Uncle Gamal* (Arabic) Arfan Library, Cairo, n.d.
___________, *Revolte Sur le Nil*, Pierre Amiot, Paris, 1957.
___________, *In Search of Identity*, Collins, London, 1978.

Shamir, Shimon, *The Jews of Egypt: A Mediterranean Society in Modern Times*, Boulder: Westview, 1987.

Tignor, Robert, *State, Private Enterprise, and Economic Change in Egypt*, (Princeton: Princeton University Press.

Tyldesley, Joyce, *Ramses: Egypt's Greatest Pharaoh*, Viking/Penguin Books, 2000.

Shuaibi, Dr. Azmi, *"Elements of Corruption in the Middle East and North Africa: The Palestinian Case,"* Paper Presented at the 9th International Anti-Corruption Conference.

Sivan, Emmanuel, *Radical Islam: Medieval Theology and Modern Politics*. Enlarged edition. New Haven & London: Yale University Press, 1990.

Springborg, Robert. *Mubarak's Egypt: Fragmentation of Political the Order*. Boulder: Westview, 1989.

_______________. *'Patterns of Association in the Egyptian Political Elite". In the Political Elites in the Middle East*, ed. George Lenczowki. Washington, D.C.: American Enterprise Institute for Public Policy Research, 1975, pp. 83-99.

Tamesis, Pauline, "Different Perspectives of International Development Organizations. *In the Fight against Corruption," in Corruption and Integrity Improvement Initiatives in Developing Countries.*

United Nations Development Program and the Arab Fund for Economic and Social Development, Arab Human Development Report 2002: Creating Opportunities for Future Generations. New York: UNDP. 2002.

Vatikiotis, P.J. *The History of Modern Egypt: From Muhammad Ali to Mubarak*, The Johns Hopkins University Press; 3rd edition (May, 1986).

Waterbury, John, *The Egypt of Nasser and Sadat: The Political Economy of Two Regimes*. Princeton Studies on the Near East, (Paperback - May 1983).

Weaver, Mary Ann, *A Portrait of Egypt*. New York: Farrar, Straus & Giroux, 2000.

INDEX

ABOUT THE AUTHOR

Aladdin Elaasar is a lecturer and author of "Silent Victims". He is a former professor of Arabic Language and Area Studies at the Defense Language Institute, and the Monterey Institute of International Studies. Born, raised and educated in Egypt and the United States, Elaasar is an expert on Egypt and the Arab world. Elaasar has been a frequent commentator on the Middle East on American TV and Radio networks and co-hosted a radio talk show in Chicago. His columns were syndicated through the Tribune/NightRidder covering current events and Arab/American issues. Coverage about him and his books have been published in: The Chicago Tribune, Middle East Quarterly, Forbes, USA Today, Wall Street Journal, Fox News, Monterey Herald, Voice of America, Swiss Info, The Daily Herald, La Presse, CarnegieEndowment.org, and others. In 2005 he was nominated as a candidate for the presidential elections in Egypt. His campaign gained worldwide media coverage.

www.ingramcontent.com/pod-product-compliance
Lightning Source LLC
Chambersburg PA
CBHW060958280326
41935CB00009B/749

* 9 7 8 0 6 1 5 3 0 0 7 0 2 *